P9-DDU-385

THE STATES AND THE NATION SERIES, of which this volume is a part, is designed to assist the American people in a serious look at the ideals they have espoused and the experiences they have undergone in the history of the nation. The content of every volume represents the scholarship, experience, and opinions of its author. The costs of writing and editing were met mainly by grants from the National Endowment for the Humanities, a federal agency. The project was administered by the American Association for State and Local History, a nonprofit learned society, working with an Editorial Board of distinguished editors, authors, and historians, whose names are listed below.

EDITORIAL ADVISORY BOARD

James Morton Smith, General Editor
Director, State Historical Society
of Wisconsin

William T. Alderson, Director
American Association for
State and Local History

Roscoe C. Born
Vice-Editor
The National Observer

Vernon Carstensen
Professor of History
University of Washington

Michael Kammen, Professor of
American History and Culture
Cornell University

Louis L. Tucker
President (1972–1974)
American Association for
State and Local History

Joan Paterson Kerr
Consulting Editor
American Heritage

Richard M. Ketchum
Editor and Author
Dorset, Vermont

A. Russell Mortensen
Assistant Director
National Park Service

Lawrence W. Towner
Director and Librarian
The Newberry Library

Richmond D. Williams
President (1974–1976)
American Association for
State and Local History

MANAGING EDITOR

Gerald George
American Association for
State and Local History

BANKS HIGH SCHOOL LIBRARY

New Mexico

A Bicentennial History

Marc Simmons

507643

W. W. Norton & Company, Inc.
New York

American Association for State and Local History
Nashville

Author and publishers make grateful acknowledgment to the following for permission
to quote from archival material and previously published works.

The Spanish Archives of New Mexico, Santa Fe, New Mexico, for permission to
quote from the letters of Teodoro de Croix, Document No. 719.

Copyright © 1977
American Association for State and Local History
All rights reserved

Published and distributed by W. W. Norton & Company, Inc.
500 Fifth Avenue
New York, New York 10036

Library of Congress Cataloguing-in-Publication Data
Simmons, Marc.
  New Mexico.

  (The States and the Nation series)
  Bibliography: p.
  Includes index.
  1. New Mexico—History. I. Title. II. Series.
F796.S54   978.9   77–585
ISBN 0–393–05631–7

Printed in the United States of America
2 3 4 5 6 7 8 9 0

For

Frank Turley,

a good man at the anvil

Contents

Illustrations

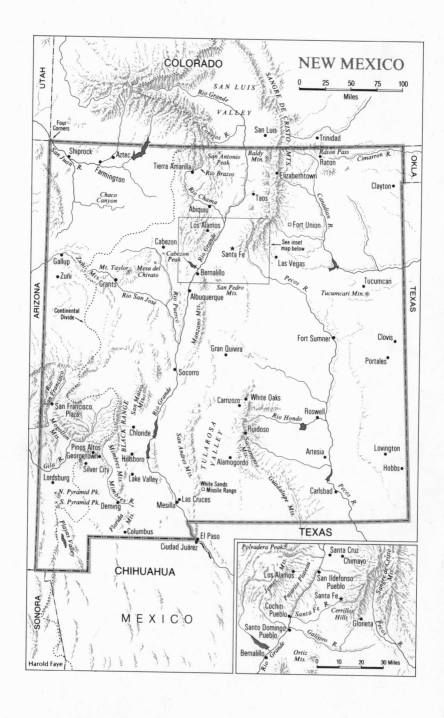

NEW MEXICO

COLORADO

UTAH

0   25   50   75   100
Miles

SAN LUIS

Rio Grande

VALLEY

Four Corners

San Luis

• Trinidad

SANGRE DE CRISTO MTS.

OKLA

Shiprock   • Aztec

San Juan R.

Farmington

Conejos R.

Tierra Amarilla

San Antonio Peak

Rio Brazos

Baldy Mtn.

Raton Pass

Raton

Cimarron R.

Chaco Canyon

Rio Chama

Abiquiu

Elizabethtown

Clayton •

Canadian R.

• Taos

Los Alamos

□ Fort Union

ARIZONA

Cabezon

× Cabezon Peak

Rio Grande

★ Santa Fe

See inset map below

Gallup

Zuni Mts.

Mt. Taylor

Mesa del Chivato

• Zuñi

Grants

Rio San José

Bernalillo

Las Vegas •

Pecos R.

Tucumcari •

San Pedro Mts.

Continental Divide

Albuquerque

Rio Puerco

Manzano Mts.

Tucumcari Mtn. ×

TEXAS

Gran Quivira

Fort Sumner

Clovis •

Portales •

Socorro

Rio Francisco

San Francisco Plaza

Mogollon Mts.

Black Range

San Mateo Mts.

Carrizozo

• White Oaks

Rio Hondo

Roswell

Chloride

Gila R.

Pinos Altos
Georgetown

Silver City

Mimbres Mts.

Hillsboro

Lake Valley

San Andres Mts.

TULAROSA VALLEY

Ruidoso

Sacramento Mts.

Alamogordo

Artesia

Lovington •

Hobbs •

Lordsburg

× N. Pyramid Pk.

× S. Pyramid Pk.

Deming

Florida Mts.

Mimbres R.

Mesilla

White Sands
□ Missile Range

Las Cruces

Guadalupe Mts.

Carlsbad

Pecos R.

Playas Valley

• Columbus

El Paso

TEXAS

Ciudad Juárez

CHIHUAHUA

SONORA

M E X I C O

Harold Faye

Inset map

Polvadera Peak

Santa Cruz

Chimayo

Los Alamos

Jemez Mts.

Pajarito Plateau

San Ildefonso Pueblo

Santa Fe ★

Santa Fe R.

Sangre de Cristo Mts.

Cochiti Pueblo

Cerrillos Hills

Gloneta

Santo Domingo Pueblo

Bernalillo

Rio Grande

Ortiz Mts.

Galisteo R.

Pecos R.

0   10   20   30 Miles

Invitation to the Reader

IN 1807, former President John Adams argued that a complete history of the American Revolution could not be written until the history of change in each state was known, because the principles of the Revolution were as various as the states that went through it. Two hundred years after the Declaration of Independence, the American nation has spread over a continent and beyond. The states have grown in number from thirteen to fifty. And democratic principles have been interpreted differently in every one of them.

We therefore invite you to consider that the history of your state may have more to do with the bicentennial review of the American Revolution than does the story of Bunker Hill or Valley Forge. The Revolution has continued as Americans extended liberty and democracy over a vast territory. John Adams was right: the states are part of that story, and the story is incomplete without an account of their diversity.

The Declaration of Independence stressed life, liberty, and the pursuit of happiness; accordingly, it shattered the notion of holding new territories in the subordinate status of colonies. The Northwest Ordinance of 1787 set forth a procedure for new states to enter the Union on an equal footing with the old. The Federal Constitution shortly confirmed this novel means of building a nation out of equal states. The step-by-step process through which territories have achieved self-government and national representation is among the most important of the Founding Fathers' legacies.

The method of state-making reconciled the ancient conflict between liberty and empire, resulting in what Thomas Jefferson called an empire for liberty. The system has worked and remains unaltered, despite enormous changes that have taken

ix

place in the nation. The country's extent and variety now surpass anything the patriots of '76 could likely have imagined.
The United States has changed from an agrarian republic into a
highly industrial and urban democracy, from a fledgling nation
into a major world power. As Oliver Wendell Holmes remarked
in 1920, the creators of the nation could not have seen completely how it and its constitution and its states would develop.
Any meaningful review in the bicentennial era must consider
what the country has become, as well as what it was.

The new nation of equal states took as its motto *E Pluribus
Unum*—"out of many, one." But just as many peoples have
become Americans without complete loss of ethnic and cultural
identities, so have the states retained differences of character.
Some have been superficial, expressed in stereotyped images—
big, boastful Texas, "sophisticated" New York, "hillbilly"
Arkansas. Other differences have been more real, sometimes instructively, sometimes amusingly; democracy has embraced
Huey Long's Louisiana, bilingual New Mexico, unicameral Nebraska, and a Texas that once taxed fortunetellers and spawned
politicians called "Woodpecker Republicans" and "Skunk
Democrats." Some differences have been profound, as when
South Carolina secessionists led other states out of the Union in
opposition to abolitionists in Massachusetts and Ohio. The result was a bitter Civil War.

The Revolution's first shots may have sounded in Lexington
and Concord; but fights over what democracy should mean and
who should have independence have erupted from Pennsyl-
vania's Gettysburg to the "Bleeding Kansas" of John Brown,
from the Alamo in Texas to the Indian battles at Montana's
Little Bighorn. Utah Mormons have known the strain of isolation; Hawaiians at Pearl Harbor, the terror of attack; Georgians
during Sherman's march, the sadness of defeat and devastation.
Each state's experience differs instructively; each adds understanding to the whole.

The purpose of this series of books is to make that kind of understanding accessible, in a way that will last in value far
beyond the bicentennial fireworks. The series offers a volume
on every state, plus the District of Columbia—fifty-one, in all.

Each book contains, besides the text, a view of the state through eyes other than the author's—a "photographer's essay," in which a skilled photographer presents his own personal perceptions of the state's contemporary flavor.

We have asked authors not for comprehensive chronicles, nor for research monographs or new data for scholars. Bibliographies and footnotes are minimal. We have asked each author for a summing up—interpretive, sensitive, thoughtful, individual, even personal—of what seems significant about his or her state's history. What distinguishes it? What has mattered about it, to its own people and to the rest of the nation? What has it come to now?

To interpret the states in all their variety, we have sought a variety of backgrounds in authors themselves and have encouraged variety in the approaches they take. They have in common only these things: historical knowledge, writing skill, and strong personal feelings about a particular state. Each has wide latitude for the use of the short space. And if each succeeds, it will be by offering you, in your capacity as a *citizen* of a state *and* of a nation, stimulating insights to test against your own.

James Morton Smith
General Editor

Preface

$\mathcal{T}$HIS book is based on my own study of New Mexico extending over a period of twenty-five years. It represents a summary of those themes and events which, for me, seem most important in conveying a true sense of the state's rich and chromatic history. Well-informed readers will soon discover that some prominent names and famous episodes from the past have been omitted. Working under a strict requirement that the long story of New Mexico be compressed into something just over two hundred pages, I have chosen to be selective rather than inclusive. In other words, instead of hastening to register mention of every significant person and happening, catalogue fashion, I have ambled along at moderate pace, singling out for treatment certain high points that help make New Mexico's complex history understandable and meaningful.

In the writing of this book, I have incurred many obligations. For practical assistance in the typing of the manuscript and for efficient help and critical comments during the long year that the volume was in preparation, my first and largest debt is to Susie Henderson of Cerrillos, New Mexico. Others who assisted in various ways and to whom I remain indebted are State Historian Myra Ellen Jenkins, Albert H. Schroeder, Lois Simmons, J. M. Simmons, Margaret and Alfonso Ortiz, John L. Kessell, David J. Weber, Frank Turley, and Virginia Gillespie. Special thanks are owed to Gerald George, a patient and tactful editor.

Finally, a word of recognition is in order for that older generation of New Mexican historians who have contributed so much toward an understanding of the state's past. Three of those scholars have offered me both inspiration and encouragement over the years, and I here acknowledge them with gratitude. They are Eleanor B. Adams, Fray Angelico Chavez, and France V. Scholes.

MARC SIMMONS

Los Cerrillos, New Mexico
November 1976

New Mexico

Introduction

$\mathcal{F}$OR Spanish colonists in New Mexico, the year 1776 was memorable, but for reasons having nothing to do with events in Philadelphia or the activities of General Washington. While patriots rallied to the call of the Second Continental Congress, the New Mexicans, who would one day be Americans, were spinning out their lives hardly aware of the fighting in the East. They were distracted instead by problems that go with trying to maintain life on a difficult frontier: Indian raids, pestilence, drought, corrupt government officials, and the unending sense of isolation. Yet, several events set that year apart, so that, afterward, 1776 loomed as an important date in New Mexico history.

For one thing, two Franciscan friars undertook an extraordinary journey. Fathers Francisco Atanasio Domínguez and Silvestre Vélez de Escalante traveled almost two thousand miles in a wobbly circle from Santa Fe through the deserts and canyonlands of the Far West. They viewed peoples and country never before seen by white men, collected geographical information useful to Spain, battled bitter winter weather, and crossed the Colorado River above the Grand Canyon after searching thirteen days for a passage—all this, while the British had been capturing Long Island and Fort Washington on the Hudson, and General Arnold had been slowing Burgoyne's forces on Lake Champlain.

It began in March, when Padre Domínguez, canonical inspector, reached the capital of Santa Fe to begin an official examination of New Mexico's missions. All visits by churchmen of rank were a rarity in that remote province of the Viceroyalty of New Spain, so the arrival of Father Domínguez created a stir. Members of the socially elite hastened to fete him; in the central plaza, masses of the faithful surrounded him to stare. He bore their veneration with commendable tolerance, but the wretchedness of the town itself was another matter. Fray Domínguez viewed Santa Fe with the eye of a man long accustomed to the courtly cities of central Mexico. And this poor adobe nothing of a capital scarcely possessed the semblance of a street.

There were no tree-lined thoroughfares. No gleaming palaces or mansions. No gold-encrusted churches. Not a single gushing fountain, so beloved by every Spaniard. No blanket of tiled roofs glowing red in the sunset. No arched porticos or covered marketplace. No twisted and scrolled grilles adorning any window. No throng of traffic. No crowds of elegant ladies or swarms of idle, dandified young men. It was a place at the end of the world, mournful in appearance and lacking, in the judgment of Father Domínguez, anything that might lift the spirit.

True, a so-called Governors Palace, made of mud bricks and adzed timbers, hunkered low on the north side of the plaza. But to any visitor from outside the province, it scarcely seemed possible that such a rude structure could house a representative of the Spanish empire and one, at that, who presided over hundreds of square leagues of His Majesty's domain.

True, in the center of town stood a parish church, also of adobe, and with an altar screen of common pine. Boys climbed to the choir loft by a ladder because there were no stairs, and the faithful had to stand or sit on the packed-earth floor because benches were lacking. At first glance, the governor's armchair, gracing one wall, seemed to lend a touch of elegance with its upholstery of crimson velvet, gold fringe, and tasseled foot-cushion. A closer look showed its regal magnificence much diminished by the poor light and primitive surroundings.

True, there existed a friar's *convento* and a couple of smaller chapels—one for the soldiers and another, dedicated to San

Miguel, for residents who lived across the thin trickle of the Santa Fe River. There were private houses, many of them merely huts, called *jacales,* scattered at random among the gardens and orchards that encroached almost to the plaza. But when that had been seen, there was little more.

Unless one found pleasure in contemplating the backdrop of sandy hills studded with piñon pine, and, in the distance, the soaring heights of the Sangre de Cristo Range. Unless the visitor could appreciate a sky more luminescent than the richest turquoise, or the puffy banks of dark summer clouds that boiled out of the sierra to bathe the brown houses and fields, leaving the air redolent of new-washed earth. Unless a stray traveler who had come over the parched wastes threaded by the Camino Real could discover beauty in the platinum bracelet of a stream that Santa Fe citizens, in their enthusiasm, had elevated to the rank of river. Unless some stranger warmed to unbounded hospitality, unless he discovered comfort in simple houses whose walls afforded coolness in summer and warmth in winter, unless he admired lighthearted people, hard-working and stoical. Unless he did—then, like Father Domínguez in the early spring of 1776, he saw Santa Fe as a trifling place.

During April and May, Domínguez inspected the spiritual and economic condition of missions in the hinterland. Even then, he was looking toward a larger project that formed part of his purpose in coming here. His religious superiors had instructed him to go in search of a route that would link New Mexico with the recently founded province of California, and while about it, to discover new fields for missionary work among the Indians.

Father Escalante, minister of Zuñi Pueblo and a man with knowledge of western trails, entered Santa Fe in early June. He had been summoned by Domínguez to share leadership in the pending expedition. The two made preparations, enlisting eight local citizens to go as an escort, and setting July 4 as the date of departure. Delays arose. The fourth passed. It was month's end before the party got under way.

The course selected by Domínguez and Escalante toward Monterey, their ultimate destination, was a roundabout one. They traveled north and west of Santa Fe up the Chama valley and into present western Colorado, through lands previously visited by Indian traders from New Mexico. Then they veered due west into unknown country of the Ute tribe in central Utah and finally angled southwest toward the Virgin River. By early October, snow fell, sealing the mountain passes, and the two friars reluctantly abandoned their quest. Swinging south, they forded the Colorado River at a spot above the Grand Canyon, known thereafter as "The Crossing of the Fathers." Late November saw them at last in the shelter of Zuñi, after nearly four months in some of the most difficult and breath-taking wilderness on the continent. They had failed to get near California, and the Indians seen were too distant to make missions practical, but a notable chapter had been added to the history of western America.

An ominous fact of life in New Mexico during that watershed year of 1776—and one readily seen by Father Domínguez when he first came to the province—dealt with the terror spread by nomadic Indians: occasionally the Ute, often the Navajo, always the Apache and Comanche. Almost every family mourned lost relatives. Towns and ranches lay in ruins. Once-vast flocks of sheep had dwindled to remnants. Caravans moved infrequently and only under heavy guard. The devastation was appalling, and it posed a formidable question. Simply stated: Could New Mexico survive?

The knotty problem had long engaged the attention of the king and his colonial officials, for the danger was not confined to that province alone. It menaced the existence of every Spanish settlement and mission stretching from Texas to the Gulf of California. A variety of military solutions had been tried and a string of peace plans, often with friars as their agents and implementers, put forth. All ended on the scrap heap. Military forces were too skimpy, the missionaries too few, provincial officials too weak, money from the royal treasury too scarce to tackle the immense job in anything like an effective manner. On this outlying frontier, Spain was vastly overextended, and to ward off disaster, she needed a new approach.

In 1776 Charles III believed he had found one. By royal decree, he separated the northern region from the old viceroyalty and created a new military department, to be called the Commandancy-General of the Interior Provinces of New Spain. Its success or failure in handling the Indians rested with a commandant-general, an officer vested with extraordinary powers, who would serve on the spot to formulate frontier policy. In May of that year, the king appointed to the post Don Teodoro de Croix, an able Fleming long in the service of Spain. Several years actually elapsed before Croix was able to get a grip on his task, but the infusion of new blood and fresh ideas eventually brought some relief to New Mexico and other hard-pressed regions along the border.

While Croix was traveling north from Mexico City to assume command of the Internal Provinces, a perfect oak of a man, Don Juan Bautista de Anza, rode at the head of 240 colonists across the deserts of Sonora toward California. One result of that march was the founding of the city of San Francisco in September 1776. At the time, New Mexicans had scarcely heard of Anza, but within two years, his name would become a household word. Croix named him in 1778 to the governorship of New Mexico with seemingly impossible instructions: win an alliance with the powerful Comanche and then make mutual war on the Apache. Over the next nine years, Anza not only achieved that goal, but he also compiled a truly remarkable record as an administrator, explorer, soldier, and Indian agent.

Thus, as durable veterans of the Continental Army watched a red-coated general surrender his sword at Yorktown and wondered vaguely what the future held for their fledgling nation, a tough and capable Spanish governor beyond the distant prairies was quietly, competently putting New Mexico's affairs in order. Not a sign did he have that, within a matter of decades, rule of this land along the Rio Grande would pass into the hands of tumultuous republican sons who called themselves Americans.

Across the centuries, the interplay of natural and human forces have made New Mexico the distinctive state that it is. No general agreement exists as to what influence has been the strongest, although many writers lean toward the overriding fact of aridity and the ceaseless struggle of men to lay claim to scarce waters. Others believe that New Mexico's persistent and vital Indian cultures, healthier here than perhaps anywhere else in the United States, contribute most toward defining the source of the state's particular élan and charm. Still others see the early introduction and the enduring life of Hispanic institutions as the chief determinant affecting the region's history. A case could be made, too, on the negative side, that poverty of both land and people through the years has done more than anything else to shape New Mexico's story.

To arrive at an understanding of why New Mexico is different, one can best begin by considering the Spaniard. It was his attitude and conduct toward the Indian and later toward the Anglo-American that governed the way human society developed along the upper Rio Grande. And it was his custom and law that established the first formal procedures for dealing with the essential issues of land and water rights.

Spain ruled over New Mexico twice as long as the United States has ruled, to date. For something like 225 years, Hispanic colonists worked and died here in comparative obscurity, their accomplishments and failures known only to a handful of government officers and missionaries. Through their own distinctive brand of pioneering, they imposed their culture on the wilderness and upon the Indians occupying it. The legacy of that work survives to this day and perhaps more than anything else endows the modern state with an exotic flavor.

New Mexico was the oldest, most populous, and most important province on the outer rim of the old Viceroyalty of New Spain. That distinction is easily forgotten, now that her sister provinces of Texas and California, so feeble in colonial times, have raced ahead by all standards of measurement, since becoming part of the United States. That earlier prominence explains the stubborn persistence of New Mexico's Spanish language and culture, which elsewhere in the Southwest have lost much of their standing.

The colony of New Mexico was dedicated, not to mining, industry, or exploitive agriculture, but to subsistence farming, herding, and evangelization of the Indian people. Life ebbed and flowed for centuries; the population crept upward; towns and ranches proliferated. And all the while, New Mexico stayed a frontier province with the dangers, hard labor, privations, and rough edges that characterize any frontier.

The Spanish pioneers who built adobe homes and missions here possessed a far different outlook from men who swung their axes and primed their long rifles east of the Mississippi. Part of the difference resided in the nature of the frontier itself. In the eastern woodlands, a brave and enterprising soul could raise a cabin, put in a crop, and rear his children. He fought off the Indians and, if lucky, kept them at bay. All the while, he fought and farmed on the assumption that, after a decade or two, the frontier would move on, leaving him a measure of tranquility in his old age and secure property to bequeath to his offspring. That situation bred its own attitude of mind.

New Mexico was not so fortunate. From its formal founding in 1598 down to the defeat of Geronimo's marauding Apaches in 1886, it suffered constant invasion by enemies. They swept, not across a frontier line, but out of every mountain chain and sheltering canyon that encircled the province. No town was so large as to be completely secure from raiders; no traveler ever left home without wondering if he would ever see it again.

The prominent Mendoza family, living on a ranch south of Albuquerque, lost thirty of its members at one swoop during the holocaust of the 1680 Pueblo Revolt. On another occasion, Pablo Vialpando left a spacious hacienda in the Taos valley to go on a business trip. In his absence, hundreds of Comanches stormed the house, killing his family and neighbors who had fled there, and carrying fifty-six women and children into captivity. Señora Vialpando died defending the main gate with a lance. Manuel Antonio Chaves, a leading frontiersman of the nineteenth century, could name two hundred relatives, near and distant, who had perished at the hands of Indians. The state of insecurity was an abiding one, generation after generation, and it bred in the New Mexicans both a deep sense of fatalism and a particular kind of inner toughness. In bravery, they could match the Anglo-Americans; and in sheer grit, tenacity, and fortitude, they had no peers.

All frontiers have a way of shaping men's character and patterns of conduct, bringing out the best in some, the worst in others. Colonial New Mexico suffered its quota of renegades, cowards, thieves, drunkards, and corrupt officials, but in the balance they counted for little. The stout folk, frugal and enduring, who were masters at overcoming obstacles, set the tone for that frontier society.

The character and courage of the Hispano soldier and pioneer have so often been belittled that it may come as some surprise to learn that these were respected and respectable frontiersmen. General Teodoro de Croix spoke of the New Mexicans in 1778 as "faithful and valorous in battle." Thirty years later Lieutenant Zebulon Pike described them as "the bravest and most hardy subjects in New Spain," exhibiting "in a superior degree, the heaven-like qualities of hospitality and kindness." Miguel Ramos Arizpe in 1812 paid tribute to the men of the northern border as being each "a hero that is worth a hundred ordinary soldiers," and even on the roughest campaigns, "ready to subsist on snakes, rats, and saddle leather without a whimper or thought of desertion." These qualities the New Mexicans shared to some degree with their frontier brethren in the East.[1]

Sturdy American pioneers who answered the westering call wanted land free for the taking and a chance to build a new way of life. Some were looking to escape the restraints of conventional society or were simply responding to an inborn urge to move elsewhere, to roam unfettered beyond the line of settlement.

The Spaniard, advancing into new regions, was animated by motives other than simple restlessness or desire for farmland. He searched for lands to be claimed for the king, souls to be won for the Church, or precious metals that would gain him a fortune, titles, and social position. A farm plot or ranch was fairly easy to obtain—a man merely petitioned the crown for a vacant piece of ground—consequently, the Spaniard in New

1. Teodoro de Croix, February 10, 1778, Spanish Archives of New Mexico, Santa Fe, New Mexico, Document No. 2, 719; David J. Weber, editor, *Foreigners in Their Native Land* (Albuquerque: University of New Mexico Press, 1973), p. 37; Nettie Lee Benson, translator, *Report of Dr. Miguel Ramos de Arizpe* (Austin: University of Texas Press, 1950), pp. 16–17.

Mexico never experienced that intense hunger, that compulsive acquisitiveness for land that dominated the westward-moving Anglo-American.

The pioneers who came north with oxcarts and mule trains up the valley of the Rio Grande were not out to build a new society, but to transplant an old one. Their Hispanic traditions of government, religion, and material culture they intended to root firmly in the arid wastes of New Mexico. Nor was this a helter-skelter movement of individual family heads, seeking better homes and led northward by their own enterprise and initiative. Rather, it was a well-organized migration, orchestrated and closely directed by the royal government, with the royal will and purpose as its motivating force.

The contrast is important. For Spain, the frontier offered vast potential for expanding the effective limits of her empire. Conquest of the wilderness was strictly controlled, its settlement was meticulously planned, its development rigidly supervised. If Spanish custom did, indeed, undergo some transformation in New Mexico and the other northern provinces, it occurred as a natural consequence of a distinctive geography and climate and of a society in isolation. There was no intent on the part of these frontier people to be other than Spaniards in the traditional mold.

For all his reputation as abuser of the Indian, the Spaniard developed, for his day, an enlightened view toward native subjects and enthroned it as a firm policy. Following the bloody conquests of Mexico and Peru, forces for humanitarian reform led by Father Bartolomé de las Casas succeeded in affirming certain basic rights for the Indians and establishing the mission of the colonists as one of a civilizing guardianship. Ancient Spanish law regulated the conduct of war, even with those tribes perpetually hostile, so that the end was never lost sight of: peaceful submission and conversion of the Indians, followed by their incorporation into Spanish society. Nowhere do we find the attitude, so prevalent on the Anglo-American frontier, that the red man stood as a barrier, merely to be brushed aside or trampled under.

New Mexico's numerous Pueblo Indians, settled in prosperous farming communities, received title to their lands, protection from encroaching settlers, and access to the courts in disputes with their Spanish neighbors. The laws did not always shield them as intended, and they suffered religious persecution at the hands of overzealous friars. But the fact remains, their legal status was clearly defined within the Spanish system. At the end of the colonial period, Pueblo Indians still possessed their ancestral lands, and their native culture survived almost intact. Even the old religion continued to serve behind a façade provided by superficial acceptance of Hispanic Catholicism. When the United States scooped up the Southwest in the Mexican War, it agreed to adhere to most of the old protective policies. As a result, the Pueblos were saved from disintegration and extinction, the lot of so many other native Americans.

If one looks for a predominant theme running like a thread through all New Mexico's history, it can readily be found in the collision and mingling of cultures. Even before arrival of the white man, Pueblos alternately fought and traded with nomadic Apaches, setting the basic pattern. The Spaniards had their days of Indian fighting, often brought on by inept governors and missionaries, but they also indulged in much borrowing of native ways. Beginning in the eighteenth century, they had to contend with European interlopers who discovered trails to the Rio Grande—first a sprinkling of French traders, and then later a tidal wave of frontiersmen out of English America.

The entire history of New Mexico from 1850 to the present is interwoven with attempts by the Indian and Hispano populations to come to terms with an alien Anglo society. Through principles supplied by the Declaration of Independence, they have tried to win equality while remaining different and have sought liberty to pursue a time-honored way of life. That history also includes the long story of the Anglo-American's adjustment to things that are uniquely and engagingly New Mexican.

1

The Spaniards

*T*HE high, dry country of New Mexico is the birthplace of America's tall tale. The land's heady mixture of winelike air, sparkling sunlight, and bare-earth colors dazzles the senses and stimulates the imagination, so that the separation of fantasy from fact becomes a difficult, sometimes impossible, chore. Here, where space stretches far and often resembles the moonscape, golden mirages and extravagant yarns of lost treasure have found a compatible breeding ground. The past is pock-marked with stories of men gone a little crazy, running pell-mell after nonexistent riches. Many among the gullible came to pointless and tragic endings, but a few, in their mad scramble to chase fantastic myths, changed the course of history. Among the latter were sixteenth-century Spaniards beguiled by a now almost forgotten fable of seven golden cities. The pursuit of this wonder sent them on tremendous journeys that ultimately led to the discovery, exploration, and naming of New Mexico.

The legend of seven cities was an old one, variant of a tale long popular in medieval Spain. According to tradition, seven bishops fled their country ahead of the Moorish invasion in the eighth century. Sailing westward, they reached the island of Antilia (a name echoed today in the Antilles Islands), where they each built an opulent city brimming with treasure. Graciousus Benincasa, on his map of 1482, placed Antilia west of the Madeiras, and on it he inscribed names of the seven mythi-

13

cal cities. After Columbus made his discovery, men wondered if these metropolises might lie somewhere on the northern continent.

The earliest Spanish captains, looking at the New World through medieval lenses, fully expected to find the fabulous places described in their ancient literature. They were particularly attentive to any reference to the magical number *seven*. Persistent rumor told of seven Indian towns in the jungles of western Mexico. And the Maya of Yucatan, as well as the Aztecs of central Mexico, spoke of seven caves from which their ancestors had sprung. Then, in 1539, something of real substance surfaced: a Franciscan friar, traveling hundreds of leagues north of Mexico City to a land called Cíbola, claimed actually to have seen, from a distance, the first of the seven wondrous cities. His announcement set off a chain of events destined to form the initial chapter in the history of Spanish New Mexico.

The willingness of colonial Spaniards to put faith in romantic and imaginative tales owed much to the extraordinary experience of Fernando Cortez, the man who discovered and conquered the land we now know as Mexico. With a fleet of ships, Cortez sailed from Cuba in 1519, intending to explore the then unknown mainland to the west. Entering Mexican waters from the Caribbean, he was deeply impressed by the natural beauty of the coastline. The country so reminded him of his Spanish homeland that he decided to call it New Spain, Nueva España, and that title remained to the end of the colonial period. It also established a precedent for other European powers that later named their American possessions New England, New France, New Netherlands, and New Sweden.

Landing on the Gulf Coast, Cortez and his daredevil soldiers heard of a stupendous kingdom nestling in a high valley beyond a wall of mountains and presided over by an emperor named Montezuma. An epic march took the Spaniards inland to the edge of the Valley of Mexico and to their first glimpse of Tenochtitlán, the treasure-laden capital of the Aztecs. What they beheld was one of the world's great cities, its inhabitants numbering in the hundreds of thousands, of whose existence until that moment Europeans had been wholly unaware. Awestruck, these knights of Spain gazed at magnificent palaces, temples, and towers, and at the glitter of a welcoming committee headed by Montezuma's nephew, who rode in a gold litter adorned with jewels and green plumes. The incredible picture reminded them of nothing less than the enchanted scenes described in fanciful novels of medieval chivalry. "To many of us," wrote one of the soldiers afterward, "it seemed doubtful whether we were asleep or awake . . . for never yet did man see, hear, or dream of anything to equal the spectacle which appeared to our eyes on this day." [1]

Over the next two years, Cortez made himself master of the land and, in the process, destroyed both the Indian empire and Tenochtitlán. Upon the ruins of the native capital, he built a new Spanish metropolis called Mexico City, after *Mexica,* the Aztecs' name for themselves. In the vernacular of the day, the word *Mexico* became synonymous with riches beyond reckoning and served as the yardstick by which future discoveries were measured.

The stunning conquest of the Aztecs and their fabulous state placed such strains upon the imagination that, for long afterward, the Spaniards were prepared to accept every absurd tale that reached their ears. Given the improbable events that had already come to pass, it was natural that their minds should conjure up even more fantastic possibilities beyond the horizon. If one Mexico, one storehouse of treasure, could exist, why not another, perhaps tucked away in the mountain-and-desert fastness of the far north? In time, the quest for a new Mexico would draw conquistadors like a magnet toward the frontier of the Rio Grande and beyond.

In the defeat of the Aztecs, Cortez reaped a fortune and gained a title of nobility from the king. But he failed to win what he coveted most: the right to rule over lands he had seized

1. Hubert Herring, *A History of Latin America,* 3rd edition (New York: Alfred A. Knopf, 1968), p. 131.

for Spain. The crown looked with wariness upon men of ambition and strength, and it moved to clip the wings of Fernando
Cortez.

In 1535, the vast domain stretching from Central America to
the misty unknown north was organized as the Viceroyalty of
New Spain, under a royal official who bore the title of viceroy.
Cortez, with his record of accomplishment, expected to be
named to the post; but it went instead to a man sent out by the
king, Antonio de Mendoza. The aging conquistador accepted
his eclipse with grace and made plans to turn his energies to
new projects of discovery in western and northern New Spain.
But his main effort was finished, and, in the quest for another
Mexico, he was forced to make way for younger swashbucklers.

The search was suddenly given focus in 1536, when four destitute figures, more scarecrows than men, appeared in Culiacán,
the outermost settlement northwest of Mexico City. They were
the only survivors of the resplendent Narváez Expedition that
had set sail from Cuba in 1528 to colonize Florida. After a
series of disasters that brought the enterprise to ruin, these four
alone, shipwrecked on the Texas coast, had managed to make
their way westward from one Indian tribe to another across the
lower Rio Grande to eventual safety. It was a harrowing odys-
sey that carried them—the first Europeans—through the interior
wilds of the North American continent.

Leader and spokesman of this party of three Spaniards and a
black slave was Alvar Nuñez Cabeza de Vaca, the original expedition's treasurer. What he and his companions had seen of
value in the remote and sterile country sounded meager enough:
some cotton shawls of the Indians, beads, coral from the South
Sea (Pacific), turquoise, and five arrowheads made of
"emeralds," which were probably malachite. More to the point
were things of which they had heard but failed to see, notably a
populous country to the north whose people possessed large
houses and traded in turquoise and other desirable goods. It was
a mere scrap of information, but one quickly seized upon by
eager Spaniards. Could this be a clue to another Mexico?

His Excellency Don Antonio de Mendoza, Viceroy of New
Spain, meant to find out. He proposed a small reconnaissance

party to go and probe the secrets of the northern mystery, for more definite information was needed to justify a full-scale expedition of conquest. Thus it was that a Franciscan friar was picked for the mission which, in a matter of months, would lead to the finding of the seven cities of Cíbola.

The friar was Father Marcos de Niza, an adventuresome cleric who had been with Francisco Pizarro during the conquest of Peru and who had served afterward in Guatemala. Both his experience and his religious calling seemed to qualify Fray Marcos as a truthful reporter. Moreover, to the viceroy's way of thinking, a friar would not stir up the Indians along the way, nor would his simple wants entail unnecessary expense for the royal treasury in the event that his hunt came to nothing.

In March of 1539, Fray Marcos set out, escorted by friendly Indians and guided by one of the castaways who had accompanied Cabeza de Vaca. His guide was Estevanico, the black slave, a man considered resourceful at finding a trail or dealing with the natives.

The precise route taken and the ultimate point reached by Fray Marcos have been much debated by historians. His own account of the journey is sketchy, and, within a year after his return, what he claimed to have done and seen was brought into serious question. But existing evidence allows the following story to be pieced together with some color of certainty.

Fray Marcos, Estevanico, and their Indian retainers walked up the west side of Mexico, angled through the sun-drenched desert of southern Arizona, and approached the cluster of pueblos belonging to the Zuñi people, located just inside the modern New Mexico boundary. They had found the fabled province of Cíbola, about which natives farther south had spoken with awe. Estevanico, ranging ahead in his role as scout, entered the first Zuñi town of Hawikúh. The tribesmen proved hostile in this, their initial encounter with a man from the Old World. His strange appearance may have pegged the black man as a sorcerer, for even today the Zuñi maintain a healthy regard for spellbinders and witches. Or perhaps it was the liberties Estevanico took with the women, or his appetite for turquoise. In any case, the Indians slew the fearsome scout and, for good measure, cut his body into pieces. Several members of Estevanico's escort escaped and carried word of the deed back to Fray Marcos.

The friar had been moving ahead rapidly, but the dire news brought progress to a sudden halt. Natives in his own band threatened to kill him in reprisal for relatives and friends lost with Estevanico. Fray Marcos calmed them with kind words and distributed small trinkets. Then he hastened on again until he entered the limits of Cíbola and glimpsed the pueblo of Hawikúh from afar. Fear kept him from going closer.

So it happened that the clear, rarified New Mexico air, heightening the illusionary effects of light and space, played its trick and showed the eager Franciscan what he wanted to see. Of Hawikúh, aglow with sunlight, he later informed the viceroy: "It appears to be a very beautiful city; the houses are . . . all of stone, with their stories and terraces, as it seemed to me from a hill whence I could view it." [2] His own Indians told him it was the least of seven cities, and that another, far larger than any in Cíbola, lay beyond. Called Tontonteac, it possessed so many houses and people that there was no end to it.

A skeptical man might have lingered awhile longer on the fringes of Cíbola; he might even have skirted it and gone on to seek the mystery of Tontoneac. But Fray Marcos had seen enough to confirm in his mind what he and other Spaniards had already imagined. So, with his Indian followers arguing for retreat, prudence overrode skepticism. The friar, after claiming the land for his sovereign, turned south toward the capital with all speed to tell the viceroy what he had found.

The news that Fray Marcos brought of the discovery of seven cities spread like wildfire and grew in the telling. In no time, the embroidered tale included mention of abundant gold and of civilized people who had weights and measures, wore woolen clothes, and rode on strange beasts. Some urgency existed in laying claim to the new prize, for it was known in Mexico that Hernando de Soto, governor of Cuba, had won royal approval

2. Herbert E. Bolton, *Coronado, Knight of Pueblos and Plains* (Albuquerque: University of New Mexico Press, 1949), pp. 35–36.

to explore the mysterious land of Florida. And, given the imperfect notions of geography that prevailed, no one knew whether Cíbola lay close to Florida.

Francisco Vásquez de Coronado was the young governor of the western province of Nueva Galicia. He happened to be at home in his primitive little capital of Compostela during late June of 1539, when Fray Marcos de Niza made a stopover on his way from Cíbola to Mexico City. Thus, Coronado was among the first to get word of the seven cities and to be stricken with gold fever. He went on with the friar to the viceregal capital, listened to the formal report made to Antonio de Mendoza, and shared in the excitement that followed.

Viceroy Mendoza, up to this point, had moved cautiously. Now, with the favorable disclosures of Fray Marcos, he was ready to act. Someone must go at the head of a full-blown expedition to unlock the secrets of Cíbola and conquer what surely would be another Mexico. The viceroy toyed briefly with the idea of assuming leadership himself, but the demands of his office kept him chained in Mexico City. Next best was to send a close and trusted friend, one who could carry his own weight and command men. The eager governor of Nueva Galicia seemed to meet the requirements.

Mendoza invested heavily in the expedition's costs for outfitting both an overland party and a co-operating fleet of three ships to be sent up the Gulf of California. Coronado, for his part, added fifty thousand pesos, a sum that would represent now perhaps a million dollars. The two men took as an article of faith that the seven cities of legend had been found and that each was a bursting cornucopia.

Fray Marcos, of course, would go as guide. By now he was something of a celebrity, his story all the rage in New Spain. Some three hundred men enlisted as soldiers, many of them of noble blood, and a host of Indian allies and servants were added to the train. Five friars, in addition to Fray Marcos, joined the group, both to minister to the company on the march and to preach to the Cíbolans and other people that they might discover. The viceroy made clear in his instructions to Coronado that Indians in the new land should be treated with fairness and civility, so that "the conquest might be Christian and apostolic and not a butchery." [3] From earlier experience, the Spaniards had learned something.

On Sunday, February 22, 1540, exactly 192 years to the day before the birth of George Washington, Viceroy Mendoza was on hand at the outpost of Compostela to conduct a grand review and muster of Coronado's company. The following morning, amid pageantry and soaring hopes, the glittering cavalcade departed. Not a man there could foresee that the hour of glory at the launching would be the high point of the expedition and that the year ahead would be overspread with bitterness and weighted with defeat.

The march north was anything but a holiday outing. As the company crossed southeastern Arizona, provisions grew short, and tempers became frayed as men and animals wore thin. After six hard months on the trail up from Mexico, Cíbola began to take on new importance as a place where food and rest could be found.

Then Hawikúh, westernmost of the Zuñi towns, came into sight, and luster faded from the dream. The shock of Fray Marcos was as great as that of anyone else. Instead of a dazzling city, there, perched on a flat and sandy hill, was a rock-and-mud pueblo "all crumpled together." Eatables it might contain, but that was the extent of its treasure. In anger, the Spaniards heaped curses upon Fray Marcos, and shortly Coronado wrote to the viceroy, informing him acidly that the padre "has not told the truth in a single thing that he has said, for everything is the very opposite of what he related except the name of the cities." [4]

Worse, the people of Hawikúh proved belligerent, and the first of the seven cities had to be taken by storm. But once it was in Spanish hands, a deputation arrived from the remaining towns to make peace. A count showed that the Zuñi had only six pueblos; Fray Marcos had been mistaken even in that. In desperation, Coronado began casting glances beyond Cíbola.

3. Bolton, *Coronado*, p. 75.
4. Bolton, *Coronado*, p. 128.

Perhaps something worth their trouble still lay hidden in the wide and sunlit land.

A detachment under Pedro de Tovar headed for Tusayan, the Tontonteac about which Fray Marcos had heard the year before. Upon investigation, that province, inhabited by the Hopi Indians of northern Arizona, presented an even poorer appearance than Cíbola. Another wing of the army, captained by García López de Cárdenas, went farther and came upon the Grand Canyon, but even the massive grandeur of the world's greatest gorge could not offset disappointment over the paltriness of the "seven cities."

Then expectations soared again. Several Indians, led by a chief the Spaniards nicknamed "Bigotes"—"Whiskers"—reached Hawikúh from the east. They had learned of the bearded strangers from Zuñi messengers and were curious. Bigotes, a handsome and well-proportioned young man, presented Coronado with gifts of finely tanned buckskin and received beads and small bells in return. More important, Bigotes was full of information about a new province called Tiguex, where numerous pueblos lay strung along the wide rope of a river. That stream, one the Spaniards would soon call the Rio del Norte, is what we know today as the Rio Grande.

Past the eastern pueblos, Bigotes related, there stretched a limitless plain that melted into the sunrise, a country mysterious and little known. It was tenanted by immense herds of "woolly, humpbacked cattle," ferocious animals whose horns and hooves had felled many an Indian hunter. If the Spaniards wished to travel east and see for themselves, they would find a welcome, and Bigotes would serve as guide.

With the illusion of Cíbola in tatters, Coronado seized upon Bigotes's recital as some small promise of better things ahead. Three hundred irritable young bloods needed action; and, if nothing else, exploration consumed surplus energies. Hernando Alvarado, one of Coronado's subordinates, went ahead with a picked body of men to sound out prospects for the main army. He paused briefly at Acoma, the pueblo that, to this day, resides 380 feet in the air atop its incredible rock; pushed on to Tiguex and other Rio Grande pueblos; continued to Bigotes's native village of Pecos; and made a hurried excursion onto the Buffalo Plains, where he followed the Canadian River for one hundred leagues before turning back.

Coronado, biding his time in Cíbola, felt some relief when a message arrived from his lieutenant, suggesting that the expedition move to Tiguex and take up winter quarters. If the land held any opportunities, clearly they lay in the east.

On the Rio Grande, the Spaniards found twelve Tiwa (or Tigua) pueblos clustered in the area north of present-day Albuquerque, and other villages lay both north and south. Like those of Cíbola, the towns resembled multistoried apartments, with ladders or notched logs giving access to upper levels. Cubical rooms in each huge complex shared common roofs and walls and were piled upon one another stair-step fashion, sometimes up to seven stories. With several hundred souls crowded inside, they were not only cozy dwellings, but formidable fortresses.

The piece of river valley where Coronado stopped is still one of the most congenial spots in all New Mexico during the summer and fall. The air is bracing, and the sun is plentiful. Cottonwoods and willows shade the banks of the Rio Grande, casting a latticework of shadow on the roiling waters. Indians work with hoes to open small ditches that irrigate patches of green corn and melons. And they cast frequent glances, just as their ancestors did in Coronado's day, toward the curved hump of Sandía Mountain to the east.

The beauty of this peak, whose timbered summit rises more than ten thousand feet above sea level, dominates the river and the surrounding countryside. The Tiwa call it Oku Piñ, South World Mountain. Among its craggy battlements near cloud level dwell important deities like the Twin War Gods; like Wind Woman, who raises the spring dust storms; and like Spider Woman, whose friendship to the Pueblo people is commemorated in ancient legend.

In wintertime, when Sandía Mountain is crowned with snow and a cutting wind rattles the withered cornstalks, life in the valley is not so pleasant, as Coronado and his company found out. With considerable presumption, they obliged the Tiwa to vacate one of their villages—Alcanfor—to provide lodging for the army. The Indians left grudgingly. Later Coronado requisitioned grain from native stores and imposed a levy of blankets, so that his men, used to the tropics, might have some protection from the severe weather. The expedition's chronicler justified such highhandedness with the age-old refrain that necessity knows no law.

Other incidents followed. The Indians rebelled. Two pueblos were laid waste, and refugees streamed toward Oku Piñ, a welcome sanctuary even in the dead of winter. It was the worst sort of diplomatic bungling, necessity aside, and for his part in it, Coronado would later be called to account.

Had it not been for an Indian named "the Turk" and his extravagant yarns, the winter of 1540–1541, with its hunger and biting cold, would have witnessed the smothering of Spanish hopes. On his trip east the previous fall, Alvarado had taken an Indian in tow at Pecos Pueblo and had dubbed him the Turk, "because he looked like one." [5] That Indian, born of some Plains tribe, became a new prophet of glory. Through signs, he told of a distant kingdom, ruled over by an emperor who slept under a tree festooned with golden bells. In a river six miles wide floated galleons with gold ornaments at the prows, and in the water swam fish bigger than horses. Gold and silver were so plentiful, claimed the Turk, that wagons would be needed to cart it all away. How many of these fabrications were his own and how many the Spaniards invented from his telling is impossible to say. The Pueblos had a hand in it also, for it seems that they encouraged the fellow to make such talk in the hope of drawing the troublesome white men out of their country.

From the beginning, Coronado's quest for mythical cities possessed all the trappings of a medieval adventure story. His band of knights in burnished armor needed only some monumental success to transmute legend into reality, and the Turk's golden kingdom on the prairies, which they were now calling

5. George Parker Winship, *The Coronado Expedition, 1540–1542,* Fourteenth Annual Report of the United States Bureau of Ethnology, Part 1 (1896; facsimile reprint edition, Chicago: Rio Grande Press, 1964), p. 216.

Quivira, seemed to fulfill the requirements and to promise a happy conclusion to the fable. The episode was to prove again that the more preposterous a tale, the more apt it is to be believed.

The following spring, Coronado set out for Quivira in a last bid to refurbish his tarnished star. Following directions of the Turk, he steered northeast across the Staked Plains of the Texas Panhandle and was brought at last to the end of the rainbow. In central Kansas, he discovered the grass houses of the Wichita Indians, and a chief who prized a copper plate worn about the neck because that was the only metal he had ever seen. This was the much-vaunted Quivira. The deceitful Turk was executed on the spot, and the dejected Spaniards, after erecting a cross to mark their farthest advance, retraced their steps to the Rio Grande.

In his own mind, Coronado now admitted failure. Some with spirit among the expedition favored continuing the search, and they asked permission to establish a settlement. Also, several of the friars expressed a wish to remain and begin missionary work. Coronado denied their requests, and, in April 1542, turned his party toward New Spain. Two of the clergy, nevertheless, overrode his authority and, with several Indian servants, elected to stay behind. They were never seen again.

In terms of its original goals, Coronado's march was a fizzle. He and his backers suffered financial loss, and the rigors of the trail broke both his spirit and his health. A cold reception by his patron, the viceroy, awaited him in Mexico City. And more. In September 1543, charges were raised against him, alleging abuse of the Tiguex Indians and contending that he passed up an opportunity to enlarge the realm by founding a settlement on the Rio Grande. Lengthy investigation by Mexico's high court acquitted Coronado of misconduct, but the verdict did little to restore his reputation.

Time has dealt with him more charitably. Seen in the perspective of centuries, his expedition stands as the grandest ever to invade the American West. Coronado expanded enormously the geographic knowledge of North America's heartland and first gave to the world some notion of the continent's interior vastness. His men were the first Europeans to view the Grand Canyon, the first to penetrate the interior of Puebloland, the first to recognize the Continental Divide, the first to cross the oceanic plains. Throughout a journey marked by unparalleled hardship and disillusionment, Coronado provided courageous leadership that alone brought his army intact back to Mexico. In spite of his mishandling the Indians and his failure to find gold, his record remains a remarkable one.

The career of Coronado and that of Hernando de Soto, who explored at the same time Florida and the lower Mississippi valley, have left an indelible, if sometimes negative, impression on American history. They served as models by which people, centuries later, came to judge all Spaniards. How many American schoolboys, for instance, have had the phrase "Spaniards lusting for gold" drummed into their heads? It is simple to say that the men of Spain lost all reason with the mention of gold, that the merest hint of a new bonanza was enough to send them skittering off to the wilderness on some bootless and harebrained enterprise. But like most stock images, that one distorts the truth. The fact is that the Spaniard was no more—or no less—prone to lose his wits over the search for treasure than was any other European. For what fairness can be found in condemning Spanish adventurers with one breath and, with the next, approving the mindless stampede of the forty-niners to California or the swarming of American prospectors into the Black Hills that had been granted by treaty to the Sioux?

The Coronado expedition is practically the only New Mexico episode to find its way into American history books. While its spectacular character and perennial interest cannot be denied, for the sake of balance, we should recall that that event was scarcely more than a brief prologue in the long story of Spanish activity on the Rio Grande.

Actually, the era of the gold-seeking conquistador, with all its smoke and thunder, was brief and transitory. Before a single English colonist had set foot on the mainland, conquest almost everywhere in New Spain had given way to productive settlement. Mexico City, by the 1570s, held a population of fifteen thousand, possessed refined public and private buildings, and supported a university that conferred degrees in law and theology. Other cities stretching toward the northern frontier flourished as important outposts of European civilization. The conquistadors, with all their foibles, were the men who made this possible.

The next chapter in New Mexico's story was added some forty years after Coronado marched home to disgrace, and it involved a flurry of four lesser expeditions. These are little known, but they are significant, for in their unfolding, more myths were dispelled. And, in their place, the notion arose that New Mexico was a country worth settling.

To reach Cíbola, Fray Marcos and Coronado had leapfrogged across some five hundred leagues of forlorn and desolate wilderness. They labeled one section in Arizona the *Despoblado,* the Uninhabited Place, because even the Indians shunned it. When no rich cities appeared at the end of the northern trail, Spaniards for a time became content to push ahead the frontier line above Mexico City in a more orderly fashion.

This is not to say that the lure of the north had altogether lost its magic. Enough unknown country stretched beyond Cíbola and Quivira to excite wonder and to lead the imagination to conjure up new mysteries. Most seductive was the belief in a continental passage, the Strait of Anian, giving access to the Pacific. For two hundred years, that vision charmed the Spaniards, until the true geography of North America was puzzled out and finally understood. During four decades, however, following Coronado's wayfaring, lands on the Rio Grande and beyond saw no horses or bearded knights. Interest in the Pueblo country and search for the strait had suddenly taken second place to more impelling events farther south.

In the year 1546, soldiers on an Indian campaign chanced upon a spectacular silver deposit at a place called Zacatecas, northwest of Mexico City. The strike brought a stampede of miners and prospectors to the frontier. Scouring the country in an ever-widening arc, determined men with picks made additional discoveries that allowed the creation of the new provinces of Nueva Vizcaya (modern Durango and Chihuahua), San Luis Potosí, and Nuevo León. The flow of metal created mining barons overnight and made the Mexican peso one of the most sought-after coins in the world. And it had another result, for it sparked a new interest in the lands seen by Coronado.

Some of the soldiers who had gone on that epic journey recalled in later years that the bare, rock-ribbed mountains flanking the Rio Grande resembled the sierras in the south that were now yielding up fortunes in silver. Was it not possible, and even likely, that those lands that had appeared so sterile and had turned out so disappointing in 1540 might actually be filled with riches? The enticing prospect was one to ponder and to build new dreams upon. By the 1580s at the latest, the idea had taken hold and had fathered a revival of the old hope of another Mexico. From that time forward, Spaniards referred to the vast northern interior as New Mexico, and the name clung, even when the country continued to prove a burying ground for visions of easy wealth.

Another force was at work, drawing attention northward, and it was one more potent than any inspired by fanciful silver mines or mythical straits. Bedded deep in the conscience of all Spaniards lay the conviction that their nation was chosen to convert the heathen of the New World. The source of that missionary impulse resided far back in Spanish history. During the Middle Ages, when Christian knights had struggled to free their Iberian homeland from the African Moors of Islamic faith, Spanish Catholicism had assumed a militant quality unparalleled in Europe. Priest and soldier worked in concert for centuries to achieve a common aim: drive the infidel back across the Strait of Gibraltar. The clergy raised money for the war effort, ministered to the spiritual needs of the soldier, and furnished him a noble reason for fighting.

In Spain, the man of the sword, profiting from that cooperation, became pre-eminently a crusader. The relationship continued when another theater of conquest opened in the New World. The triumph over Islam at home and the discovery of America confirmed Spaniards in the belief that the Almighty had found their performance pleasing and that He wished them to extend their mission to the pagan Indians in the wilderness.

That conceit bred an enormous self-confidence and fueled

superhuman efforts that allowed the Spaniard to explore and claim some of the world's most forbidding deserts, mountains, and jungles in the space of a few short decades. It also contributed to the formation of the most popular image of the Spaniard handed to us by history: that of the armored conquistador moving fearlessly into some howling wasteland, with a robed and sandal-shod padre striding humbly by his side. As far as New Mexico is concerned, at least in the early years, that image is not unsound.

It was in fact a Franciscan lay brother, not a prospector after silver nor an explorer questing for the Strait of Anian, who set off the chain of events that brought about the rediscovery and ultimately the colonization of the land of the Pueblos. His name was Fray Agustín Rodríguez, and, in 1580, he was saving souls among the Conchos Indians of southern Chihuahua near the outpost town of Santa Bárbara. Hearing stray reports of an advanced agricultural people who lived to the north, Fray Agustín perceived a splendid opportunity to expand the field of the church. He knew a little of Coronado's earlier exploration, but initially, it seems, he failed to connect it with the land he was now proposing to enter.

After receiving permission from the viceroy, the friar put together his expedition, comprised of two additional Franciscans, nine soldiers, and some nineteen Indian servants. The soldiers were volunteers, animated in some measure by a desire to carry out their ancient role as protectors and supporters of the clergy. But, as several of them had experience in prospecting, it is easy to guess that they intended to keep a sharp eye peeled for promising signs of minerals.

The party got off on June 5, 1581, pushed down the Conchos River to its junction with the Rio Grande, then ascended that stream to the villages of the Pueblo Indians in New Mexico. The friars were exuberant. The potential harvest of converts exceeded all expectations. Hernando Gallegos, a member of the escort, expressed a thoroughly favorable opinion of the Pueblo people. He saw them as clean, handsome, and industrious, and he felt that if interpreters had been available, some would have quickly become Christians.

The inquisitive band of Spaniards probed the secrets of this strange country, visiting Taos in the far north, the buffalo range beyond the Pecos River, and the western homes of the Acoma and Zuñi. One of the friars, Father Juan de Santa María, was so elated with what he saw that he set off alone to carry a report to Mexico. But the Pueblos, whose docility was more apparent than real, believed he was going to fetch more soldiers; warriors therefore followed his trail for three days and killed him. The mischief done by Coronado's men two decades before bore bitter fruit.

Francisco Sánchez Chamuscado, captain of the soldier contingent, decided they had dallied in that quarter long enough. Not so Fray Rodríguez and his remaining companion, Father Francisco López: they were not about to leave when before them loomed the kind of prospect every missionary dreamed of. They would stay and build a mission at the Tiguex pueblo of Puaray; the soldiers were free to go home.

Chamuscado died of a fever just a few leagues before reaching Santa Bárbara; but his men, including Hernando Gallegos, went on with news of what had been done. Of immediate concern was the safety of the two friars left in New Mexico. Frontiersmen spoke of a rescue, and they were encouraged by a certain Fray Bernardino Beltrán who wished to go and aid his fellow Franciscans.

A colonial merchant and man of circumstance, Antonio de Espejo, agreed to finance and lead an expedition. After recruiting fourteen soldiers, he and Fray Bernardino set a course for the Rio Grande in November of 1582. They were too late. The friars at Puaray had been slain, evidently soon after their escort left. At that discovery, Espejo showed his larger motive: he was interested in a rumored lake of gold and in mines hinted at by the Indians. Brushing aside complaints from Fray Bernardino, he went pelting off into the tablelands west of the Rio Grande. The golden lake was a phantom; but, casting a wider loop than had any Spaniard before him, Espejo uncovered, near modern Prescott in central Arizona, outcroppings of copper that displayed a little silver. In his own mind and in later writings, he magnified the importance of his find enormously. Returning to the Rio Grande, he encountered hostility among the Indians at Puaray, so he sacked the pueblo and executed sixteen captives. The people of Tiguex were learning again what it meant to oppose the reckless Spaniards.

Espejo's exaggerated recital of New Mexico's potential richness, given upon his arrival home, stirred up sleeping dogs left lying since Coronado had punctured the myths of the seven cities and Quivira. Plenty of stout souls were still willing to risk their necks for a chance at fortune. But the matter rested with the king, and his pious majesty, who saw himself as the supreme crusader, cared more for extending the dominion of the church than in listening to embellished tales of treasure. It was the large number and quality of the Pueblo Indians that titillated his interest. That consideration led him to issue a royal decree (dated Madrid, April 19, 1583) directing the viceroy of New Spain to arrange a contract with some responsible citizen to go, at his own expense, to settle and pacify the land now known as New Mexico and to see to the conversion of the native people. After much scrambling among a legion of contenders, the prize finally went to Juan de Oñate of Zacatecas.

During the years when the Spanish bureaucracy was shuffling papers and moving at a snail's pace toward the appointment of Oñate, two wholly unauthorized expeditions left for New Mexico. The first was led by Castaño de Sosa, the second by Leyva de Bonilla. While their influence on history was slight, they do illuminate the workings of a new Spanish law that governed exploration and conduct toward the Indians.

In the interval since Coronado and de Soto had marched to conquer, the entire concept of conquest had been called into question and was found wanting in morality. As a consequence, His Spanish Majesty had issued a set of Royal Ordinances in 1573, outlawing the use of violence in dealing with the Indians, except in a few specified cases, such as when they offered submission and then later rebelled. The measure set strict standards of conduct for soldiers, colonists, and friars, and bade them use gentleness and persuasion with the native people. The repugnant term *conquest,* which seemed to give license to strong-arm tactics, was now replaced by *pacification.* The juggling of words was more than an idle formality designed to appease Spain's critics. It meant that the king firmly intended to protect his Indian subjects.

Proclaiming worthy laws in Madrid was one thing; enforcing them under the stern realities of life on a far frontier was another. And the crown knew it.

So it added a key feature to the Ordinances in hopes of insuring their observance. In the future, no Spaniard would be allowed to undertake discovery and settlement of new lands on his own responsibility. Such enterprises, vital to the affairs of empire and church, could only proceed under strictest supervision and with personal authorization of the king. The viceroy might review qualifications of those interested in leading expeditions, might make a preliminary selection and draft a contract defining privileges and restrictions under which they were to operate. But the final decision in all these matters remained that of the sovereign. If only men of proven loyalty and high quality received admission to the frontier—and they were bound by tight laws—the king reasoned that expansion of his New World realm could advance at a more serene pace and that maltreatment of the Indians would abate.

The idea was noble, if unrealistic. Certainly it left no room for bold individualists to go their own way. Pioneers in English America would have found such restrictions not only meddlesome but intolerable. Spaniards, on the other hand, viewed the ordinances with the same reverence they attached to all the king's commands. Outwardly, at least, most tried to conform. The few who did not paid for their folly.

A fraudulent silver assay and the first wagon train to cross a portion of what is now the United States figured in a testing of the Royal Ordinances during the years 1590–1591. Gaspar Castaño de Sosa, lieutenant-governor of Nuevo León in northeastern New Spain, was the man who stirred up the tempest, when he decided on his own initiative to settle New Mexico.

Ruling Nuevo León in the absence of a governor, this ambitious and restive Spaniard looked about for some way to carve a name for himself. The small silver-mining town of Almadén, where he maintained his headquarters, offered slim prospects.

The original strike had burned itself out in a matter of months, and the residents were left almost destitute. All goods had to be carried in on muleback over rough trails, and few could afford their exorbitant cost. Almadén was a place without a future. Not so New Mexico. Every man of the frontier, Castaño de Sosa included, knew that there lay the next utopia whose mountains and mesas offered certain reward. Why not pack up the people of Almadén—men, women, and children, numbering some 170 souls—and break for that shining land? The plan, in its sheer audacity, was a novel one. In aim, it foreshadowed the movement of countless American pioneers who, in later centuries, would leave home to seek more fertile pastures.

Unfortunately, there was a hitch. The law of 1573 stood in the way. Could it be circumvented?

At that very moment, Oñate and other influential men were petitioning the crown for permission to invade and pacify the northland, as Castaño de Sosa was probably aware. No matter. He would ride out anyway, and as justification for his action, he settled upon a technicality. New Mexico was not a new country waiting to be discovered. Coronado, Fray Agustín, and Espejo had explored it and made effective Spain's claim. So his colony would go forth, pretending confusion, because rules in the Ordinances referred to ''new discoveries.''

It was a shaky point, the lieutenant-governor well understood, since prevailing law prohibited travel anywhere without official sanction. Therefore, to show conformity with the law, he would request permission of the viceroy, but only after measuring a good start on the trail. A bold push might carry the project through. If it succeeded and he colonized New Mexico, his superiors would likely accept the fact and give grudging endorsement. At least that was his hope.

Another problem arose, less formidable than the legal one, but more immediate. Some of the Almadén people, whether out of fear of the unknown or from mere inertia, failed to warm to the idea of migration. Resourceful Castaño de Sosa, with the cleverness of a magician, produced some Indians from the north who happened to be toting a load of rock threaded with gleaming metal. He made an assay, attended by much hullabaloo, and before it was finished, he slipped a silver mug into the pot, without anyone being the wiser. The upshot of his little deceit was predictable. At the completion of the assay—when a small, rough ingot of silver passed from hand to hand—the majority raised a clamor to be off at once. For the benefit of a tiny handful who still held back, the leader announced airily that any man not joining would be executed as a traitor to the king. In the end, all tagged along. So once more the celestial vision of a treasured kingdom furnished grist for another installment in the early history of New Mexico.

The struggling colonists from Nuevo León cast themselves adrift without a map, much less a road over which to roll their ten wagons and carts. Castaño de Sosa knew vaguely of the Pecos River, and he guessed its valley might offer a convenient avenue to their destination. He directed his path across the thorny shrub and cactus flats of south Texas, where the hard and pebbly soil wore out twenty-five dozen horseshoes in a matter of days.

Plagued with thirst, the Spaniards reached the Pecos to find its waters pregnant with bitter alkaline salts, but the valley opened above them through diminutive forests of greasewood and pointed the way they wished to travel. When the terraced walls of Pecos Pueblo at last rose to view, on December 30, 1590, they had been on the trail for five months, an epic trek accomplished with nerve and daring. Scarcely known today, their journey marked the first passage of wagons upon ground destined to become part of the American nation. Though the people spoke Spanish and moved north instead of west, they deserve credit as forerunners of that tidal wave of settlers in prairie schooners who would one day pour across trails of the Far West.

For the next two and a half months, Castaño de Sosa wandered among the Pueblos along the Rio Grande. He exacted promises of obedience to God and king and conducted himself with restraint, just as the Royal Ordinances demanded. Some of his followers, who had never developed much heart for the undertaking, became disquieted and began to whisper of mutiny. Their poking about in the mountains revealed no silver mines, and nothing else in that desolate region excited their interest.

When the sword fell, however, it was not from within. Out of the south, a troop of fifty soldiers suddenly appeared, bearing an order of arrest issued by the king and the viceroy. Flinty Castaño de Sosa accepted the document, placed it over his head in token of submission, and with supreme dignity received the iron fetters that he was to wear back to Mexico City. Like others before him, he had gambled on the reputed riches of New Mexico and lost.

A second incident offers more evidence of the Spanish government's hostility toward illegal expeditions. Not long after the Castaño de Sosa episode, a Captain Francisco Leyva de Bonilla led his troop of soldiers against renegade Indians who were attacking cattle ranches along the Nueva Vizcayan frontier. The campaign stretched into weeks and carried the men farther north than they had ever been before. Almost before they were aware of it, the lower reaches of New Mexico opened ahead of them. The pull of opportunity proved overpowering. Without any shadow of authority, Captain Leyva announced his intention to continue on to the Rio Grande. If anything worthwhile lay hidden there, he would find it.

The venture carried the small party of Spaniards and their Indian servants north to the pueblo of San Ildefonso, above the site of Santa Fe. There they remained for a year, parts of 1593 and 1594, living off the local people. When the Indians' patience wore thin, they dredged up the shopworn, but still useful, tales of populous kingdoms tucked away on the outer margin of the Buffalo Plains. Captain Leyva and his men left in a cloud of dust kicked up by their horses. And they did not return.

Years later, one of the native servants, Jusepe, found Oñate on the Rio Grande and related the terrible sequel. The little company had gone east to a great settlement, probably the same seen by Coronado in Kansas, where one of the soldiers, Antonio Gutiérrez de Humaña, quarreled with Leyva and killed him. Afterward, Indians overran the camp, and Jusepe, escaping, fled toward New Mexico, where he was picked up by roving Apaches. His information allowed the Spaniards to close the books on Captain Leyva, whose misdeed had provoked an order for his apprehension. The king remained unyielding: exploration was far too important to be left to law-breakers and soldiers-of-fortune.

Spaniards had now entered New Mexico on at least six distinct occasions. None of them stayed and settled, for the moment was not right, and all their comings and goings scarcely left a trace on the sprawling land. Then, in the bench-mark year of 1598, matters took a different turn.

Don Juan de Oñate, governor and *adelantado,* came with horsemen, livestock, and families in wagons. His caravan was attended by the rumbling, rattling, bawling, thumping medley of sounds that betray homeseekers on the wilderness roads of every new frontier. These reverberations spelled the beginning of change for New Mexico and the end of somnolent days in which the Pueblo Indians had lived and worked in perfect independence. For them, the time when centuries were allowed to drift evenly by, one almost indistinguishable from another, was definitely over.

About Juan de Oñate, founder of New Mexico, certain facts are plain. He was born in 1552, in the mining town of Zacatecas, which his father, a Basque, had helped establish six years before. Juan and his brother Cristóbal were twins, the latter named for their sire. The pair grew to manhood enjoying the advantages and prestige that came with being sons of a silver baron. But they shared in the hard knocks that were the lot of every youth weaned on the savage frontier beyond Mexico City.

Early in his teens, Juan de Oñate went as a soldier with the viceroy of New Spain to wage war against the ferocious Chichimecs of the north, who skinned Spaniards alive and left their bodies hanging along the roadways. For twenty years he fought them, becoming a seasoned campaigner; and, as head of his own expeditions, he won extensive new lands for the royal domain.

Juan married Isabel Cortez Tolosa, daughter of a mine owner and descendant, on her mother's side, of Fernando Cortez. By her, he had two children. When Isabel died prematurely, in the late 1580s, the husband was overcome with grief, and friends, in the following years, claimed that his loss caused him to begin looking toward New Mexico as a place to forget his troubles.

These spare details we have. What is missing is the essence of the man—knowledge of his thinking and mood, understanding of the full scope of his motives. Even his physical appearance eludes us; we know only that, at the time of going north, he had reached his late forties and wore a beard, threaded with gray and neatly trimmed. No portrait survives of Oñate, nor indeed for any figure prominent in the affairs of New Mexico during that period—with a single exception.

Gaspar Pérez de Villagrá, one of Oñate's lieutenants and a most vocal supporter, published in Spain, in 1610, a volume entitled *A History of New Mexico*. In epic verse, it recounts the dry and miserable march of the settlers northward, the planting of a settlement above Santa Fe at San Gabriel, and the week-by-week existence of the colony's first troubled months. As literature, it lacks distinction, but as the personal record of a crucial period in New Mexico history, the work stands unique. Furthermore, its printing came ten years before the landing of the Pilgrims and fourteen years before publication of Captain John Smith's much-quoted history of Virginia.

From a heavy-lined woodcut, which serves as a frontispiece, stares forth Pérez de Villagrá, bearded, his balding head framed by one of the outsized fluted collars of the day. The austerity, the inner toughness, the dignity, and the natural grace so often attributed to Spaniards radiate from this simple portrait. It leads us to believe that something of the same qualities must have been apparent in the features of Juan de Oñate. What is known of his career in New Mexico confirms the suspicion.

The whole venture started badly. For three years—from 1595, when he began putting the pieces together, until his departure for New Mexico early in 1598—Oñate did battle with the ponderous bureaucracy that wanted each detail spelled out in advance. And at every turn, he had to fend off envious rivals who hoped to discredit him and grab the honors that went with the founding of a new province.

In the end, his perseverance won through. The viceroy and the king approved, after some modifications, the contract he had submitted. The most telling points were these: Oñate himself was to bear practically the entire expense of the project, including recruiting and equipping two hundred soldiers and their families, the assembling of livestock, and the purchase of supplies needed to build new homes on the Rio Grande. For his part, the

king granted Oñate titles of governor, *adelantado* (purely hon-
orific), and captain-general of New Mexico; a salary of six
thousand ducats yearly; and the right to distribute land and Indian tribute to his followers. Since the main purpose of this occupation, at least in the eyes of the crown, was to pacify and
Christianize the Indians, the royal treasury stood the cost of five
missionaries and a lay brother.

Oñate received a set of instructions reminding him that the
work of the Church had first claim on his attention. Pointed
mention was made of the Ordinances of 1573, and a curious
requirement was included, directing that a survey of New Mexico's coastline and harbors be made. Everyone assumed that
once this new bastion of settlement was installed at the core of
the continent, the elusive Strait of Anian would providentially
turn up. While all these considerations weighed on Governor
Oñate, they failed to keep him from considering his own profit
and glory. Into his personal stock of supplies went heavy mining tools and forges, bellows, and crucibles for smelting—just
in case New Mexico yielded any silver.

After six months on the long trail from the south, Oñate's
cavalcade lumbered into the shelter of the Tewa pueblo of San
Juan, astride the Rio Grande. Thirst and hunger and vast dis-
couragement had worn the colonists ragged. Only constant
prayer, much kneeling at open-air Masses, and the unbounded
energy of the governor brought them through. But here was a fit
place to build a capital.

San Juan stood in the midst of a narrow though fertile valley
near the Chama River's junction with the Rio Grande. East and
west, lofty peaks marched in line across the horizon; one of
them, Tsicomo, served as a sacred shrine for all the Tewa people. Reports of the Castaño de Sosa expedition had mentioned
the hospitality of the residents of San Juan (in contrast to the Indians of Tiguex farther south, who had learned to despise the
Spaniards) and the abundant surpluses of corn their irrigated
fields produced. Oñate desperately needed friendship and food
to face the coming winter.

Amiable relations were established almost at once. The San
Juans lived up to their reputation, even offering to share their

homes with the newcomers—at least that is Captain Villagrá's testimony. One of the friars remarked that they were the best infidel people he had ever seen.

In the short space of two weeks, the Spaniards hastily threw up a church, large enough to contain every member of the colony. Their original intention was to construct a town adjacent to the pueblo, which they had come to call San Juan de los Caballeros. Within a few months, that plan was abandoned. Oñate ordered everyone to remove to the west bank of the Rio Grande, where there was more room to expand. On a low hill some three harquebus shots above the Chama, they began work on the villa of San Gabriel, New Mexico's first capital.

The frustrations Oñate experienced in his decade as governor were all foreshadowed by a series of unnerving events during the initial months of occupation. Division in his ranks brought the first trouble.

More than he would have admitted, the governor was banking on some spectacular mineral discovery early in the game to give his men and his own hopes a needed lift. Almost at once he began visiting the shadowy corners of the province to obtain the allegiance of outlying pueblos and to search for ore-bearing rock. But his prospecting merely confirmed what others before him had already found out. New Mexico was not Zacatecas.

The small grain of enthusiasm that had survived the rigorous journey to the new country rapidly waned. Some men plotted mutiny; four others stole valuable horses and scurried south toward Santa Bárbara. Pérez de Villagrá pursued the deserters, caught two, and returned to San Juan with the gloomy tidings that he had beheaded them on the trail.

Then a greater disaster broke: massacre and retribution, the frontier's twin scourges. Though it pulled the colonists together, weeks passed when survival of the tiny Spanish enclave by the Rio Grande appeared in doubt.

It started innocently enough in the late fall of 1598. Oñate took a squad of soldiers and rode southeast to survey a group of pueblos situated near some salt lakes beyond the Manzano Mountains. From there he decided to go directly west and find the seacoast, assuming that it lay within easy march. He sent a messenger to Juan de Zaldívar, his nephew and second-in-command, with orders to collect reinforcements and catch up with him on the trail. With luck, they would meet somewhere near Zuñi.

Young Zaldívar never made it. His party camped one evening at the foot of the great rock upon which Acoma Pueblo perched. Here dwelled some of the most independent-minded and openly hostile Indians in New Mexico. A military strategist would have judged their sky village to be the stoutest native stronghold in North America. On all sides, sheer walls rose abruptly hundreds of feet above the surrounding plain. Steep and narrow trails, at places mere toe holds pecked out of the rosy sandstone, provided the only way to the top. Above, on the flat surface, a fortified pueblo offered another perimeter of defense. Certainly the Acomas felt safe, else they would never have taken measures— which, through hindsight, appear foolhardy—to oppose the Spaniards.

Zaldívar and some of his men were lured to the summit, and a horde of painted and befeathered warriors fell upon them. One after another, the sword-swinging Spaniards went down, until the few who remained were driven to the edge of the cliff. There was no choice; they jumped. Twenty-year-old Pedro Robledo smashed against the rocky wall, his body tumbling to the base like a broken doll. Three other soldiers landed in sand dunes swept up by winds against the foot of the mesa. They were gathered up, dazed, by members of the horse guard who had remained below.

Oñate got the news as he was moving slowly over the trail west of Acoma. His nephew and ten of the men dead. Several more injured. The Acomas in revolt. Other pueblos showing hostility as word spread. The colony teetering on the brink of catastrophe.

When Pérez de Villagrá wrote later in his *History* that no men have ever yet been able to count upon good fortune and a lucky fate to order their affairs, he expressed a truism familiar to all Spaniards. For them, personal valor and a strong faith, demanding direct confrontation with problems, were the hallmarks of manhood. Trusting in chance or in the healing salve of time to

resolve matters was not their way. That course only served
weaklings.

And Juan de Oñate was no weakling, although persons unaccustomed to the behavior of Spaniards might have judged him
so, if they had seen him pass that first night, after receiving the
tragic news from Acoma, alone in his tent weeping and praying
before a cross. Yet the succeeding weeks left no doubt of the
man's nerve or of his determination to hold the colonists
together.

From his camp in the west, the governor beat a hasty path
back to San Juan under a leaden December sky, arriving a few
days before Christmas. The next weeks passed in feverish activity as war councils hummed and arms were readied with much
clanking and polishing. Every Indian in New Mexico watched
and waited to see what the Spaniards would do.

Oñate wanted to head the attack against Acoma himself, but
on that, every soldier in the company voted against him. In the
event that something went awry, he would be needed at home to
take the surviving colonists out of New Mexico. Hence, leadership passed to Vicente de Zaldívar, younger brother of the slain
Juan.

In mid-January, seventy men, with weapons glinting in the
winter's sunlight, departed for Acoma like a medieval army
bent on a crusade. Of the monumental battle that took place—
Spaniards scaling the walls in brutal assault; Indians pelting
them with a hail of arrows and stones; the sheer blind courage
of attacker and defender locked arm in arm in combat; the firing
of the pueblo and appalling slaughter of its inhabitants—of all
this on that battle-seared promontory, scarcely an American
today knows a single detail. The Spaniards had their victory,
but it was a heartbreaking day for humankind.

Oñate rejoiced, not so much in the ruination of a people and
their home but in the salvation of his colony, for the terrible fate
of Acoma effectively cooled the passion for war in other pueblos. But he meant to nail down the message with one last
hammer-blow. Vicente de Zaldívar had returned to the Rio
Grande, triumphant, leading a pathetic string of captives.
Hundreds of Acomas were dead, but the governor still intended

to hold these survivors accountable for the massacre of his nephew and his men. After a lopsided trial, conducted in mid-February 1599, Oñate handed down the sentences. Perhaps through clemency, he condemned no warrior to death. Yet the punishment was so harsh that almost four hundred years after the fact, it still strikes us with horror: men over twenty-five to have one foot cut off and to spend twenty years in personal servitude; young men between the ages of twelve and twenty-five, twenty years of personal servitude; women over twelve, twenty years of personal servitude; sixty young girls to be sent to Mexico City for service in convents, never to see their homeland again; and two Hopi taken at Acoma to have the right hand cut off and to be set free so they might convey to their people news of the retribution.

It would be pleasant to relate that, after the misfortunes of that first winter, Juan de Oñate got a firm grip on matters and was able to construct a solid foundation for the New Mexican colony. But such was not the case. In spite of his dedicated effort, the project slowly fell apart.

From the viceroy, Oñate was obliged to request military reinforcements, since, after Acoma, he dared not go on lengthy expeditions without a strong garrison to leave behind and defend San Gabriel. The plea for aid in itself alerted the crown that all was not going well on the Rio Grande. Red tape promoted the inevitable delays, so that the new contingent of soldiers, along with much-needed supplies and six additional friars, did not reach the capital until Christmas Eve, 1600. Thus strengthened, the governor was ready to resume the search for those things needed to give stability and glory to his frontier government: mines, the Strait of Anian, harbors on the South Sea.

First he looked toward Quivira as offering the greatest promise. He possessed a competent guide in Jusepe, the Indian who appeared from the plains with information on the fate of the Leyva de Bonilla party. But though the governor led eighty men down the Canadian River, across Oklahoma, and explored the gilded land of Quivira, like Coronado, he found nothing to stir the imagination or lend foundation to wispy legend.

Returning to his struggling settlement, Oñate received a

crushing blow. San Gabriel was practically deserted. The majority of colonists, soldiers, and friars, sick to death from disappointments and angered by the governor's strict rule, had taken advantage of his five-month absence and had gone back to New Spain. Many of the men had been aristocrats, living in comfortable circumstances before coming to New Mexico; and when heaven failed to drop immediate riches in their laps, they grew fussy and lost interest in the bleak little colony. Defection of the friars was the result of dissatisfaction with Oñate's oftentimes stern policies toward the Indians. Yet they themselves had displayed a lack of zeal, staying at San Gabriel and offering excuses for not going to assignments at remote mission stations. They had emerged, in fact, as the ringleaders in the movement to abandon the province.

In face of this new setback, the governor stubbornly clung to the hope that, with the few loyal people remaining to him, he could somehow put things back together. While he sent Vicente de Zaldívar to Mexico and then to Spain in an effort to raise new money and recruits, the governor attempted one last search for the Golden Fleece. In the fall of 1604, he picked up the trail westward to the South Sea, the route he had been forced to quit in mid-stride at the time of the Acoma trouble. Even some small success might disperse the cloud gathering over his name, for he knew that the deserters, upon reaching New Spain, had accused him of incompetence and mismanagement.

With thirty men, less than half his Quivira expedition, Oñate struck across the heart of Arizona by way of the Hopi villages. He encountered the Colorado River and followed it to the head of the Gulf of California. Then he scouted about in a futile attempt to find rumored pearl fisheries. He listened to Indians who beguiled him with tales of a tribe of unipeds, of giant Amazons, and of people who slept under water. And he finally reckoned that nothing existed in these parts that could possibly benefit his province of New Mexico. Even the sea was too far away to be of any use. With this final throw of the dice, his last pinch of optimism faded.

New Mexico had become a millstone around Oñate's neck. Gold and silver deposits, if he had but known it, lay within reach—in Colorado, in Arizona, in Nevada, and even in New Mexico. But he, and every Spaniard before and after him, missed them; the vast riches kept their secret safe until American prospectors broke open the vault in the late nineteenth century.

Had the Spaniards experienced a gold rush or silver boom anywhere along the frontier, a flood of miners and settlers might have raised a permanent center of Hispanic civilization that would have changed the course of history in western America. Oñate, when that seemed a real possibility in the beginning, had entertained visions of a new northern viceroyalty, with himself at the head, which would spread over the upper continent and guard the approaches to the Strait of Anian, when that marvel should be found. But none of that was to be. That fate, in which Captain Villagrá put so little stock, blasted Oñate's dream and marked his efforts a failure.

Yet not entirely. For he fathered a province that lived long after Oñate and his heirs were dust. And if it failed to flower as a viceroyalty, at least New Mexico matured to become the main anchor of Spanish power along a fifteen-hundred-mile frontier. Could the first governor have returned two centuries later, to view the thirty thousand inhabitants distributed in towns, villages, and ranches, with their homes and fields, herds and flocks, all supported by a chain of missions, he would have seen that his years of misery and privation had not been wasted. It has always been in the nature of things that some men build so that others may reap the benefit.

In 1607, the same year that Englishmen laid the foundations of Jamestown, the Spanish crown suspended Oñate from office. The king flirted briefly with the idea of withdrawing the colonists and giving up the sickly outpost in Puebloland. Before such a drastic step could be taken, an encouraging report came from Franciscan friars who had gone out to replace the faint-hearted deserters. The Indians were beginning to respond, and eight thousand converts could already be counted. In view of that, it was unthinkable that the king, committed to spreading the faith, should abandon New Mexico. Instead, he made provision for taking the province under royal patronage, meaning that he, or the viceroy of New Spain, would, in the future, appoint succeeding governors, to serve a term of four years, and that all of the province's expenses—civil and religious alike—would be borne by the treasury. The period of flamboyant treasure-seekers and empire-builders ended with this announcement of New Mexico's new status.

Early in 1610, Oñate's successor as governor arrived on the upper Rio Grande. Don Pedro de Peralta carried not only his appointment to office but an order directing removal of the colonists from San Gabriel to some better location. It is probable that the viceroy had decided that Oñate's settlement lay too close to San Juan and infringed upon the croplands of the Indians. Or he may have been aware that, in the event of hostilities, its exposed and vulnerable position posed a serious danger to the Spaniards.

As near as investigation can determine, Governor Peralta inaugurated construction of the new *villa* of Santa Fe in the late spring of 1610. The name? Peralta may have called his capital after the city of Santa Fe in Spain, built on the Roman grid plan by Ferdinand and Isabella and designated as the prototype for New World municipalities. Or he may have simply got the idea from his formal instructions, which commanded him to extend the *Santa Fe,* the Holy Faith, among the Indians.

The site was a congenial one: high, above seven thousand feet, on the banks of a narrow stream that flowed from the towering Sangre de Cristos and disappeared in a southwesterly direction toward the Rio Grande. Best of all, the handsome little valley was unclaimed by any Indian pueblo, although a scattering of low dirt mounds indicated that the native people had once lived and farmed there.

Peralta and the first members of an elected town council, the *cabildo*, superintended the marking of municipal boundaries, the assignment of house and garden lots to citizens, and the selection of space for a plaza and for official government buildings. Throughout all this activity prevailed a feeling of permanence and solidity that had been lacking in the establishment of San Gabriel. The Spaniards pegged their claim to their new ground, and now, they meant to build for the future.

2

The Pueblos

IF any people belong completely to New Mexico—and New Mexico to them—it has to be the Pueblo Indians. They occupied this tawny land for a thousand years or more, and they still occupy it. Everyone else, by comparison, is a Johnny-come-lately, even the nomad Apache and Navajo who reached the Southwest not long before the Spaniards.

Archeologists, beginning with Adolph Bandelier in the 1880s, have pried open an uncountable number of ruins belonging to the Pueblos' ancestors, the Anasazi, and, in their digging, have laid bare a long and fascinating record of human activity in the Southwest. The story revealed by tumbled walls, stone tools, and fragments of pottery is, of course, a partial one. But some gaps can be filled by consulting accounts of early Spanish chroniclers, who often commented at length on Indian ways, and by reference to modern studies of anthropologists whose work describes ritual patterns and social customs little changed by the centuries.

To most New Mexicans today, the Pueblo Indian is a person who peddles his handicrafts on the old plazas at Santa Fe and Albuquerque, or one who dances with feathers and rattles at appointed times of the year. He is rarely seen in any depth as a representative of a rich and honored culture that has flourished and suffered on these same deserts and mesas since before the time European crusaders marched to Jerusalem.

Such want of knowledge sometimes produces curious incidents. One is the case of a young surgeon in an Albuquerque
hospital who asked an Indian nurse to help him communicate
with a patient who spoke no English.

"Sorry. I can't help you," she told him. "That man is a
Navajo, and I am a Pueblo."

And the doctor's puzzled reply?

"But you both speak 'Indian,' don't you?"

His misconception—absurd in that there are better than five
hundred different Indian languages in North America—is more
widely held than it should be. For benighted innocence, it must
rank alongside the popular belief, shared by a surprising number
of Americans from the East, that a person needs a passport to
enter New Mexico.

The fact is that no Pueblo Indian can communicate with a
Navajo or an Apache, both of whom speak Athabascan; nor can
they understand the Ute of New Mexico's northern border,
whose language is Shoshonean. There is not even a tongue common to all the Pueblo. Each village falls into one of four distinct
linguistic groups: Keresan, concentrated in the area north of
Bernalillo and including the western Laguna and Acoma;
Zuñian, an enclave south of Gallup; Shoshonean, of a dialect
different from the Utes, spoken by the Hopi of northern Arizona; and Tanoan, whose speakers extend from Taos south to
Isleta and include the people of Jemez. For members of one
group, the speech of any other remains unintelligible.

That situation calls attention to another point of confusion.
The term *Pueblo* refers not to a single tribe but to a group of
people who share a common culture and follow a similar way of
life in which all are tillers of the soil. To the first Spaniards, the
five- and six-story, terraced dwellings of these Indians made the
sharpest impression. Incredible apartments they were, unlike
anything the newcomers had encountered before in America.
With simple logic, they therefore lumped all the native urbanites
together, even while recognizing linguistic differences, and
called them *Pueblos,* meaning "Townsmen." Each village they
called a *pueblo.* Today, the stepped buildings are gone, except
at Taos and a few other places where remnants survive. Even

so, the Indians are still "Townsmen," though they may live in scattered, single-family units—mobile homes, for instance, or houses built by the government.

It is doubtful whether any white man has ever comprehended the full scope of Pueblo belief and thought. Such understanding rests upon knowledge of the inner workings of religion, which pervades and dominates all aspects of Pueblo life. And the Indians, through four hundred years of bitter experience, have learned to resist intrusion into that sacred area. Piecing together fragments provided by historian and anthropologist allows us to say something that is general and true, so far as it goes, about Pueblo habits and capacities of mind. It does not permit those deeper insights necessary for authentic sympathy and accurate judgment.

Sixteenth-century Spanish chroniclers were the first to draw a picture of the Pueblo mode of life. Like most men, they were quick to note the obvious, to single out the strange for special mention, and to interpret all in light of their own experience. For example, these swaggering soldiers, a scant two generations removed from the Moorish wars in Spain, first looked at the Pueblos as if they were related to the infidels defeated by their forefathers in the Old Country. Their descriptions frequently compared Pueblo practices with those of the Moors and, incredibly, *mosque* was the word that they initially attached to the Indian ceremonial chamber that we now term a *kiva*.

Since what we get from these chroniclers is all one-sided—information filtered through their own prejudices and preconceptions—it cannot be accepted as completely trustworthy. Yet because they were curious and were much given to writing in detail to the viceroy or to the king, their words provide a valuable glimpse of the externals of Pueblo life as seen by the first Europeans.

In 1540, Coronado's men found some seventy or more rock-and-mud villages scattered over northern New Mexico and extending westward in an irregular line to the outlying pueblos of the Hopi. Most of the communities were centered on one or more square plazas, with terraced apartments rising on each side. Well-built, whitewashed, and clean, they evoked wonder and admiration in the Spaniards. Interior walls bore painted designs and murals of a religious character on their whitened surfaces. Each plaza held two ceremonial rooms, partially underground, with entry provided by a ladder through the roof. In addition to their religious function, these rooms, or kivas, also served as lodging for visitors. Two other features distinguished the pueblos: large turkey pens—one for each family—capable of holding a hundred birds; and dog houses, constructed below ground level, to shelter the peculiar shaggy canines of the Indians.

Scarcely less telling than the architecture were Pueblo handicrafts, which the Spaniards compared favorably to those seen among the Aztecs. Skilled potters created artistic masterpieces of painted bowls, water jars, and ladles. Jewelers produced magnificent necklaces and inlaid pendants of shell and turquoise. Weavers used native cotton, as well as fibers from wild plants, to manufacture blankets, shirts, belts, and skirts, some of which were embellished with colored embroidery. Leatherworkers turned out sturdy moccasins with hard soles of buffalo hide and uppers of finely tanned buckskin. Over and over, Spanish writers emphasized that the people wore clothes and shoes, a trait which, in their view, showed them to be superior to other Indians met in northern New Spain.

Agriculture was the mainstay of the Pueblo economy, and the Spaniards said that, for the Indians, corn was God. Corn or Indian maize was the only native grain. It formed the principal crop, supplemented by plots of beans, squashes, melons, cotton, and tobacco. In good years, pueblo roofs were weighted with drying produce. The surplus went into tightly sealed interior rooms or into storage cists under the floors, where it might lie secure up to six or seven years until needed in time of famine.

Some of the western Pueblos, and those on the eastern slope of the Manzano Mountains, managed to get by with dry farming, but the majority of villagers employed flood-farming techniques or developed extensive irrigation systems. Where ditches and small dams were used to get water from rivers and streams into planted fields, the work became a community project, requiring the entire labor force of the pueblo.

Hunting and the gathering of wild vegetable products contributed to Pueblo foodstuffs. Seasonally, parties traveled to the plains to hunt buffalo, returning with dried or "jerked" meat and hides. At least seventy different plants growing nearby provided not only food but medicines and dyes. Saline lakes in the Estancia Valley and south of Zuñi offered a ready source of salt. Through their own industry in farming and by taking advantage of nature's bounty, the Pueblo Indians managed to present a picture of prosperity at the opening of the historic period.

The large number of scattered villages, averaging no more than several hundred people in each, suggests that the Indians had mastered an important principle. They must have learned that restricting population density prevented an overtaxing of natural resources. Soil depletion was always a threat; to combat it, the Indians dispersed people and communities and rotated their crops, fertilizing them with human waste and possibly turkey dung. In those locations where flood-farming was practiced, river silt served to replenish the fields.

At the time of the Spanish conquest, each pueblo, surrounded by its farmlands, composed an autonomous political unit. No shadow of any league or confederacy existed to tie even villages of the same language together. Community independence was jealously guarded, and frequent instances arose of open conflict between towns. In spite of the enduring myth that portrays the Pueblos as meek and unwarlike, they were as quick to take up bow and club as any other people, when outraged or offended. They performed war and scalp dances and undertook devastating raids, which sixteenth-century Spanish records indicate were most often directed against their neighbors. The defensive nature of Pueblo architecture, it seems, was first developed as a protection against their own kind rather than nomad Apaches.

Religion formed the core of Pueblo life and molded its distinctive configuration. The entire fabric of social, economic, and political activity within each village was stitched together by a common religious thread. The Indians saw the cosmos as personal and humanlike, a place where spiritual forces took an active interest in and ruled over the material world. Supernatural sanctions governed a strict moral order, providing rules for proper conduct and defining what was good in life. Elaborate ritual, filled with color and suffused with reverence for holy powers, expressed in dance and song the people's aspirations for universal harmony and life-giving rain.

Such government as the Pueblos had was strongly theocratic. The native priesthood directed all phases of village life, acting through clans, or in some cases, through medicine societies. Many of the pueblos had a head priest or chief, who governed with the aid of a council of lesser religious officers; others, notably the Tewa, possessed dual chiefs, equal in authority, who ruled alternately during the summer and winter seasons.

One of the most conspicuous phases of ceremonialism involved activities of the *Katcina* (or *Kachina*) cult. The Katcinas, ancestral spirits who brought moisture and good health, were impersonated by costumed and masked men. Upon arrival of the Spaniards, dances of the cult were openly performed in the village plaza. The use of masks, however, so repelled the newcomers, who saw them as manifestations of devil worship, that the entire cult at once became an object of persecution. In a literal sense, the Katcina rites were driven underground, where they are performed in secret to this day.

The picture of Pueblo society, as given by Coronado and the men who followed him, can never be enlarged to show what the Pueblo people were really like, how they felt, and how their small, isolated world looked to them. The Spanish chroniclers had little talent for catching the subtleties that might have provided authentic clues to the Indians' inner life. They could generalize about what they saw, then praise or condemn, but they could not grasp and record the fundamental truths that composed the matrix of Pueblo thought and belief. Their failure to reach a deeper level of understanding led, in the seventeenth century, to monumental disaster for both peoples.

All that the Spaniards discovered and observed in Puebloland, beginning in 1540, rested upon a cultural tradition that extended backward hundreds of years. Of that past, the invaders had no knowledge, nor did they possess the means to learn about it, had the interest existed. Only in recent decades have archeologists succeeded in unraveling some of the mysteries that surround the origin and development of Pueblo culture during the long and obscure years of prehistory in the Southwest.

Men, of unknown type, inhabited New Mexico long before the Pueblolike people emerged. A Negro cowboy, George McJunkin, while riding up Wild Horse Gulch in 1908, discovered the first trace of them. The spot lay close to the little village of Folsom in the northeast corner of the state. Along the walls of the gulch, McJunkin spied bones, large and bleached, and mingled with them were curious flint points of superb workmanship. When the find came to the attention of scholars in 1925, the bones proved to be those of extinct giant bison, and the now famous Folsom points offered first proof that man lived and hunted in North America, during the Ice Age, eight to ten thousand years ago. Subsequent discoveries, including those at Sandía Cave near Albuquerque and at the Clovis site north of Portales, pushed back the antiquity of human occupation still further.

The Ice-Age men who flaked the fine spear or dart points and hunted big game on the grasslands of eastern New Mexico seem to have had little or no relation to the forebears of the Pueblos. For that, we must look west of the Continental Divide to an archaic desert culture which archeologists know as the *Cochise*. These people possessed an economy based upon the collecting of wild foods and the hunting of small game. When severe drought resulted in the concurrent disappearance both of big game animals and the Folsom hunters, about 5,000 B.C., the Cochise gatherers adapted to the new environmental conditions and, in so doing, furnished the base from which Puebloan farming cultures developed.

The introduction of agriculture here, just as in the Old World, represented a turning point in man's struggle to advance his material well-being. Cochise artifacts, in association with small, primitive ears of corn dating between 2,000 B.C. and 3,000 B.C., were excavated at Bat Cave in west-central New Mexico, beginning in 1949. Until that discovery, no proof existed of the practice of agriculture in the United States before the Christian era. We suppose that that earliest corn, along with squash and the gourd, was a borrowing from Mexico, and that later diffusions brought beans, other crops, and finally, the knowledge of pottery making.

These innovations transformed the simple Cochise way of life so that, about 100 B.C., a new, more sophisticated southwestern tradition emerged. The Mogollon people, centered in the southern uplands along the present New Mexico-Arizona border, were its earliest representatives. In the first centuries after Christ, they became the cultural leaders in the Southwest, living in pit-house villages, worshipping in ceremonial lodges, farming mesa tops and stream valleys, and producing ceramics of consummate artistry.

Mogollon influence gradually seeped northward into the canyonlands of the Four Corners, the area where New Mexico now meets Colorado, Utah, and Arizona. Here, a desert people— gatherers known as Basketmakers, for the profusion of superbly woven baskets that they left behind in dry caves—began their own march toward a cultural summit. Advancing in a manner similar to the Mogollon, though at a later time, they evolved, by A.D. 700 to A.D. 800, into the Anasazi (a Navajo word for "the Ancient Ones") who were the direct ancestors of the historic Pueblo.

By the close of the first millennium, the Anasazi began to surpass the achievements of the older Mogollon. They built large urban centers comprised of towering apartments, some of which contained as many as five hundred rooms. These, one day, would give Pueblo culture its name. They resorted to more intensive farming and effectively utilized irrigation devices for watering fields. Religious practices, particularly those related to weather control, assumed more elaborate form. Ceramics flowered, and potters achieved new heights of excellence with clay and paint.

In Chaco Canyon, where a massive communal dwelling sheltering twelve hundred people was raised at Pueblo Bonito, the Anasazi produced a totally unexpected marvel of engineering. They built a complex system of roads extending from the canyon in four directions to other towns or ceremonial centers. Some highways were twenty to forty feet in width, cleared of rubble, leveled, and lined with ditches or stone borders. Their builders coped with cliffs by installing masonry or rock-cut stairways. One road led unwaveringly due north in a straight line for forty miles to the San Juan River. Nothing else quite like that exists elsewhere in the United States. It tells us, for one thing, that the Indians of Chaco had a highly developed social organization, one that could mobilize the huge labor force such a project must have required. But the roads also present a question. Travel was by foot, since there were no wheeled vehicles or draft animals; why therefore did they bother with all that strenuous building? We can only guess that the roadways had some symbolic meaning or perhaps facilitated the running of ceremonial races.

The prodigious towns of northwestern New Mexico, contrived of expert masonry and embellished with pillars and towers, were scarcely outshone by the cliff cities of other Anasazi who dwelled at Mesa Verde, Colorado, or in the Kayenta region of Arizona. In the years from the eleventh through the twelfth centuries, all these ancient people experienced a golden age that has come to be called Classic. Then, during the 1200s, and seemingly in orderly fashion, the great Indian communities, one by one, were abandoned, and their populations migrated elsewhere. No one yet has been able to offer a clear-cut explanation. Drought, erosion, and soil exhaustion may have played a part. Invasions by enemy raiders or the ravages of epidemic disease could have contributed to the exodus. More likely, internal tensions or feuds, of the kind common among the Pueblos in historic times, dealt a deathblow to the outsized towns, causing their residents, perhaps in piecemeal fashion, to desert and move to new country. Since they left no record of their reasons for going, modern experts are reduced to speculation and to endless dispute among themselves.

Some of the Indians drifted south out of the Four Corners and founded new centers, as at Zuñi and Hopi, which survive to the present day. Others, probably the majority, shifted eastward across the Continental Divide and settled alongside rustic country cousins who already inhabited the Pajarito Plateau near Los Alamos and the valleys of the Rio Grande and its tributaries. Here the Spaniards found them, prosperous and secure, in the sixteenth century, farming as they had always done and trading with the Apaches of the plains.

"No one comes to America to plow and sow, but only to eat and loaf." [1] So wrote the viceroy of New Spain to the king in 1608. His letter dealt with affairs in New Mexico, and he was distressingly concerned with the prospects of placing that distant province on a solid economic footing. His statement bore some exaggeration, for one important class of Spanish subjects, the missionary friars, ate moderately and were little given to idleness. However, the clergymen shared one belief with the gluttons and loafers: the Indians, for their own good and for the benefit of His Majesty's realm, should be put to work. By that was meant that their energies should be rechanneled—for the Indians already worked like beavers to feed and shelter themselves—toward tasks deemed useful by those Spaniards, laity and clergy, who proposed to live off the Indians' sweat. Such a notion of enforced labor dominated the thinking of colonial New Mexicans fully for eighty years and promoted increasingly abrasive relations with the Pueblos.

Initially, in almost every case, the Indians received the Spaniards hospitably, opening homes and religious ceremonies to them and making generous gifts of hard-won food. The Rodríguez-Chamuscado party, passing through the Piro Pueblos near Socorro in 1581, had such a quantity of tortillas, cornmeal mush, squash, and beans pressed upon it that every day enough was left to feed five hundred men.

Such liberality, of course, could not continue. With permanent colonization in 1598, the Pueblos found their voluntary sharing insufficient to appease the appetites of hungry Spaniards. Oñate's settlers, the documents tell us, dug irrigation

---

1. George P. Hammond and Agapito Rey, editors and translators, *Don Juan de Oñate, Colonizer of New Mexico, 1595–1628,* 2 vols. (Albuquerque: University of New Mexico Press, 1953), 2:1068.

ditches and put in their crops, but we can guess they drafted San Juan Indians to do most of the physical labor. In any case, these fields failed to supply all their needs, and very soon the governor began to impose levies of corn and other products upon the scattered villages and to send squads of soldiers to enforce collection.

Later, Oñate established the *encomienda* system, by which heads of Indian households were required to pay a yearly tribute in corn and blankets to the Spaniards. That put affairs on an orderly basis, since the Pueblos now knew exactly what their obligation was, but it made the burden no more palatable. The tribute or tax, as the seventeenth century wore on, came to be fixed at one Spanish bushel of corn and a small cotton blanket. The Indians could easily meet that modest assessment in years when bountiful rainfall brought bumper crops, but, given a dry season or two, the tribute worked genuine hardship. What other effects it produced upon a people who, through incalculable ages, had never seen a tax-gatherer, we can only surmise.

Indian grain and Indian weaving, collected under the system of *encomienda*, contributed to feeding and clothing the Spaniards. Still another institution, the *repartimiento*, mobilized native labor and forced the Pueblos to till the white man's fields and tend his livestock. Any Spanish landowner could apply to the governor for a body of laborers, and the governor then made a levy of up to a hundred Indians on some nearby pueblo. These workers were to be paid a daily wage and rations, and the term of their enlistment was limited by law. It was believed, with some authority, that only by obliging the Indians to work could the tasks necessary be accomplished. The Spanish settlers, at least at the outset, looked upon themselves as gentlemen, and men of the upper class in traditional society did not soil their hands at menial work.

From the European point of view, the *repartimiento*, or forced-work levy, was an expedient both logical and just. If it violated any natural rights of the Indians, the Spaniards were unaware of it. Had the laws regulating the system been adhered to with regularity, the Pueblos might have borne this added imposition with equanimity. Yet, as in any relationship involving subject people, the *repartimiento* cloaked a host of abuses. Many Spaniards avoided paying wages; they held out on rations; they demanded stints longer than the limits allowed; they often took the Pueblos at harvest time, when the Indians were desperately needed for work at home; and, most oppressive of all, they offended native women. Such vexations, never successfully dealt with by the viceregal government, built a hard kernel of resentment among the Indians, a resentment that grew with the passing years.

The legislation on tribute and labor did not relieve the suffering Pueblos, mainly because of the irresponsibility and inadequacy of some of the men who served as governor during those early decades. The worst among them not only failed to curb abuses of the colonists, but used their own high office to exploit the Indians for personal profit. They came from Mexico City, puffed-up with self-importance and eager to make a killing, so that, at the end of their term, they could go home rich. Unhappily, the only way they could manage that in a barren land like New Mexico was by exploiting the native people. Their methods were crude and all quite illegal: pressing gangs of Pueblos into service to weave and sew in miserable sweatshops set up in the governor's own palace; forcing them to scour the mountains collecting piñon nuts; using them as beasts of burden to carry bags of salt from the saline lakes to Santa Fe; requiring them to go onto the plains as agents of the governor and trade with the Apache; and the list goes on. Whatever goods were manufactured or gathered by the Indians went south by wagon caravan to be sold in the mining communities of northern New Spain, and never a cent of profit did the worker see.

The notorious Governor Bernardo López de Mendizábal, who was indicted in 1661 after he left office, faced an attorney for the Indians who claimed he owed more than twenty-four hundred pesos in unpaid wages. The high court of Mexico City found the former governor guilty on the general charge of illegal use of native labor and, among other penalties, fined him three thousand silver pesos. His case was not exceptional.

One could reasonably suppose that the missionary friars would have intervened to prevent mistreatment of the Pueblos by corrupt officials and colonists. Indeed, they made a show of so doing—their damning letters to superiors in Mexico City are particularly revealing—but their motives in defending the new converts were not altogether noble. If they showed resentment when the Indians were overtaxed and overworked, it was because they wished to turn more of that wealth and labor into the mission program. In the long run, demands of the friars and their interference in native affairs weighed far more heavily upon the Pueblos than did all the irritations raised by the colonists.

The seventy years in New Mexico history following the founding of Santa Fe in 1610 has properly been called "the Great Missionary Era." Some 250 friars of the Franciscan Order worked among the Pueblos during these decades, and the crown spent upward of a million pesos on salaries, supplies, and the building of massive churches. The expenditure of so vast a sum on what was purely a humanitarian undertaking underscored the king's commitment to the spread of the True Faith. The friars, it is accurate to say, played the primary role in bringing Hispanic civilization to the upper Rio Grande, but their work returned not a single peso to the royal treasury.

The Franciscans, through their network of missions stretching from Pecos on the edge of the plains to the western villages of the Hopi, created their own private realm that operated practically independently of New Mexico's civil government. They even had their own ecclesiastical capital at Santo Domingo Pueblo, a dozen leagues south of Santa Fe. There resided the *custos,* head of the Order in New Mexico and agent for the Inquisition. The *custos* was a man of sufficient power and prestige to challenge, when he thought it necessary, the authority of the governor.

The strength of the clergy was centered in the scores of churches and smaller chapels distributed among the Pueblos. These structures often formed part of a walled compound that also contained the priests' quarters, workshops, storerooms, and stables. When the imposing ruins of these buildings are viewed today, at Pecos or Gran Quivira National Monuments, for example, it is at once obvious that the tight cluster of Spanish buildings dominated the original Indian town. That was the effect, of course, that the friars were trying to achieve.

Each mission, the center of a *doctrina,* or native parish, was meant to indoctrinate its dependent Indians, not only in religion but in Hispanic economic and social customs. The padres were versatile men who could give instruction in catechism, music, Latin, painting, blacksmithing, carpentry, weaving, and a dozen other subjects. They taught some of their charges to play small pipe organs that had been brought with much labor in wagons from Mexico. Other Indians learned to be actors and performed in little plays that carried a religious theme.

Surrounding every Franciscan establishment there existed a perpetual hum of activity. The Pueblos had known hard work before, but the new kinds of labor imposed upon them possessed an intensity and a cheerless character wholly outside their experience. Every task the friars thought up seemed to require an army of Indians to get it done. They were assembled in huge throngs to do the original construction of church and compound, and thereafter they provided cooks, maids, servants, gardeners, stock-herders, and maintenance men. The endless round of religious services required other Indians as sacristans, bell-ringers, porters, and *fiscales,* the last appointed to enforce compulsory attendance among the villagers. The slightest lapse of duty brought swift and severe punishment—whipping, a term in the stocks, or a head-shaving. Loss of one's hair was considered by the Pueblos as a colossal indignity, and some of those who suffered such punishment became so distraught that they fled to the mountains. As a consequence, the viceroy had to order that harsh bit of discipline stopped in 1620.

Pueblo men experienced further humiliation when the padres attempted to badger them into building walls. The division of labor in native society prescribed weaving, hunting, and making war as proper male activities, and adobe work was considered to be a womanly pursuit. "If we try to oblige some man to make a wall," Father Alonso de Benavides tells us, "he runs away from it, and the women laugh." [2] This otherwise observant and

2. Mrs. Edward E. Ayer, translator, *The Memorial of Fray Alonso de Benavides, 1630* (Albuquerque: Horn and Wallace, 1965), p. 33.

quick-witted friar, who served as *custos* for the New Mexico missions from 1626 to 1629, was evidently amused by such behavior. Like most missionaries, he had small tolerance for Indian custom and etiquette, and little understanding of the degree to which daily violations of it pained the Pueblos.

Father Benavides wrote a famous *Memorial* to the king in 1630, painting a rosy picture of spiritual conquest on the Rio Grande and asking for more funds and priests to expand the work. Through tinted glasses, he saw the Indians so contented and pious that "they seem Christians of a hundred years' standing." [3] Could the good friar have pushed aside his illusions, even momentarily, he would have been appalled at the embers of hatred and discontent smoldering beneath the surface.

Franciscan policy assumed a more militant tone in the years following 1630, after Benavides had returned to Spain. It was not that the Pueblos failed to go through the proper religious motions or to proclaim themselves faithful converts. The difficulty lay in their refusal to throw out the old gods and their persistence in dancing, singing, handling venomous snakes, wearing masks, and sprinkling sacred cornmeal. To the Spaniards, all that smacked of idolatry and devil worship. Having established so potent an institution as the Holy Office of the Inquisition to root out heretics among their own kind, there was no way the Spanish mind could accept the coexistence of Christianity and "pagan practices" among the Pueblo disciples. As they saw it, every mote of paganism must be banished.

The Indians looked at their situation in a very different light. For them, religion, above all, meant establishing harmony with the cosmos; and if that could be more effectively accomplished by joining their rites with the strange, new creed introduced by the Spaniards, so much the better. They were quite willing to accept Christianity and to integrate it into the native religious structure. They achieved that, to a degree, by incorporating several saints—St. James, St. Isidore, and St. Rafael, for example—into the assembly of *katcinas*. Christ they received as a bringer of light and a culture hero similar to their own figure Pohé-Yemo; and to the color and sound of Catholic ritual, they

3. Ayer, *The Memorial of Benavides*, p. 34.

responded with genuine enthusiasm. The Hopi, on first meeting Coronado's lieutenants, entertained the notion that a new era was dawning in which faiths of the two peoples would be united in one religion leading to a greater brotherhood. The Rio Grande Pueblos may well have harbored the same idea. If so, they suffered an ungentle awakening, for the Spanish padres would have none of it.

Ever since Father Bartolomé de las Casas set the tone in the mid-sixteenth century, the church had held that souls of the Indians must be won peacefully, by example and instruction. Many missionaries followed that rule with saintlike patience. Yet even the mildest among them lost their good humor when faced with Indians who, year after year, clung stubbornly to the ancient ceremonials of their grandfathers. By the end of the first quarter of the seventeenth century, New Mexican friars began to sense that the Pueblos had no intention of abandoning the old faith. Hence, they concluded that if kindly persuasion and moderate discipline could not root out "heathen practices," then strength of muscle must do the job. It was a decision fated to bring unspeakable tragedy upon the head of every person residing in the sunny province of New Mexico.

The padres, digging in with unparalleled industry, launched assault after assault upon the foundations of the Pueblo religious structure. The principal objects of persecution were the native priests, whom the missionaries condemned as sorcerers. Unable to discredit them in the eyes of the Indians, the friars took to flogging and hanging. Understandably, it was from the Pueblos' priestly class that leaders of rebellion ultimately came.

The friars took particular offense at the kivas and masked dances seen in every pueblo. With Spanish soldiers to back them, they raided the sacred chambers, defiling altars and murals, and gathering up masks, prayer plumes, fetishes, and other holy paraphernalia, which they burned in the plazas. The destruction and a strict prohibition against public dancing seemingly put an end to the *katcina* and other ceremonies. In reality, it merely drove the Pueblo religion into hiding.

One may wonder why the Indians, saddled with such an oppressive load and enjoying the advantage of numbers, simply did not rise at once and throw the Spaniards out. But to do that they would have had to form some kind of union, and such an idea proved slow in maturing. Not only was co-operation among villages foreign to the Indian way of thinking, but social forces also worked against the emergence of leaders who might bring it about. Tightly knit Pueblo communities functioned under a strict rule of conformity, with every person bound to a common code of behavior. No room existed for a strong-willed individual who deviated from the norm or who worked to outshine others. In such an atmosphere, no one desired to lead—it was bad form and brought public censure—so no one led. Decision-making fell to the hierarchy of native priests, which formed a general consensus on every issue. When that failed, as occasionally happened, the pueblo might be torn by factional dispute, with the weaker party splitting off to found another village.

Internal feuds and social divisions were not confined to Pueblo society. The Spaniards of the seventeenth century fell prey to a factionalism so bitter that it tore the colony of New Mexico apart and contributed to the opening of a wedge that allowed the Indians at last to gain an upper hand. The struggle was joined between Church and State and the issue was one of jurisdiction over the Pueblos. That a succession of governors and a band of friars could come to physical blows and wage open war upon one another appears unimaginable to us today. It proved no less mystifying to the Indians, who became pawns in the affray.

Seeds of conflict lay in the two overlapping spheres of influence—civil and religious—that the Spaniards established in each pueblo. When Oñate discovered that the Indians possessed no single leader or chief who could speak for individual villages, he remedied that by introducing in every place the office of petty governor (*gobernadorcillo*) and the lesser positions of lieutenant-governor, sheriff (*alguacil*), irrigation boss (*mayordomo*), and church warden (*fiscal*). These men, elected for one-year terms by people of the pueblo, formed, in effect, a small municipal government handling minor political and judicial affairs. In time, a council of elders, or *principales,* was added to

serve as an advisory body, its membership composed of all
former governors and lieutenant-governors.

When Oñate wrote the king that he had founded many *repúblicas* in New Mexico, he was referring to these representative pueblo governments. Under the Spanish system, the *república,* or municipal domain, was the only area in which
citizens were permitted direct participation in politics. Electing
town officials gave them a fleeting but welcome taste of democracy. By allowing the Pueblos to set up their own *repúblicas,*
the Spaniards hoped to hasten the Indians' integration into
Hispanic society. The intent, however, was frustrated by the native priesthood, which remained in firm control behind the
scenes. Those holy men designated the persons who were to be
"elected" to the Spanish offices and governed through them.
Each pueblo, to this day, has its governor, who continues, as in
former times, to represent his village in dealings with outsiders.
And, in that role, he remains a front man, manipulated by the
religious powers who stay hidden in the wings.

The Indian *república* was designed to introduce the Pueblos
to Spanish political forms, just as the *doctrina,* or native parish,
was intended as an agency for the implanting of Christianity.
These institutions might have worked well enough, had the governor in Santa Fe and the missionary friars been able to agree
upon the part each was to play in their development. Instead,
the parties fell to petty squabbling over jurisdiction and authority, causing a rift that all too soon led to fierce competition for
the allegiance and services of the Indians.

The yearly voting in which the Pueblos selected their officials
was a case in point. Repeatedly, the governor and the friars,
contrary to law, meddled in the election process, each trying to
curry favor or gain influence over the Indians chosen. The scandal reached the ears of the viceroy, who issued an order in
1620, guaranteeing the Indians in their *repúblicas* full liberty to
elect their own officers on January 1 of each year. The governor's only legitimate function in these matters, the viceroy
pointedly noted, was to approve and confirm the native officials
after the people had expressed their will, while the friars were to
provide no more than nominal supervision over the balloting. In
spite of the order, interference in Pueblo elections continued.

At a dozen other points involving the Indians, the New Mexican governors and the clergy came to blows. The ascendancy of greed and overweening pride sundered the traditional partnership between Church and State. Discord often erupted in violent quarrels that, on occasion, led to bloodletting, so that the entire period from 1610 to 1680 was one of intermittent civil war. The story, pieced together some forty years ago by historian France V. Scholes from scattered documents in the archives of Spain and Mexico, is as melancholy as it is fascinating. A brief look at the career of one governor, Luís de Rosas (1637–1641), will provide a fair sampling of the travail through which Spaniards and Pueblo Indians passed in this troubled period.

By all accounts, Luís de Rosas was a blunt and uncompromising man, given to sudden furies, who ruled New Mexico with an authoritarianism that bordered on tyranny. He arrived in Santa Fe in the spring of 1637 with the regular caravan that brought supplies to the settlers and missions. The friars hoped, as they did with the appearance of each new governor, that Rosas would prove a weak and pliant tool in their hands. But, as always, they were doomed to disappointment. Within weeks, the governor discovered the means used by his predecessors to exploit the Indians; he was out for profit, and woe to those who got in his way.

Filled with arrogance, he went among pueblos neighboring the capital, demanding that their residents weave blankets and other textiles to be delivered to him. In Santa Fe, he put together a workshop and forced Christian Pueblos to sweat alongside unconverted Apache and Ute captives under abject conditions of servitude. To Pecos Pueblo on the eastern frontier, he went with boxes of knives, ordering Indians there to trade them to the Apaches for buffalo hides and meat. When that venture failed to produce the profit expected, he blamed the Pecos friars, arrested one of them, and carried him off to Santa Fe a prisoner. The governor then promised the Indians of Pecos permission to revive their traditional dances if they furnished him more blankets and hides.

Every action Rosas took caused the Franciscans additional distress. They claimed he was out to destroy all Church privi-

lege and influence. His statements and conduct seemed to bear
out the charge. Once, while attending Mass, the governor listened in simmering rage while the padre delivered a sermon
rebuking those who disobeyed God's law. Well aware that the
remarks were intended for his ears, Rosas jumped to his feet,
shouting, "Shut up, Father! What you say is a lie!" [4] Then he
stalked from the church with his soldier escort meekly following.

The Pueblos who heard of the episode were scandalized, and
they asked one another how they could believe what the friars
taught when the governor himself had branded one of them a
liar. Rosas aggravated the issue by ordering the Indians not to
obey their missionaries and by going to several villages where
he scolded the resident priest in public. His highhanded ways
slowly began to have effect, and the viselike grip the friars held
upon the Pueblos loosened.

After more altercations with the church, Rosas expelled the
clergy from Santa Fe early in 1640. In a bid to bring the cho-
leric official to his senses, two friars returned to the capital with
an appeal for peace. Rosas met them near San Miguel Chapel
and beat both men mercilessly with a stick until they were
bathed in blood. After that mad display of savagery, the Franciscans lost all desire to compose their quarrel with the governor, and they sent out a body of settlers and soldiers who had
joined them to pillage his ranch. In retaliation, Rosas dispatched
squads of men to rob and desecrate some of the distant mission
churches that had been abandoned by the padres. The vendetta
continued for months, ending only when a new governor arrived
from the south to replace Rosas. When the former governor was
slain shortly afterward by a jealous husband, there were few to
mourn his passing.

The dreadful Church-State rivalry through the years eroded
the Spaniards' ability to exert any real control over New Mexican affairs and left them practically no time to confront the calamity fast overtaking the Pueblos. Adding to their other woes,
the Indians suffered periodically from epidemic diseases brought

4. France V. Scholes, "Church and State in New Mexico, 1637–1641," *New Mexico Historical Review* 11 (1936):303.

by the Europeans. Against smallpox, measles, whooping cough, and cholera, they had no natural resistance, and they died in droves. Crowded together in small, airless rooms of their pueblos, they were fearfully susceptible to contagion. In 1640, at the height of Rosas's ignominious reign, smallpox killed three thousand Indians, or something more than 10 percent of the entire Pueblo population. Other epidemics in the 1660s further thinned their ranks.

To make matters worse, the weather turned sour. During the first half of the seventeenth century, New Mexico was blessed with abundant rainfall, a fact that doubtless aided the Spaniards in establishing and maintaining their colony. After 1650, a definite falling off in moisture became noticeable, and, by the middle of the following decade, the province found itself in the throes of drought. Starvation now added to the toll of Pueblo deaths.

In the three years from 1665 to 1668, no crops were harvested. Travelers saw the bodies of Indians who had perished from hunger lying scattered about their villages and along the roads. At Humanas Pueblo (now Gran Quivira National Monument) east of the Manzano Mountains, 450 Indians starved to death, and that place, as well as neighboring villages, had to be abandoned in the 1670s.

Famine hit the Spaniards equally hard, and many were reduced to eating toasted cowhides. On the plains, the grass withered, game became scarce, and the Apaches, well-acquainted with New Mexico's weak defenses, swept through like a bloody scourge looking for something to eat. It is scarcely surprising that the Pueblos attributed much of this misfortune to the Spaniards, especially to the friars who had raised so many impediments against performance of the rain-making ceremonies.

Friction between Spanish officials and the clergy abated after 1670 in the face of common exhaustion; but, for the Pueblos, the truce only meant that their enemies had leisure again to renew the unholy crusade against native religion. The friars took up the cudgel with vehemence, completely oblivious to the fact that their new persecutions, heaped upon existing stresses, were driving the Indians to the breaking point.

In 1675, Governor Juan Francisco Treviño at Santa Fe was

persuaded that stern measures against the Pueblo priests would have a salutary effect upon the missionary program. Consequently, he dispatched soldiers throughout the villages to arrest forty-seven medicine men alleged to be sorcerers and teachers of idolatry. Three of those deemed most guilty were hanged by the Spaniards, and a fourth hanged himself. The remainder felt the lash and were imprisoned.

A dramatic confrontation followed. Tewa warriors from villages north of the capital arrived, bristling with weapons. Brazenly, they invaded the apartment of the governor in his mud palace, demanding release of the prisoners. Treviño was cowed; his soldiers had ridden off to fight Apaches, and the stern demeanor of these Pueblos left little doubt that they meant to have their way, whether he put up a defense or not. The whip-scarred medicine men were set free, among them a fierce young man named Popé, who was soon to carve his name deeply in the history of New Mexico. The Indians marched out of Santa Fe, pleased with their small victory and carrying the seed of an idea they would nourish over the next five years: facing a united army of Pueblos, the Spaniards were vulnerable.

Decades of misfortune had brought New Mexico, by the late 1670s, to a tottery state. The non-Pueblo population numbered about thirty-five hundred souls, but a large proportion of these were persons of mixed European, Indian, and Negro blood whose loyalty to the government was weak. A mere one hundred and seventy professional fighting men shouldered the burden of defense for the entire province. After almost seventy years, Santa Fe was still the only real community. Most of the people lived near the missions or in walled haciendas scattered thinly from the Socorro region northward to the Taos Valley. That pattern of settlement, with families existing in islandlike remoteness from one another, compounded the problems of administering and defending the Spanish governor's sprawling jurisdiction. He did have a lieutenant-governor residing near Isleta Pueblo, who ruled over the southern district of the Rio Abajo, and a handful of lesser officials, called *alcaldes mayores*, who governed rural subdivisions. But communication and co-operation with even these few officers was difficult.

The Franciscan *custos,* Father Francisco de Ayeta, a man of generous nature and indomitable spirit, worked tirelessly in these years to restore some order in provincial affairs. It was largely through his petition, assented to by the new governor, Antonio de Otermín, that the viceroy sent (in 1676) fifty convicts, armed, to bolster New Mexico's soldiery. Ayeta was still not satisfied, for more than anyone else, he perceived the ominous build-up of storm clouds. The following year found him in Mexico City, pleading for an additional fifty soldiers and funds to build a presidio, or fort. The viceroy demurred. New Mexico's costly needs seemed never-ending. He would refer the matter to the king.

In the meantime, Ayeta superintended the provisioning of a supply caravan for the missions; and, when it was well stocked, he started for New Mexico. Through months of toil and ankle-deep dust, he brought his jolting carts to the small mission outpost of El Paso del Norte on the Rio Grande. While he was camped there, government couriers on lathered horses rode in from the north. The unthinkable had happened. New Mexico's Pueblo people had thrown off their traces and unleashed a frenzied war. The countryside was aflame. The missions lay sacked and burned. Governor Otermín, together with all the people of Santa Fe and beyond, were presumed dead, and the lieutenant-governor, Alonso de García, was marching out from the south with the stricken remnant of colonists and friars. The Spanish realm founded by Oñate eight decades before had dissolved.

Elsewhere in the western world in that year of 1680, men went about their affairs unmindful of New Mexico's woeful spasm. France's Louis XIV, nicknamed the Sun King, was at the peak of his power, strutting and posturing for all his partisans and enemies to see. In French territory on the upper Mississippi River, the explorer La Salle was busily laying the groundwork for an expedition that two years hence would make possible the first descent of that notable waterway to its mouth. In England, the visionary Quaker, William Penn, accepted a grant of land west of New Jersey from the Duke of York, in repayment of a debt owed his father. And English Carolinians in the same year led an army of three hundred Indians against Spanish outposts that had crept northward out of Florida.

In Spain during the month of June, the Inquisition staged one of its periodic public spectacles for the punishment of heretics. The macabre event unfolded in Madrid's Plaza Mayor, in the presence of the king and his court. Amid the pomp and glitter of the procession that carried the condemned to center stage, little evidence could be found that Spain was wracked by a plague, sunk in the depths of economic depression, and starved as a result of bad harvests. Universal misery among the common people appeared to be no excuse for deferring punishment of religious criminals.

Wearing cardboard caps upon which their crimes were written and surrounded by fifty guards garbed in black-and-white robes marched twelve men and women, ropes about their necks, torches in hand. They were followed by twenty others of both sexes, some destined to be strangled, others to be burned alive. Mingling with the file of Inquisition officials and nobles could be seen a body of charcoal merchants armed with pikes and muskets, men who had furnished the huge quantities of wood for the execution pyres. The ceremony continued interminably, sentences were read, and the guilty were mounted on donkeys to be carried to the stakes outside the city walls.

Through the lens of history, it is possible to detect a note of irony in such heavy-handed dealing with dissenters. A little better than a month after the parade of death in Madrid, the Pueblo Indians, themselves victims of two generations of religious persecution, brought their remote corner of the Spanish empire to its day of reckoning. The Pueblo Revolt of 1680 not only destroyed New Mexico, but it rocked the entire northern frontier of the viceroyalty and sent shock waves rippling through Mexico City and, ultimately, the mother country. The tragedy was one of the worst to fall upon Spain's dominions in America. Not until that moment had she ever lost an entire province to the Indians.

The Pueblos rose on the feast of San Lorenzo, August 10. For once, they were together—or almost so. Popé, medicine man of San Juan and one of those sent to the whipping post in 1675, had taken the lead in weaving the net of conspiracy that tumbled the Spaniards from their lofty seat. He was joined by Luís Tupatú of Picuris Pueblo, Catití of Santo Domingo, and other newly emergent leaders. Their task had been herculean. Not only did they have to overcome the villagers' natural antipathy toward confederation, they had to contend with a minority of Indians who were still loyal to the Spaniards and might betray the plot at any time. Popé, according to later testimony, killed his own son-in-law, the *gobernadorcillo* of San Juan, who opposed the revolt; and Catití, for his part, threatened to behead anyone who did not join. Reasoned argument combined with threats finally brought all the pueblos in line, except those of the Piros in the far south, who could not be reached. Knotted yucca cords, circulated by runners, served as a calendar by which each village measured time to the day appointed for taking up arms.

The gathering rumble in the countryside reached the ears of Governor Otermín at Santa Fe, but too late to head off disaster. Saturday morning of the tenth found most of the scattered settlers and missionaries unprepared and unwarned. That day and those that followed witnessed a wholesale butchery. A handful of survivors from the Santa Cruz valley to the north and from the Cerrillos Hills a few leagues south straggled into the capital with tales of horror. Bodies of men, women, and children lay strewn along the roads where they had been stopped in flight. Smoke from burning houses and missions cast a pall across the sky. In the churches, the priests had been slain at their altars and the holy furnishings torn apart and desecrated with human excrement. The Indians spent their greatest fury here, in retaliation for the destruction that their own sacred kivas had suffered.

Once the outlying districts had been thoroughly pillaged, the rebel Pueblos came together in a body and moved against Santa Fe. Not only had they found strength in union, they were now well provided with horses, harquebuses, and swords claimed from defeated Spaniards.

Under threat of siege, Otermín and his captains worked feverishly, rushing the people and what livestock had been saved into the compound of the Governors Palace. The rest of the capital was abandoned to the enemy. Rumors floated about, adding to the prevading air of hopelessness: all the settlers in the Rio Abajo, including Lieutenant-Governor García at Isleta, had perished; the revolt had spread south to El Paso, where Father Ayeta and others in the supply caravan supposedly had suffered annihilation. Otermín, grasping at straws, tried to send messengers through the Indian lines with desperate pleas for García, should he still be alive, to come to the relief of the capital. None got through.

For nine long days, the vast army of Pueblos, investing the limits of Santa Fe, hammered away at the beleaguered Spaniards. Otermín himself led several sallies outside the walls to secure drinking water from the Santa Fe River. In these, he received two wounds and lost some soldiers; but the Indians also suffered heavy casualties.

The governor knew that the fate of his people dangled by a fragile thread. Neither of the choices open to him was an enviable one: stay forted up in the smoking ruin of the capital and hope aid arrived before starvation set in; or try to break and run with a caravan encumbered by women, children, and the wounded. Necessity forced upon him the latter course.

Getting away was easier than anyone could have expected. The Pueblos had won their war; they were content to let the enemy ride south unmolested. Near Sandía Pueblo, Otermín captured an Indian in a deserted cornfield and from him learned that Lieutenant-Governor García was not dead. That official had gathered the Rio Abajo people, and believing that Santa Fe had been overrun, had begun a retreat out of New Mexico. Otermín sped a rider after him, with instructions to halt on the road until the governor's own brigade of refugees could catch up. The two parties finally linked on the Camino Real below Socorro, and with "the poor women and children on foot and unshod, of such a hue that they looked like dead people," as one account put it, they marched out, leaving New Mexico to the victors.[5]

5. Charles Wilson Hackett, editor, *Revolt of the Pueblo Indians of New Mexico and Otermín's Attempted Reconquest, 1680–1682,* 2 vols. (Albuquerque: University of New Mexico Press, 1942), 1:213.

In the days and months that followed, the Spaniards tried to paw through the mists of the past to find the cause of their unprecedented calamity. In an early letter to the viceroy, Governor Otermín, writing under a burden of grief, attributed the revolt to his own lamentable sins. On cooler reflection at a later time, he heaped blame upon the "stupid ignorance of the Indians" and upon the devil who inspired their infamy.[6] His blindness in perceiving the short- and long-range causes of the revolt was a symptom of the same malady that had afflicted all seventeenth-century New Mexican governors. They had gone about their self-serving ways, oblivious to the anguish of the Indians and unmindful of the fact that every people possess a limit beyond which oppression will no longer be endured.

In terms of modern wars and disasters, the number of Spanish casualties in 1680 appears moderate; twenty-one friars and some four hundred colonists were slain. But, at the time, the toll was regarded as staggering. Father Ayeta and the few surviving friars who joined him at El Paso mourned, not their lost brethren who had won the glorious crown of martyrdom, but the thousands of Christian Indians whose souls had been seized by Satan. For them, that was the most baleful aspect of the catastrophe.

Rid of the Spaniards, the Pueblos hoped to recover the past and go back to those days before Coronado had turned their world topsy-turvy. Popé put out firm orders. Every Indian should go to the river and scrub with soapweed to wash away the taint of baptism. Men must put aside wives taken in Christian ceremony and marry again according to native tradition. Whatever the Spaniards had brought from afar and had left behind was to be destroyed—clothing, tools, weapons, livestock, carts—even fruit trees. These instructions, given in the first flush of victory, were doomed to be ignored.

Time cannot be recaptured, as Popé and his supporters learned, to their discomfort. During the years of Spanish rule, the Indians became something different from what they had been earlier. The transformation had come slowly and quietly,

---

6. Hackett, *Revolt of the Pueblo Indians*, 1:122.

and it was irreversible. Scarcely a Pueblo alive in 1680 could remember how affairs had stood before the Spaniards had brought them cattle and sheep, exotic vegetables and grains, iron hardware, and a new religion. In varying degrees, these things had become part of their lives. In spite of Popé's commands, many villagers retained their animals, continued to use their carts, refused to pull up their orchards, and some kept little forges in operation to work the scraps of iron and steel that were spoils of the revolt. A few who had been touched deeply by the friars squirreled away religious articles, salvaged from the churches, against the day when the Christians might return.

One thing hadn't changed and that was each pueblo's unwillingness to give up a grain of its independence. Once the Spaniards rode away, Popé's authority shriveled, and the light of union grew dim. The old and numberless feuds among villages resurfaced, and the Apaches, now handsomely a-horseback, showed by the rattling of their lances that they were still to be reckoned with. None of that meant, however, that the Spaniards could simply walk back and reclaim what they had so recently lost. Governor Otermín discovered that much when he made the attempt late in 1681.

The Spanish refugees had halted at El Paso, there to be succored by Father Ayeta's supply caravan which, after all, had not been annihilated. The area was then under the jurisdiction of Nueva Vizcaya, but the viceroy gave Otermín authority to rule as if he were still in Santa Fe, so that, with an exile government, he could hold his people together until time for a reconquest. In November, the governor led 146 soldiers and several score Indian allies—a pitifully small force—on the up-river trail to Isleta, the southernmost pueblo still occupied. The Indians, with little show of enthusiasm, rendered obedience and were welcomed back into the fold of the church. But that was the only place Otermín had any success.

As the Spaniards ascended the Rio Grande, the Pueblos fled to the mountains, many of them using the same paths followed by their great-grandfathers in escaping Coronado. Had they stayed in their villages, Otermín would have accepted a token submission and passed them by. But in anger over the leave-taking, he sacked and burned three pueblos north of modern Albuquerque. And, at every chance, he tore apart newly built kivas and destroyed *katcina* masks, the very same acts which for so long had enraged the Indians and which ultimately precipitated the revolt. Experience had taught the governor nothing.

When several pueblos threw together an army on the river south of Santa Fe, Otermín gave up. The hostility he faced, the raw winter weather, and the shortage of forage for his horses obliged him to withdraw to El Paso, to leave the retaking of New Mexico to a more propitious day.

It is worthy of note that the governor was prepared to deal leniently with the Indians, provided only that they renounced their rebellious acts and submitted anew to the discipline of the missionaries. True, his own hardheaded sternness frustrated any peaceful redemption of the Pueblos, but to his credit, he engaged in no general slaughter. He sought restoration of the province, not extermination of its native people. In spite of their own blundering and almost total inability to grasp the Indian point of view, the Spaniards' most rapacious tendencies were usually held in check by religious strictures and the king's laws. These combined to create a dramatic sense of mission that caused the best among Spanish leaders to weigh every action on the scales of moral duty.

How different were matters in southern New England after Indians ravaged the settlements in King Philip's War, 1675–1676. Avenging colonists executed chiefs in bloody fashion, and shipped boatloads of warriors off to the West Indies to be sold into slavery. That the Indian population was practically snuffed out troubled the Puritan conscience not at all.

Several reasons lay behind the Spaniards' desire to recover New Mexico. One was the simple wish to reclaim Indian souls lost to Christendom. Another, more practical, had been stated earlier by Governor Otermín, who noted that, without New Mexico as a frontier buffer, other provinces of northern New Spain stood exposed to invasion by Apaches and similar warlike tribes. Finally, there was the matter of Spanish pride. That could be restored only by winning back sovereignty over the Pueblos and their country.

The crown appointed a soldier of noble blood, Don Diego de Vargas, to the governorship in 1691, hoping that, with the limited men and resources available, he could somehow bring about the reconquest. The undertaking was viewed emotionally as another *reconquista,* paralleling, though on a smaller scale, Spain's recapture of territory from the infidel Moors during the Middle Ages. Governor De Vargas, fired with crusading zeal, felt the weight of history on his shoulders and to the task at hand, he gave heroic dedication.

First, he had to put down rebellious tribes surrounding El Paso—Sumas, Manos, Chisos, and others—for the success of the Pueblos had inspired peoples of northern Nueva Vizcaya to seize the hatchet. With peace nominally restored at his headquarters, the governor set out for Santa Fe in late summer of 1692. Trailed by two hundred soldiers and a body of chaplains, he entered the ruined capital and approached the walls of the old Governors Palace, which the Indians had remodeled and converted to a pueblo. Warriors appeared on the rooftops and peered down, dumfounded to see Spaniards once again in the streets of Santa Fe.

After a flourish of trumpets and drums, De Vargas delivered a conciliatory speech in loud tones, proclaiming that he had come, not to chastise, but to pardon and convert. And he announced that all must leave the pueblo peacefully and re-enter the fold as loyal Spanish vassals. During twelve hours, he returned time and again to repeat his soft words. The Indians were frightened and unsure whether the new governor could be trusted. Would he venture inside the courtyard as proof of his pacific intentions? De Vargas would, and both his boldness and gentleness of manner won the Indians over. In a gala ceremony, the Spaniards unfurled their banner, making New Mexico once more part of His Majesty's empire.

Diego de Vargas toured the province, repeating his speech, and received pledges of peace. Popé had died, the Apaches and Utes had grown ever more troublesome, and now each pueblo, as before, faced an army of Spaniards alone. What could they do but submit? The governor was back at El Paso in time to celebrate Christmas of 1692. His first entry had been made with soldiers only; for his second, he planned to take back a new wave of colonists.

News of De Vargas's triumph sparked a wild celebration in Mexico City. Bells pealed joyfully, the clergy sang hymns of thanksgiving, and the viceroy ordered that an official history be written to commemorate the event. But the jubilation was premature. Upon returning to New Mexico in the fall of 1693 with soldiers, seventy families, and eighteen friars, Governor De Vargas found that many of the Pueblos had renounced their allegiance given the previous year. The vision of a peaceful reconquest evaporated like a mirage.

The Spaniards took Santa Fe by storm, after passing two weeks in a futile effort to persuade the Indians to capitulate. With his base secure, De Vargas spent much of the following year in hard campaigning that brought many of the remaining Pueblos into line. In battle, he was unrelenting, but once peace had been restored, he issued pardons and sought reconcilation. In that he was encouraged by the viceroy, who gave strict instructions that punishment was to be reserved for criminal violations of the law and was not to be meted out indiscriminantly in the heat of passion. As for the Pueblos, the governor won his best marks when he left their kivas undisturbed. Burning these sacred places, as his predecessors had always done, produced nothing but turmoil, and De Vargas recognized its folly at last.

Yet peace was elusive; much of New Mexico remained in a troubled state. Governor De Vargas observed that most of the Pueblos entertained no sincere wish to take up the Christian path, and any show of friendliness was simply a sign that they wanted to resume the trade in European goods that had been interrupted in 1680. Many villages split into pro- and anti-Spanish factions, and some Pueblos, unable to reconcile themselves to the resumption of alien rule, fled to the wilderness to live among the Apache and Navajo.

Several villages staged a minor revolt in 1696, resulting in the deaths of five missionaries and twenty-one other Spaniards. The governor put down the disturbance with a vigorous hand, showing little of the charity he had displayed earlier. But, by century's end, the reconquest was virtually complete. Only the

Hopi in the Far West remained free from Spanish authority, and they would continue so in spite of repeated attempts to woo them back in the following century.

What had happened to the Pueblos during the first one hundred years in which they were obliged to share their homeland with the Spaniards? Of greatest significance was the drastic reduction in their population. At the opening of the historic period, they may have numbered as many as forty thousand to fifty thousand. The toll taken by disease, famine, Apache attacks, and conflicts with the Spaniards left them with probably no more than fourteen thousand by the year 1700. As a corollary, the number of villages declined by more than half.

As we have seen, new crops and manufactured articles introduced by the Spaniards contributed to the Pueblo economy and eased domestic life, while superficial acceptance of religious and political forms worked some changes in the routine of village affairs. Further, the Spanish language had begun to win acceptance as a *lingua franca,* a useful second tongue by which the Indians could communicate not only with friars and government officials but also with other Pueblos speaking unrelated languages.

The lesson found in a century of upheaval was not lost on either Pueblo or Spaniard. The reconquest proved to the Indians that their independence was irretrievable, and that henceforth, some accommodation must be reached with the new lords of the land. The need for compromise dawned more slowly upon the Spaniards, but it came to them, too, in the course of the following century, as a series of fresh problems showed distinctly that royal interests in New Mexico could best be served by collaboration with the Pueblo people.

3

More Spaniards . . . and
a Few Frenchmen

N the spring of 1704, New Mexico's reconquistador Don Diego de Vargas, then sixty years of age, led a force of soldiers and Pueblo scouts against Apaches who had been raiding in the middle Rio Grande Valley. From Santa Fe, the governor marched his men downriver as far as the village of Bernalillo, where he picked up the enemy's trail and followed it southeastward through the foothills of the Sandia and Manzano mountains. In the midst of the pursuit, one of the soldiers fell ill with a sudden fever and had to be sent back; then another was stricken, and another. Finally, De Vargas himself came down with the malady and had to be carried to Bernalillo by his men. There, on April 8, after drawing up a will and giving instructions for his elaborate funeral, he died.

The passing of Diego de Vargas marked the end of one phase of colonial New Mexican history and the opening of another. During the seventeenth century, Spaniards on the Rio Grande had concentrated their attention inward on provincial affairs—the missionary program, relations with the Pueblos, petty squabbles between religious and civil factions—and they scarcely ever cast a glance outward to events taking place elsewhere in America or in Europe. But in the years following the death of Governor De Vargas, a plague of problems from afar began to crowd in upon the New Mexicans and force them to reckon with circumstances developing beyond the limits of their own province.

One of the first of these arose out of the intense rivalry between Spain and France for possession of the vast wilderness in the interior of North America. The Frenchmen Joliet and Marquette, moving down the Mississippi from Canada, had discovered the mouth of the Arkansas River in 1673, and they were followed by fur traders who soon established posts in the Illinois Country. Then Robert Cavelier de la Salle laid plans for colonizing the mouth of the Mississippi and, with the backing of the French king, he set out in the summer of 1684 with four boatloads of settlers. Perhaps because of faulty maps, he missed his original destination and landed instead on the Texas coast, deep within country claimed by Spain.

La Salle put up a flimsy fort near the head of Lavaca Bay, but Indian attacks and an epidemic rapidly reduced his colonists to a mere handful. While attempting to march overland and find the Mississippi, he was slain by some of his own men in the pine forests of east Texas.

The French invasion, feeble though it was, thoroughly aroused the Spaniards, who sent eight separate expeditions by land and sea to scour the Gulf Coast for signs of the intruders. By the time La Salle's fort was discovered, it lay deserted, in ruins. But soldiers from New Spain did find several survivors scattered among the Texas Indians and bore them off to Mexico City for interrogation. At least two of these French captives eventually became Spanish subjects and were allowed to emigrate to the province of New Mexico, after its reconquest from the Pueblos. They were Jacques Grolé and Jean l'Archeveque, who, as Santiago Gurulé and Juan de Archibeque, founded families that today number hundreds of descendants.

The La Salle episode offered a clear warning to the Spaniards that the northern frontier of the viceroyalty was in jeopardy, and it led them, in the years after 1700, to plant missions and forts in Texas, an area that they had long claimed but neglected to settle. At the same time, New Mexico began to assume importance as a buffer colony protecting the valuable mining districts farther south. Indeed, royal officials in the last half of the colo-

nial period came to regard New Mexico as a defensive bastion
of Spanish power in the far north, and they pushed into the
background the province's missionary program, which had earlier occupied such a prominent place.

Before his death, Governor De Vargas had heard stories of
French traders from Illinois and Louisiana moving among the
Plains tribes, bartering with them and winning alliances. Such
rumors persisted into the opening years of the eighteenth century, and they aroused a towering fear in the Spanish viceroy
and king. It is not surprising, therefore, that they directed New
Mexico's governors to keep a sharp watch for evidence of
French infringement on the outer border. Along with that command went a decree forbidding Spanish subjects on the Rio
Grande to engage in any trade with foreigners. That was part of
an old and well-established policy of Spain to safeguard her empire.

In the spring of 1720, a young lieutenant of the Santa Fe
presidial garrison, Don Pedro de Villasur, headed a force of
forty-two soldiers, Pueblo Indian militia, and several private citizens on an expedition northeast toward the Platte River in
present Nebraska. He had orders from New Mexico's Governor
Antonio Valverde to check on disturbing reports that large
numbers of Frenchmen were operating among the Pawnee, a
powerful and potentially dangerous tribe dominating the central
plains. With Villasur marched Juan de Archibeque, who now,
more than thirty-five years after his arrival in America with La
Salle, was serving the Spaniards as scout and interpreter.

The expedition moved up the east side of Colorado within
sight of the Front Range and past the supernal peak that would
one day bear the name of another young lieutenant, Zebulon
Pike. On the Platte, the Spaniards ran into a large village of
Pawnee. Villasur attempted to open communication, dispatching a note written in French by Archibeque; then he went into
camp amidst tall weeds along the river bank. Near daybreak of
August 14, the Indians fell upon the expedition, firing muskets
obtained from their French allies and unleashing a cloud of arrows. Villasur and Archibeque were among the first to fall. In
all, more than thirty soldiers perished, leaving a few of their

comrades, all gravely wounded, to carry news of the disaster back to Santa Fe.

The destruction of the Villasur expedition caused much consternation among officials in New Spain and spurred plans for strengthening defenses on New Mexico's eastern rim. Investigation showed that Governor Valverde had been at fault for sending an unseasoned lieutenant on such an important and dangerous mission, and he was fined fifty pesos to pay for charity Masses for the souls of the dead soldiers. The Spaniards suffered added anxiety because the expedition's official journal had been lost at the time of the attack. If found by the Pawnee and delivered to the French, it would, they feared, provide their enemies with an invaluable record of the watering holes and trail leading back to Santa Fe.

And French traders were indeed interested in reaching Santa Fe. They figured that, if the legal barriers could be broken down, a ready market awaited them and that their goods could be paid for in silver brought from the Chihuahua mines. By the late 1720s, they were trading in the camps of the Comanche who had moved into New Mexico's eastern plains; and in 1739, the first small party of Frenchmen entered Santa Fe. It was led by Pierre and Paul Mallet, residents of Illinois. With a half-dozen companions and a stock of wares, the Mallets had braved the rigors of prairie travel in hopes of opening the Spanish market. The Santa Feans rang mission bells in welcome and eagerly snapped up the French trinkets and cloth, much to the perplexity of the Spanish governor, who was under orders to prevent just such a thing from happening. In something of a quandary, he sent off a hurried message to the viceroy informing him of the Mallets' arrival and requesting an easing of restrictions so that trade might be opened between New Mexico and the Mississippi valley.

The viceroy's curt reply was not unexpected. He sternly reminded the New Mexicans that the frontier stood closed to foreigners. The king would not tolerate trade across his borders, no matter how much his subjects might desire it. The Mallet brothers were disappointed by the rebuff but cannily perceived that the law in New Mexico could easily be evaded. The entire province was so starved for manufactured goods that it seemed likely a few Frenchmen could slip in each year to do business, counting on the local authorities to look the other way. While risks were great, they were far outweighed by the chance to reap immense profits.

The Mallets left Santa Fe, returning eastward by way of the Arkansas River and thence continuing down the Mississippi to New Orleans, where they made a favorable report to the French governor. During ensuing decades, a number of traders traveled regularly between Louisiana and New Mexico. Occasionally they suffered arrest when a strict governor was in office at Santa Fe, but often they sold out quickly and got away with their hard-earned fortunes in bullion and furs. That small but steady traffic across America's midlands was a forerunner of the flourishing commerce Anglo-Americans would establish in the following century. When that later breed of traders carved out the Santa Fe Trail, beginning in 1821, they had no idea that they were following in the footsteps of enterprising Frenchmen, who two generations before had pursued the same shining vision to New Mexico.

Franco-Spanish competition for territory in North America ended in 1763, with the conclusion of the French and Indian War. In that conflict, which pitted England against France, the latter got a sound drubbing and lost all of her colonial empire on the American continent. Sensing the inevitable in 1762, the French had ceded the vast and rich Louisiana Territory to Spain, to keep it from falling into English hands. With that windfall, the Spanish boundary, so long defended on the limits of New Mexico and Texas, leaped all the way to the Mississippi. Since the aggressive Anglo-Saxons were still largely confined to the eastern seaboard beyond the Appalachians, the Spaniards for the time being could dismiss the problem of foreign intruders on the northern edge of New Spain. That was just as well, for they had other troubles in abundance to preoccupy them.

Concurrent with the French threat to New Mexico, the Spaniards after 1700 had been forced to contend with warring nomad Indians whose challenge in the long run proved far more costly. The magnitude of the suffering and destruction experienced by colonial New Mexicans can scarcely be imagined today. In the Spanish archives at Santa Fe are still preserved the officials' reports, with their faded ink and brittle paper, that recount in grisly detail the killings, the robberies, and the acts of wanton destruction by parties of Indian raiders, sometimes numbering upward of a thousand men. Now that all is serene, who among us can conjure up any authentic picture of the mood of stark terror that overlaid the New Mexican countryside two hundred years ago?

The principal offenders included several tribes. On the far northeastern frontier, assorted Apache bands, who had coalesced to become the Jicarilla, created disturbances in the first years of the eighteenth century. Below them, on the southeastern plains, other Apaches, known in time as the Mescalero, launched raids against the middle Rio Grande district. It was the Mescalero who had brought about the depopulation in the 1670s of the Pueblo communities on the eastern slope of the Manzano Mountains. All along the southern limits of the province and extending into the cactus-studded wastes of Arizona ranged the ferocious Gila Apache, a perennial menace to every traveler and sheep-raiser south and west of Albuquerque. Finally, the Navajo, whose territory took in the mountains and mesas of the west, completed the ring of enemies hemming in New Mexico on every side.

If we can judge by their descendants, all the Apaches and the Navajo were born with a strong love of personal freedom. Heredity and a roving life disposed them toward a durable individualism and a peculiar imperviousness to hardship and pain. These qualities made them formidable warriors and—after suffering abuse from the Spaniards in the seventeenth century— implacable foes. Understandably, repeated attempts by friars to congregate them in missions never got off the ground. Nomadism was in their blood, and once they acquired the horse and a new mobility, soft words of missionaries or the feeble efforts of Spain's scant soldiery could do little to check their predatory ways.

Following the Pueblo Revolt and the Spanish reconquest of New Mexico, another fierce people, the Comanche, suddenly appeared like a thunderbolt out of the northern mountains. They

NEW MEXICO

A photographer's essay by Joe Munroe

Photographs in sequence

Shiprock.
Albuquerque skyline.
Albuquerque at dusk.
Carlsbad Caverns National Park.
Nuclear fusion project, Los Alamos.
Fence near Chama, early morning.
Rio Grande near Las Cruces.
Trinity Site near Alamogordo, marking spot of first atomic explosion.
Indian family, Shiprock.
Mission of San Francisco de Asis near Taos.
Porch of the Palace of the Governors, Santa Fe.
Building an adobe house near Chimayo.
Painter Georgia O'Keeffe, Abiquiu.
Painter Peter Hurd, San Patricio.
Sheep ranch near Roswell.

first raided the Jicarilla Apache about 1706, a foray that revealed the inviting plains filled with game lying northeast of Taos. One look and the Comanche knew that there was a country to be claimed as their own.

For a while they set up their camps in the San Luís valley near the head of the Rio Grande, alongside their mountain cousins, the Utes. From that base, the two tribes sent war parties against the Jicarilla and occasionally against the Pueblos and Spaniards. By the late 1730s, the Jicarilla had been so badly mauled that they abandoned their hunting grounds on the plains and fled west to the vicinity of Taos and Pecos pueblos, seeking refuge. As the Jicarilla retreated, the Comanches moved in and occupied the lush grasslands of eastern New Mexico. From there, they launched devastating raids against the Rio Grande settlements for the next fifty years.

The merciless war forced upon New Mexico by the plains and mountain tribes inevitably pulled the Spaniards and Pueblos closer together. In the early decades of the eighteenth century, they evolved a system of mutual support that shored up provincial military defenses and kept both peoples from being overwhelmed. The Pueblos formed militia companies to march alongside regular troops on campaign duty and opened up their villages as a haven to Spanish settlers forced from their homes by marauders. Such co-operation, unthinkable prior to 1680, was made possible by a new spirit of tolerance shown by the Spaniards following the reconquest.

New Mexico's great missionary era had come to an end with the Pueblo Revolt, for in the period of resettlement that followed, the Franciscans failed to regain their earlier strength and influence. Some, though not all, of the destroyed missions were rebuilt. But while the friars resumed work, they no longer displayed the uncompromising zeal that had poisoned their relations with the Pueblos during the seventeenth century. The governors in Santa Fe, at one time the scourge of the Pueblos, now became sympathetic to Pueblo problems and attentive to complaints against an occasional friar or settler who abused them. The Indians' co-operation and good will, they had finally recognized, was essential to the maintenance of the province.

The conciliatory attitude of clergy and government officials, a strong recollection of the consequences of their futile revolt, and the new threat posed by Comanche and Apache attack led the Pueblos to accept the Spaniards as rulers and allies. There was little else they could do. After 1700, settlers from New Spain flowed into New Mexico in a small but steady stream, establishing towns, farms, and ranches. As a result, Spaniards and *mestizos* (mixed-bloods) soon outnumbered the Pueblos, who for the first time found themselves in the minority.

General Diego de Vargas, shortly after the recovery of Santa Fe, had established the new town of Santa Cruz de la Cañada in a small fertile valley near the Tewa Pueblos. Albuquerque became a municipality in 1706, when thirty-five families marked out a plaza among giant cottonwoods near the east bank of the Rio Grande. These two towns, together with the capital and El Paso far to the south, remained New Mexico's four principal communities or *villas* for the rest of the colonial period.

The bulk of the new Spanish population lived in a sprinkling of hamlets along the Rio Grande, the lower Chama River, and in the Taos valley, eking out a living on small irrigated plots or tending flocks of sheep. The rural character of this society meant that the people, scattered and isolated, had little opportunity to unite for defense. In some of the larger villages, they were able to form enclosed quadrangles with defensive towers and embrasures on the walls, but even these were not as effective in repelling attack as the fortified Indian pueblos. Several of the eighteenth-century governors attempted to force the dispersed farming folk to join together in more easily defended communities; but they stoutly resisted such pressure, claiming they needed to be near their fields to protect them from bears and robbers.

The mainstay of New Mexico's defenses rested with two presidios or garrisons of regular troops, one created at El Paso in 1683 (withdrawn after 1772), the other at Santa Fe in 1693. Unfortunately, the king was so plagued with troubles in Europe and worried by first the French and later the British intrusions elsewhere in America that he was of little mind to heed the chorus of pleas from New Mexicans for adequate troops and military supplies. In the 1720s, for example, the Santa Fe presidio had only eighty men to garrison the capital and patrol hundreds of square leagues of Indian country. Such a meager force would have proven wholly unequal to the work but for the support of large numbers of citizen militia and Pueblo Indian auxiliaries. Even when the Comanche and other tribes stepped up their devastating war after mid-century, the crown showed more interest in reducing expenses on the frontier than in providing the additional outlays needed to relieve the beleaguered colonists. One of His Majesty's inspectors, upon surveying the immensity of the problem and listening to the clamor for military aid, concluded that "the treasury of Midas would not suffice" to produce an improvement in the situation.[1]

Through long experience, the Spaniards had worked out a sequence of steps for dealing with nomadic Indians. They began with the peaceful approach, using missionaries to extend the olive branch and to argue the merits of settling down under the tutelage of Spanish friars and officials. When that failed, as it often did, the next step was a resort to total war, or "war by fire and blood," in the quaint phrasing of the period. If that course proved futile or too expensive, the royal government was not above bribing or buying off the untamed tribesmen. That strategy often proved singularly effective.

The time for parleying with all the tribes, friendly and hostile, came annually at the great Taos trade fair. In the autumn, parties of Comanches, Utes, Apaches, and occasionally Navajos streamed toward the Taos valley, laden with buffalo hides, buckskins, jerky, and horses to exchange for Spanish hardware and Pueblo foodstuffs. During the fair, a universal truce prevailed, observed even by the wildest warriors, so that any person felt safe traveling the trail to Taos. For the Spaniards, it was a welcome break from the constant round of war that filled the rest of the year. Moreover, the fair gave them a chance to send missionaries and other envoys among the unruly guests, presenting arguments in behalf of a permanent peace.

But diplomatic maneuvering always took second place to

1. Alfred Barnaby Thomas, *The Plains Indians and New Mexico, 1751–1778* (Albuquerque: University of New Mexico Press, 1940), p. 13.

business and unrestrained revelry. Cavalcades of Indians in holiday finery mingled with a host of Spanish citizenry bearing their
wares on burros or oxcarts. Often the governor came from Santa
Fe, attended by a spirited retinue, to impose what loose order he
could on the boisterous throng. His presence was also needed to
prevent his own subjects from cheating the Indians and to arbi-
trate the dozens of small quarrels that developed in the course of
the bartering. Then there were captives to be ransomed: an occasional Spaniard taken from some distant province, or, more
commonly, Pawnee and Wichita slaves brought from the central
plains. For that purpose, the king provided the governor a special mercy fund.

The brilliant, noisy pageant lasted day and night—a picturesque and turbulent spectacle, rivaled in the history of the
American West only by the trading rendezvous of the mountain
men in the nineteenth century.

About the fair, a curious twist: once the last hide and steel
awl had changed hands, the participants parted amiably and returned to their homes—there to lay plans for resuming the brutal
war that had been suspended for matters of commerce. Weeks,
sometimes only days, after leaving Taos, Comanche or Ute
freebooters might swoop down with their ear-splitting war cries
and run off the same horses they had so recently traded away.

This deadly seesaw game continued for decades, with New
Mexico suffering thunderous volleys from its enemies. The conflict reached a crescendo in the 1770s and threatened to reduce
the province to complete poverty and ruin. Leafing through
reports on raids and casualties for these years, the modern
reader is provided a doleful reminder of the savagery of frontier
warfare. Examples: Comanches numbering one thousand ravaged the Chama valley and the country around Santa Clara
Pueblo in July 1774, killing seven persons, wounding others,
and kidnapping three boys. Late in the month, another two
hundred warriors of the same tribe attacked Albuquerque, slay-
ing Spaniards and their Indian allies and making off with a great
flock of sheep and the town's entire herd of horses. Little defense could be mustered against that particular assault, for the
district militia was away campaigning against the Navajo. That

tribe had recently run off many of the sheep grazing south of Albuquerque, deliberately leaving behind just enough animals so that, with the natural increase, they would find something worth stealing when they returned the next year.

From early May to the end of July 1775, forty-one people were killed during incursions by Comanches, Gila Apaches, and Navajos, thirty-three of the fatalities being Indians of Sandia Pueblo. Many towns and pueblos lost their entire stock of horses, making any kind of retaliation impossible. Up and down the Rio Grande, people were abandoning their ranches and villages and moving to the few places that offered some measure of safety. During that trying time, the population of Santa Fe more than doubled, as refugees fled the countryside. Father Francisco Atanasio Domínguez, who inspected the condition of New Mexican missions in 1776, found Taos Pueblo so heavily fortified that it resembled "those walled cities with bastions and towers that are described to us in the Bible." [2] Inside, he saw blocks of houses inhabited by Spanish settlers who had joined the pueblo for protection.

The entire province lay under a virtual state of seige, leading Governor Pedro Fermín de Mendinueta to inform the viceroy of his inability to guarantee the continued survival of New Mexico. That was alarming news. All of New Spain's frontier provinces bled from the effects of the appalling Indian war, but none was so exposed and open to trespass as New Mexico. If it should succumb, a gaping hole would be left on the northern border and the terrible spoilers could pour southward like a flood. The prospect was unthinkable.

Alert at last to the dimensions of the crises, the king set aside his penny-pinching game and took a forceful step to strengthen the outer reaches of his North American dominions. In 1776 he created the military jurisdiction in northern New Spain known as the Commandancy General of the Interior Provinces and placed it under General Teodoro de Croix. With a competent

---

2. Fray Francisco Atanasio Domínguez, *The Missions of New Mexico,* translated by Eleanor B. Adams and Fray Angélico Chávez (Albuquerque: University of New Mexico Press, 1956), p. 110.

leader in the field, the crown hoped that the battered colonists would take hope and work with the government toward developing new policies to discourage Indian attack. As a further sign of royal concern, Croix received a favorable response to his request for two thousand soldiers as reinforcements for the wobbly frontier line stretching westward from the Gulf of Mexico to Sonora.

In 1778, at the city of Chihuahua, General Croix convened a council of prominent officials to study the latest reports on the condition of frontier defenses. Governor Mendinueta, now retiring from his post in New Mexico, attended, together with Don Juan Bautista de Anza, who having made a name for himself in Sonora and California, was on his way to assume the governorship at Santa Fe. From all sides, Croix received gloomy accounts. Weighing the testimony, he swiftly reached the conclusion, as he wrote to Spain, that if the important barrier of New Mexico was lost, nothing could stop the Indians from making themselves masters of the entire border country. It fell to Anza, therefore, to prevent that from happening.

What Croix proposed was use of the time-tested stratagem of divide-and-conquer. Break down the hostility of the Comanche, he instructed Anza; bring them into a firm alliance with the Spaniards; and then, using them as auxiliaries, as the Pueblos were, wage a war of no quarter against the Apache. It was a bold and imaginative plan, certainly, and one long considered by the Spaniards. But could it be carried out?

An affirmative answer to that question depended upon the courage and ability Don Juan Bautista de Anza brought to the governorship of New Mexico. As it turned out, he possessed an abundance of both qualities, which, together with his tremendous energy and inflexible will, stood him in good stead in facing the troublesome assignment given by Croix. When posted to Santa Fe, Anza's only thought was to go and get a difficult job done— overcome the hostility of the Comanche and cement a military alliance with them. At the beginning, a gambler would have hesitated to bet a ducat on his chances, for the Comanches' surliness and preference for war were too well known. But then, Anza, born on the Sonora frontier and raised on a steady diet of

Indian fighting, was accustomed to facing unpalatable realities. His initial task was to win the Comanches' attention and respect, an aim best achieved on the battlefield. As quickly as possible, after getting settled in Santa Fe, he began taking the measure of his foes, sizing up both their firebrand leader, Cuerno Verde, and their sanctuary on the plains that stretched from Colorado across eastern New Mexico. Anza's past experience led him to see with clarity what he had to do: invade the Comanche homeland and vanquish Cuerno Verde on his own ground. That was the only argument, he believed, that the Indians would understand.

Chief Cuerno Verde, or Green Horn (a name derived from his painted buffalo-horn headdress), hated the Spaniards with cold fury, a passion that arose after they killed his father in battle. "The scourge of this kingdom," Anza described him in a letter to General Croix, and a man "who has exterminated many towns, killing hundreds and making as many prisoners whom he afterwards sacrificed in cold blood." [3]

In mid-August of 1779, the governor readied his punitive force at San Juan Pueblo. The several score regulars he brought from Santa Fe looked sharp and formidable enough, but sight of the citizen militia and the Pueblo warriors who had answered his call was sufficient to make Anza cringe. Their scrubby, underfed horses seemed scarcely fit for campaign duty, while their motley assortment of weapons beggared description. Militiamen possessing as much as three charges of gunpowder were among the more fortunate. As best he could, Anza remedied the poverty of his volunteer soldiers, allotting a good horse to each individual and distributing military stores. He then organized the command, totaling almost six hundred men, into three divisions, sent out his scouts, and marched northward toward Colorado to find Cuerno Verde.

The governor was aware that all previous campaigns had taken the mountain pass east of Taos into the Comanche country. But that route was constantly watched, so that the enemy

---

3. Alfred Barnaby Thomas, *Forgotten Frontiers* (Norman: University of Oklahoma Press, 1969), p. 66.

had plenty of warning whenever the Spaniards approached. So Anza decided that the way to travel was up the west slope of the Rockies, with the wall of peaks on the east screening his movements. At a point even with the enemy's lair, the little army could cross the mountains and outflank the Comanche camps.

The plan worked perfectly. Governor Anza bulled his way over the ridges of the Front Range just below Pike's Peak and hit the Indians from behind. In the first encounter, he seized a number of prisoners and more booty than could be loaded on a hundred horses. More significantly, he obtained news of Cuerno Verde from the captives. The Comanche leader with his principal subchiefs had gone, days before, to pillage New Mexico and was even now returning to his main camp below the Arkansas River, where he planned a victory celebration. Anza, seeing a splendid opportunity to settle accounts if he could catch the war party by surprise, immediately put his troops in motion toward the south.

The way led across the sweeping plains, carpeted now with thick buffalo grass and sickle-headed grama, past dark juttings of the western mountains, and down to the sandy banks of the Arkansas. Below the river, Anza's boldness was rewarded. He caught Cuerno Verde in an ambush. At the first sign of the Spaniards, the chief pranced forward on his horse, spoiling for a fight. So enraged was he at finding New Mexicans in his backyard that he failed to perceive that his party had been surrounded. "Thus pride and arrogance brought him to his end," wrote Governor Anza in his official report of the affair.[4]

At the last moment, Cuerno Verde realized his mistake and tried to retreat—too late. The Indians killed their horses and, using the bodies as a barricade, made their stand. Anza observed with wonder that the chief retained his swagger to the last, disdaining even to load his own musket. He contemptuously passed it to one of his men to recharge, while in the interval exposing himself to heavy fire.

The Spaniards, for once having the advantage of numbers, rode their enemies down and that was the end of the fight.

4. Thomas, *Forgotten Frontiers,* p. 136.

Along with Cuerno Verde, there perished on the plains of Colorado his son and heir, four subchiefs, and the tribe's principal medicine man. Elated, the soldiers shouted "an infinite number of huzzas in the name of the King," and gathered up the spoils of victory. Governor Anza returned to Santa Fe, carrying as a trophy Cuerno Verde's vaunted headdress with its green buffalo horn. In all their painful years of warfare with the Plains Indians, the New Mexicans had never seen anything to match this decisive defeat of the Comanches. It was Anza's finest military exploit.

The death of Cuerno Verde produced no immediate capitulation on the part of the Indians, but it effectively stemmed the terrible raids that had plagued the New Mexicans for three-quarters of a century. And it prepared the ground for an eventual permanent peace with the Comanche nation.

The momentous event came in 1786, following a long period of skilled diplomacy by Anza. He had been unwilling to arrange a pact until all divisions of the tribe agreed to submit and to elect a single individual to represent them in Spanish councils. In February an impressive array of chiefs and distinguished warriors arrived at Pecos Pueblo, ready to join with the Spaniards in a declaration of peace. And they had a new leader, Ecueracapa, to present to Governor Anza, who had ridden the dozen leagues from Santa Fe to meet them.

There at Pecos, beneath the southernmost ranks of the Rockies, whose snow-clad summits shone in the winter's light, unfolded in barbaric splendor one of the most extraordinary ceremonies ever witnessed in the West. Conscious of the effect of good theater upon the Indians, Anza, in solemn council and with many colorful flourishes, consummated the treaty of peace. Upon Chief Ecueracapa he bestowed the lofty title "General of the Comanche Nation," and as a sign of authority granted by the king, vested him with a staff of office, a saber, and a banner.

The Comanches, accompanied by the Utes who had joined in the festivities, responded with flowery oratory, thanking the Spaniards for overlooking past hostilities and promising both to keep the peace and to join in common war against the Apache.

Then they dug a hole in the middle of the council ground and ritually refilled it, symbolizing the end to their long war against New Mexico.

Incredibly, the peace held, to become one of the most enduring ever arranged between red man and white. The Spaniards over the years showered their new allies with gifts and carried on an expanded trade. The Comanches, either in the company of soldiers or in their own war parties, rode against the still-hostile Mescalero and Gila Apaches, keeping them at bay along New Mexico's southern frontier. Comanche General Ecueracapa proved so steadfast in friendship that he asked that youths of his tribe be educated in European ways and religion. Later, in 1793, when Ecueracapa was mortally wounded on a raid against the Pawnee, the Spanish governor, Fernando de la Concha, demonstrated his high regard for the Comanche leader by dispatching New Mexico's only surgeon to the isolated Indian camp on the plains in a futile effort to save Ecueracapa's life.

The legacy of Anza's landmark treaty was still evident a century later, when the United States cavalry locked horns with the Comanches for control of the southern plains. No Anglo-American could then travel with any security through the vast distances of western Texas and eastern New Mexico. Yet, Hispanos and Pueblos moved freely, hunting and trading, and enjoying the safe passage that Governor Anza had won for them a hundred years before.

Other undertakings of Anza's administration were less dramatic than the Comanche peace, and less successful. In 1780, soon after returning from the expedition against Cuerno Verde, the governor set out on a mission of mercy to the Hopi pueblos. These people, residing atop barren, sun-roasted mesas on the western fringe of New Mexico, had been wracked by drought for three years, and Anza hoped to curry favor by bringing them relief supplies. It had been a full century since the Pueblo Revolt, and the Hopi still clung stubbornly to their independence, rejecting all overtures by government officials and missionaries to submit to Spanish sovereignty. Their present desperate plight suggested to Anza that they might at last be willing to capitulate.

Hardened as he was by a life of privation, the governor was moved to sympathy by the suffering he found. The Hopi were emaciated by starvation and many had sold their children to other tribes in exchange for food. He distributed supplies to those who would accept them and persuaded a handful to go back with him to the Rio Grande to live as Spanish subjects. But the majority sided with the *cacique,* or head priest, of Oraibi Pueblo, who told Anza that he preferred to stay and perish in his own country and that he must refuse the gifts of food, for he had nothing of value to give in return. Since he was not inclined to force anything upon the Hopi against their will, Governor Anza turned back to Santa Fe, leaving the tribe hungry but secure in its liberty.

Another project of Anza involved his attempt to open a direct road between New Mexico and the province of Sonora. That venture formed part of a larger scheme developed by the colonial government in those years to improve communication within all the northern provinces, thereby strengthening both their defenses and economies. Fray Francisco Garcés, an uncommon explorer and trailbreaker stationed at Mission San Xavier del Bac, near Tucson, had tramped through much of the desert Southwest in the mid-1770s. In fact, one of his solitary wanderings found him newly arrived in the Hopi villages on the same July Fourth that colonial revolutionaries were putting ink to paper in Philadelphia. Also in 1776, Fathers Escalante and Domínguez made their memorable journey northwestward from Santa Fe in a fruitless bid to discover a practical route from New Mexico to the California coast. These expeditions merely confirmed that geography on that section of the frontier imposed monumental barriers to travel and that more exploration was needed to discover practical lines of communication.

Sonora at that time extended northward to the Gila River (taking in an area later to be obtained by the United States in the Gadsden Purchase) and included a scattering of Spanish settlements, among them Tucson and Tubac. The country above the river, practically two-thirds of modern Arizona, then formed part of New Mexico. East of Sonora lay Nueva Vizcaya, a province tied closely to New Mexico by the Camino Real, or

King's Highway, running from the city of Chihuahua almost straight north to El Paso and Santa Fe. This road, the only real thoroughfare in or out of the Rio Grande settlements, allowed the favorably situated Chihuahuan merchants to establish a tight monopoly over interprovincial commerce, much to the disadvantage of the New Mexicans. A new, direct highway to Sonora, if Anza could find one, would give New Mexico a chance to purchase imported goods at fairer prices.

In the fall of 1780, Governor Anza left Santa Fe with a force of 150 men, setting a southwesterly course. Skirting the Black Range in south-central New Mexico, he crossed a waterless desert in the vicinity of the modern town of Deming, climbed the San Luis Pass, and, after a march of almost six hundred miles, reached the capital of Sonora at Arizpe. Unfortunately, the route he traveled was too long and difficult to be of much value to the New Mexicans, and the trip was chalked up as a failure. Notwithstanding, Anza had turned in a faithful and honest performance.

In 1787 he was relieved of his governorship because of ill health and, the following year, he died in Sonora. His career as a frontiersman easily rivaled that of a Boone or a Crockett or a Carson. But unlike those national heroes whose names today are household words, Juan Bautista de Anza and his story remain unknown to most Americans.

In the fifty years before New Spain (or Mexico) won independence in 1821, her northern frontier weathered another challenge—this one posed by British and American intruders. In Europe, Spain and England were traditional enemies, and their mutual antipathy carried over to the New World. After France was expelled from North America in 1763, the two powers were left facing each other across the wide reaches of the Mississippi, to await a day of reckoning. For the Spanish, the hour seemed to be at hand when, in 1776, the Atlantic seaboard colonies proclaimed their independence and set out with banners flying to humble mighty England. As eager as she was to see an old imperial foe brought to her knees, Spain entertained fears, and not without some justice, that success by the Thirteen Colonies might infect her own colonial possessions with the notion of rebellion. But balanced against that apprehension was the belief that an independent American nation would offer less of a threat to New Spain's frontier than would England.

By 1779, the year in which Anza defeated Cuerno Verde, Spain openly supported revolution in English America and began diverting funds and munitions from New Spain to support the patriots fighting the British in the South and West. The Spanish authorities experienced some worry that the vast Louisiana Territory and perhaps even New Mexico might be invaded, and as in the case of the French menace a generation before, they instructed the governor at Santa Fe to keep up his guard and restrain any Britishers found operating among the Indians.

With the triumph of the American Revolution and the end of war in 1783, the danger to New Mexico appeared to subside—but not that to Louisiana. Along the Mississippi, Spain now confronted a new sovereign nation, proud and eager for growth, while to the north England still held a solid base in Canada. It was from the latter quarter that the first jabs were made at the soft underbelly of Spanish Louisiana. In the twilight years of the eighteenth century, agents of England's great trading companies commenced to swarm out of Canada into the upper Mississippi and Missouri valleys, establishing posts and winning Indian allies. Spain regarded that as a blatant invasion of upper Louisiana, and she did her best to counter the thrust by sending her own traders and an occasional expedition to tribes along the middle Missouri. She also offered a bounty of three thousand dollars to the first Spanish subject who should ascend that mysterious river, find its source, and then cross to the Pacific. No Spaniard ever claimed the reward, and achievement of the feat was left to Lewis and Clark after the area had passed to the United States.

As one means to strengthen her hold on interior North America during those unsettled years, Spain made preliminary attempts to open direct communication lines between Santa Fe and outposts in Texas and Louisiana. The man in the vanguard of that effort was Pedro (or Pierre) Vial, a native-born Frenchman. He had spent a number of years as a captive of the Comanche and from them gained an intimate knowledge of wilderness paths. In 1786 and 1788, he made trail-breaking trips between the New Mexican capital and San Antonio; in 1792 and 1793, he traveled from Santa Fe to St. Louis and back, providing his Spanish employers with detailed maps of the southern plains country. The viceregal government failed to follow through and develop roads over the routes pioneered by Vial, but it was made acutely aware of the ease with which Anglo-Americans, should they ever breach the barrier of the Mississippi, might scamper up the trails pointing to the heart of New Mexico.

That barrier, in fact, evaporated in 1803. Three years before, Spain, under pressure from Napoleon, returned Louisiana to France with the understanding that the territory would never be delivered into the hands of a third power. The restriction was wholly ignored by Napoleon, who turned around and sold the entire Louisiana Territory to the United States. When the French colors were struck and the American flag run up at New Orleans late in 1803, New Spain suddenly discovered a new and formidable contest looming at her northern gates.

The immediate problem was one of boundaries. No one knew what Louisiana contained or what its limits were on the north, west, and south. Under the circumstances, it was to the advantage of both the United States and Spain to make their own claims as wide as possible, and that they proceeded to do—the former asserting rights over all lands extending to the Rio Grande, and the latter claiming the Missouri River as the northern boundary of New Mexico and Texas. Neither position was historically tenable, but each country resolved to press the issue and gain what it could.

The Spaniards were in particular dread of losing control of the Missouri, believing, wrongly, that its upper waters bowed south, giving easy access to New Mexico. In foreign hands, they thought, the river would point like a dagger at Santa Fe and the flourishing mining country below it. A Spanish agent in St. Louis gave voice to that fear when he warned in 1804 that American officials at that city were collecting every scrap of available information on possible land and water routes leading to New Mexico. He prophesied that, if something was not done to forestall invasion, plundered silver from the Mexican mines would soon be floating down the Missouri.

When it was learned in New Spain that Meriwether Lewis and William Clark had set forth at the bidding of President Thomas Jefferson to explore the Missouri and find a water route to the Pacific, alarm approached the level of panic. As had happened on so many occasions in the past, when danger loomed on the frontier, the burden of taking appropriate countermeasures was laid upon the governor of New Mexico. That official, Don Fernando Chacón, sent a small reconnaissance party northward under Pedro Vial in the summer of 1804 to gauge the progress of what he termed *"Capitán Merri'*s expedition." Among the Pawnee of Nebraska, Vial encountered a band of French traders. They had no news of Lewis and Clark, but they could relate that other Americans had already been among the central plains tribes winning their allegiance. Only the Pawnee had given them a rebuff and remained loyal to Spain.

When Vial conveyed that information to Santa Fe, it filled the governor with anxiety. Two parties were launched, in succession, each with instructions to reach the Pawnee and persuade them to seek out and attack *"Capitán Merri"* and his company. But both groups of Spaniards were turned back by hostile Indians without accomplishing their mission. Their failure left the way clear for Lewis and Clark, who had passed the winter of 1805–1806 on the Pacific shore, to return unchallenged across the continent to St. Louis.

Another American expedition, sent in 1806 to explore the southwestern corner of the Louisiana Purchase, affected the Spaniards of New Mexico more directly. Twenty-six-year-old Lieutenant Zebulon Montgomery Pike, son of a veteran of the American Revolution, had orders to search for the headwaters of the Arkansas and Red rivers. Young Pike, with twenty-three men, crossed the plains to the foot of the Colorado Rockies, where all shivered through a miserable, icy winter. In the spring of 1807, he led his stalwarts over the mountains and put up a stockade on a small tributary of the Rio Grande. He was convinced, or at least pretended to believe, that he was on the upper reaches of the Red River, and hence still on American soil. A hundred mounted Spaniards from Santa Fe who descended upon his isolated little post soon dispelled that illusion.

Bustled off to the New Mexican capital as a prisoner, Lieutenant Pike found himself treated to an intriguing glimpse of the forbidden town whose name had long becharmed frontiersmen moving west. In popular American myth, exotic Santa Fe was forever linked to Quivira and the treasure of the conquistadors; the riches of the Chihuahua mines flowed there in a silver stream and paid for graceful palaces and temples; and along its splendid streets rode haughty Spanish noblemen dressed in silk and lace. The reality of conditions in Santa Fe, Pike quickly noted, had nothing to do with the myth. The town, in fact, had experienced little improvement since 1776, when Father Domínguez had bewailed its rueful and comfortless aspect.

"Its appearance from a distance struck my mind with the same effect as a fleet of the flat bottomed boats, which are seen in the spring and fall seasons, descending the Ohio River," wrote Pike later in a summary report. By "flat-bottomed boats," he meant the "miserable houses" of adobe brick strung for a mile down the slender stream valley. The farming practices, he observed, riding through the outskirts of the town, were no more advanced than the style of architecture. "They are a century behind us in the art of cultivation . . . and I have seen them breaking up whole fields with the hoe." [5]

Severe as he was in some of his judgments, the captive lieutenant was also painfully aware of his own wretched appearance and that of his soldiers. With their bearded and haggard faces, shaggy hair, and threadbare clothing, they were something less than impressive representatives of the United States. Curious onlookers who crowded around them in Santa Fe's streets, seeing such wild and unkempt men, wanted to know if people in their country lived in real houses, or in tents like the Indians; and did they know what hats were? The little band, coming

5. Donald Jackson, editor, *The Journals of Zebulon Montgomery Pike,* 2 vols. (Norman: University of Oklahoma Press, 1966), 1:391; 2:51.

BANKS HIGH SCHOOL LIBRARY

from its ordeal in the Rockies, possessed not a single hat. Pike, by his own admission, was mortified.

As these bedraggled soldiers and New Mexican citizens took first stock of one another, they had no way of knowing the strange twists of fate that would soon bring their peoples into a conflict and eventual union. Lieutenant Pike, though he was unsuspecting of the fact, was even then helping to set in motion forces that would lead to America's economic and, ultimately, military conquest of New Mexico.

The treatment Pike received in Santa Fe was courteous, though he submitted to endless questioning by the Spanish governor regarding the motives of his expedition. His answers did not completely satisfy the provincial authorities, and as a result he and his men were sent on to Chihuahua for further interrogation. There, in June 1807, Pike learned that they would be taken north and deposited in American territory at Natchitoches, Louisiana. While the Spaniards were content to be rid of these unwilling guests, they were not prepared to have them publicize the road to Santa Fe or the details of life in New Mexico. Spain was still too jealous of her possessions and too suspicious of foreigners to want information leaking abroad. Pike was therefore sent home without his notes and maps, made first-hand as he explored the southwestern border.

Back in the United States, the lieutenant found that some of his astute countrymen were already looking beyond the Louisiana Purchase to territories stretching toward the Pacific; thus what he had seen behind the veil shrouding New Mexico was of national interest. From memory, Pike assembled a report of his experiences in northern New Spain and saw it published in 1810. The work gave Americans their first inside view of Hispanic life and customs on the Rio Grande, but of even greater weight were the references to economic conditions. In Santa Fe, Pike recorded, the cost of manufactured goods was staggering. Some fine-quality textiles were selling for as much as twenty-five dollars per yard, while, on the other hand, sheep, raised locally in abundance, went for only one dollar a head. The conclusion, for any Yankee trader, was obvious. New Mexico offered a ready market, vast and untapped, if only the stringent

Spanish restrictions on commerce and travel could be broken down.

In the years following Pike's venture, several bands of enterprising Anglo-Americans—in their slam-bang, push-ahead manner—gathered up an assortment of goods and struck out from Missouri to try to gain a toe hold in Santa Fe. But in practically every instance, they met with a hostile reception, suffering imprisonment and confiscation of their wares. Spain, having kept New Mexico's borders legally sealed to the French for half a century or more, was in no mood to throw them open now to a self-assertive people who posed an even more formidable threat. Development of commercial relations would have to await a shift of sentiment in New Spain. Already, by 1810, rumblings from the south in favor of Mexican independence could be heard, inspired in part by America's own success; and there were those in Missouri, and elsewhere on the western frontier, who speculated that the day was not far off when a new and more friendly government might be installed in Santa Fe.

Through the long years of the colonial period, when Spanish officialdom was grappling with the larger problems of empire, the New Mexicans in isolation were evolving a social order with its own distinctive stamp. The first colonists who came to the Rio Grande with Oñate had been a proud and aristocratic lot. Both men and women brought articles of fine apparel, tailored of silk and velvet, for they expected to recreate in the northern wilderness some semblance of the elegant society to which they were accustomed. But it was not long before the realities of frontier existence showed plainly that the refinements of civilization possessed little chance of surviving. Suits and dresses of fine fabric quickly gave way to those made of coarse homespun cloth and leather.

Many pioneers, those in New Mexico as well as elsewhere in America, came to feel a strong attraction for the free, uninhibited life offered by the frontier and to find the ways of the Indians more compatible than the restraints and conventions of their own society. For example, the Dutch along the Hudson, Swedes on the Delaware, and Englishmen in Carolina all saw ranks of their men become wild and shed their civilized behavior as they would shed a raincoat.

Wilderness life also tainted Hispanic culture on the Rio Grande and turned some colonial citizens toward a career of gambling, fighting, and lawlessness. Other New Mexicans, while not giving way entirely to primitive instincts, nevertheless developed an independence of spirit and a disdain for authority that was quite uncharacteristic of Spaniards. Father Juan de Morfí, writing in 1778, complained that many rural New Mexicans chose to live in remote areas because, unobserved by neighbors or civil authorities, they were free to commit immoral and criminal acts. He reported that some isolated colonists "were not ashamed to go about nude so that lewdness is seen here more than in the brutes, and the peaceful Indians are scandalized." [6] Nor were residents of New Mexico's towns immune from the virus of social rebellion. Governor Fernando de la Concha in 1788 discovered with considerable dismay that the people of Santa Fe, "churlish by nature and wedded to the perfect freedom in which they have always lived," ignored his order to move their outlying houses closer to the main plaza to provide for better defense of the capital. [7] This frontier, it seemed, like most others, promoted a spirit of individualism and weakened the hand of civilized institutions.

Throughout the eighteenth and into the nineteenth century, these frontier folk slowly expanded the limits of settlement, taking up irrigable farm plots in outlying river valleys like those of the Chama, the Pecos, and the Puerco. They lived in small clusters of flat-roofed adobe houses with packed-earth floors and mud fireplaces that smoked villainously. Their simple needs, like their dwellings, were supplied for the most part by the land. What could not be produced at home could often be obtained through barter from the neighboring Pueblo Indians or from the Plains tribes at the annual Taos fair. More fortunate rural fami-

6. Marc Simmons, editor and translator, *Fray Juan Agustin de Morfi's Account of Disorders in New Mexico, 1778* (Belen, N.M.: Historical Society of New Mexico, 1976), p. 9.

7. Marc Simmons, "Settlement Patterns and Village Plans in Colonial New Mexico," *Journal of the West* 8 (1969):18.

lies—those with large land holdings and numerous sheep, in the area below Bernalillo—even enjoyed a few luxuries brought hundreds of hard leagues up the Camino Real from Chihuahua. Lieutenant Pike expressed surprise at seeing occasional pieces of silver dinnerware, and he rubbed his hands in delight when his host at one village offered as refreshment a cup of imported chocolate sweetened with sugar.

For the most part, however, life was uncomfortable and dangerous and offered few material rewards. The majority of New Mexicans knew, at some time in their lives, the sting of want and the pangs of hunger. All citizens from the governor to the poorest peon and shepherd were familiar, too, with the taste of fear that came from facing the constant danger of Indian attack and confronting the periodic epidemics against which colonial citizens could muster little defense. Smallpox, most unrelenting of diseases, swept the province on an average of every ten years, so that the majority of the population bore its disfiguring scars.

Nor were hostile Indians and sickness the only threats to life and health. Rattlesnakes also took their toll—the death certificates attesting to that can still be seen among the records of the Spanish Church—and grizzly bears brought down many a farmer who tried to protect his corn crop from their marauding. Floods claimed other New Mexicans, as did river crossings, with their tricky currents and quicksands. And lightning during the summer rains made new widows seasonally. Among the latter, to cite just one example, was Señora María Sánchez, whose husband, a Santa Fe presidial soldier, was killed in 1805 by a lightning bolt while riding a government mule. Not only did the grieving Señora suffer the loss of her spouse, she was ordered by the unfeeling authorities to pay for the dead mule.

The ever-present specter of death nourished in New Mexicans a tragic sense of life and reinforced that attitude of fatalism that so many writers have judged to be an inborn characteristic of all Spaniards. Nowhere were these qualities more sharply manifested than in the religious paintings and sculpture of the later colonial period. Forced to decorate churches and home altars with their own art, the settlers, using gypsum, paint, and pine, produced stark and bloody images of Christ and the saints; it was as if, by dwelling upon the agony of the Church, the suffering New Mexicans hoped to forget their own day-to-day problems.

Common perils and hardships on any frontier tend to break down barriers separating social classes, but one would be mistaken to think that in such a leveling process complete equality is ever achieved. Spanish New Mexico, like the new territories on the western edge of the United States, was peopled largely by hard-working pioneers. And yet even a casual look at the colonial scene reveals several distinct layers of society.

At the top were a handful of leading government and Church officials and military officers. They were well-traveled and literate men, frequently disdainful of the primitive living conditions and backwardness of the local people. That was especially the case with some of the governors who came directly from Spain or Mexico City and bore titles of nobility. They conducted their affairs with a formality and pomp strangely out of place in the dusty and wind-buffeted capital of Santa Fe, but their attempts at social display helped remind New Mexicans that they were part of a great empire, bound together as much by tradition and ceremony as by political ties.

Of second rank were petty officials, merchants, a few artisans, and a small group of large landowners—people of substantial influence in provincial affairs, though they might be poorly educated and of only moderate wealth. Many of them could trace their family tree back to an ancestor who had come with Oñate, which in New Mexico was a social premium equal to a link with the *Mayflower* in English America.

The great mass of ordinary people, many of them mixed-bloods, were simple farmers or small stock-raisers. Such yeomen were the backbone of the province, providing through their labor a solid economic foundation and furnishing militiamen for innumerable Indian campaigns. Among citizens in that class were persons known as *genízaros,* a social category composed of Indians, originally captives or slaves of nomadic tribes who had been ransomed by the Spanish government. Parceled out among the colonists, they became domestic servants or laborers, and in time lost practically all trace of their Indian heritage. With support of the Franciscans, many of them successfully petitioned the governor in the later colonial years for permission to establish their own towns on the frontier. Thus Abiquiú, Tomé, Belén, and San Miguel began as *genízaro* settlements, serving as a defensive buffer on the outer margin of the province.

On the bottom rung of New Mexico's social ladder could be found landless persons who made their way as wage laborers: farm helpers, cattle herders, shepherds, and household servants. Some of them were able to retain their independence and move from job to job as they chose. Others became victims of a system of debt peonage, through which employers contrived to hold workers in thralldom by making large advances in money or goods for which the worker could never hope to pay.

The isolation and the vastness of New Mexico's frontier guaranteed in themselves some measure of individual freedom for colonial citizens. Nevertheless, room scarcely existed in that provincial, authoritarian society for the growth of anything resembling democratic institutions. The governor held the important right of making land grants in the name of the king. In the governor's hands also were concentrated broad political, judicial, military, and economic powers. He might provide just leadership, if he was an honest and capable man; but if he happened to be vain and corrupt, as was the case with several seventeenth-century governors, then he could easily assume the trappings of a dictator and rule by whim. In the latter instance, the few trifling rights of the common citizen went by the board, at least until such time as the viceroy or the king became aware of the situation and with their long arms plucked the tyrant from his bailiwick on the Rio Grande.

Justice was in the hands of a half-dozen or so magistrates, called *alcaldes,* who rendered decisions on the basis of common sense, local custom, or personal prejudice rather than upon any formal knowledge of the law. Governor Fernando de Chacón in 1797 tried to find qualified persons to fill two vacancies left by *alcaldes* who had died; much to his astonishment, he could discover no one in all New Mexico worthy of receiving these appointments. Appeals could be carried from the courts of the *al-*

caldes to the governor himself, and then upward—if the litigant had time and money enough—to the high courts of New Spain. The notion of trial by a jury of one's peers was unknown.

Unfamiliar, too, was the idea, cultivated by English colonists in the 1760s during their struggle over the British Stamp Act, that only a representative government should levy taxes upon the people. New Mexicans routinely paid a variety of exactions demanded by the royal authorities, including a stamp tax required for all official documents, and they did so without a whimper. These colonists had practically no experience in political participation and had little tradition, beyond the municipal level, of debating issues that affected them; so they never questioned the right of the king's officers to collect whatever revenues His Majesty wished.

At the very end of the colonial period, turmoil in Europe, growing out of the French Revolution and Napoleon's subsequent rise to power, brought changes to Spain that influenced New Mexico and the rest of Spanish America. In the mother country, liberal Spaniards created a *cortes,* or parliament, and invited each of the New World colonies to send a representative. New Mexico's delegate, selected by leading citizens in 1810, was a good-humored gentleman and merchant of prominence in Santa Fe, Don Pedro Bautista Pino. For him, the first meetings of the *cortes,* with all their awkward groping toward democratic procedures, proved an eye-opener. Here was a truly representative body prepared to acknowledge that government should respond to the needs of its citizens, and that those citizens should express their needs. Don Pedro, with a fat folder of notes under his arm, appeared before the *cortes,* which had convened in Cadiz, prepared to state the case for New Mexico.

He was, in fact, ready to do more than deliver lofty speeches and thump the table with his fist to emphasize New Mexico's wants. He put what he had to say in a little book, printed in 1812 under the title of *A Concise and Candid Exposition on the Province of New Mexico.* In it he told the *cortes* in straight terms much about the problems facing his homeland and suggested what action Spain could take to provide remedies.

New Mexico was gravely menaced, he asserted, by Americans who were eagerly pressing upon her borders, seeking an excuse for invasion. These Americans were well aware that the province had been neglected by Spain in the past, and they hoped through promises of liberal laws and open trade to wean the New Mexicans away from allegiance to the king and to encourage them to join the province of Louisiana. The provincial military should be reorganized and new forts established, Pino warned, if New Mexico was to meet this foreign challenge.

The colonial delegate asked for other things in his book: schools, a better judicial system, and a separate bishopric for New Mexico (the bishop of Durango, eight hundred miles south of Santa Fe, was then administering the province's Church affairs). He also described in some detail conditions of life among the farming and ranching folk who inhabited New Mexico's sandy stream valleys and grassy uplands. Altogether, Pino's *Exposition* offered a valuable picture of provincial affairs only a few short years before independence sundered ties with the mother country.

In spite of Pino's pleas and the good intentions expressed by the *cortes,* Spain was in no position materially to aid New Mexico. The ties of empire were weakening everywhere in the New World, and already parts of South America were breaking away to establish separate nations. New Mexico's own woes, only some of which had been touched upon by Pino, were themselves symptomatic of imperial decay. At the end of the Spanish period, the province of New Mexico found itself still isolated and adrift and moving toward an obscure future that seemed to hold little promise for improvement.

4

The Mexicans

*N*EW MEXICO is a different world . . . the Siberia of the Mexican Republic," wrote young Albert Pike, traveler and author, in 1833.[1] Like many Americans who visited the Rio Grande settlements after independence, he found the land's silent spaces and inscrutable people both fascinating and repellent. Coming from the forests of the East or the lush prairie country of the Middle West, newcomers felt awed by the enormity of the viewscape, by its rocky bleakness, by the scarcity of trees and the thinness of grass, and by the extremes of temperature. A country in which eggs could be fried on rocks in the summer and the few streams froze to granite hardness in winter indeed brought to mind a picture of Siberia.

The inhabitants of New Mexico, too, were a subject of wonder and, occasionally, of contempt. Already at that early date, some Americans had become contaminated with the virus of cultural superiority and had adopted an arrogance toward foreigners that would shortly find expression in the catchwords of expansionism—Manifest Destiny. Merchants, traders, and health-seekers from all parts of the United States brought to Santa Fe attitudes of mind appropriate for polite New England society, but singularly out of place in a rough-and-tumble fron-

1. David J. Weber, editor, *Albert Pike, Prose Sketches and Poems* (Albuquerque: University of New Mexico Press, 1967), p. 249.

107

tier capital inhabited by Spanish New Mexicans. The detractors were literate and sometimes sensitive men, but the journals they kept of their experiences in New Mexico almost always lacked that warmth and inner glow necessary for authentic understanding.

New Mexican society in the 1830s and 1840s offered to the Puritan-minded no lack of transgressions to censure. Everywhere the straight-laced Protestant merchantmen looked, they uncovered a multitude of sins, and again and again they drew a stereotyped portrait of Mexicans as "a lazy gossiping people, always lounging on their blankets and smoking cigarillos." [2] The raucous native music, produced by guitars and homemade violins, offended the traders' ears; and when the same music that had been played the night before at a riotous fandango was rendered in church on Sunday, they were consumed with indignation. In their eyes, local politics appeared wholly corrupt, and judicial proceedings were handled in so casual a manner by *alcaldes* or magistrates that no citizen accustomed to representative government could find them tolerable. The local soldiery was cowardly, shabby in appearance, and criminally short of arms and equipment. And the women, the American traders judged, were without shame or honor; they rouged their cheeks, went barefoot, and smoked cornhusk cigarettes in public. Worse were the priests, who kept the people enchained and who indulged in the same vices—strong drink, gambling, and womanizing—as their parishioners. Altogether, they saw New Mexico as Sodom on the Rio Grande.

The New Mexicans in their friendly, easygoing, rollicky, endure-all manner welcomed the dour Yankee traders, gladly bought their wares, and paid not a whit of attention to their criticisms and brusque behavior. These Hispano pioneers knew what effort had been expended to carve out and hold their small enclave of civilization on the upper Rio Grande; they remembered the many times their poorly armed soldiers—a gang of tatterdemalions, one American called them—had ridden out to fight superior numbers of hostile Indians; and they were aware

2. Weber, *Albert Pike,* p. xv.

of the worth and virtues of their own women and clergy. If haughty Easterners therefore wished to cast scorn upon them and ridicule local custom, the New Mexicans were content to remain silent and let the harsh realities of daily life in their country speak for them and set the record straight.

It was, of course, the success of the Mexican independence movement, which brought in its wake the end of restrictions on commerce and travel, that allowed Americans to enter New Mexico freely and conduct their business. In August of 1821, Mexico unfurled its banner and asserted claim to separate nationhood, but word of the change in political status did not reach remote Santa Fe until weeks later. The New Mexicans, shut off by distance and poor roads from events in the south, had no hand in the winning of independence from Spain. Yet once it was an accomplished fact, they made a show of enthusiasm: "Having heard the sweet voice of liberty," as their governor, Facundo Melgares, put it, they celebrated by ringing church bells, firing artillery salvos, and uttering patriotic speeches.[3]

For twenty-five years, New Mexico was to remain part of the Mexican nation, but as a loose appendage rather than an integral component. Self-reliance had become so inbred among her people that they tended to exhibit a combination of distrust and disinterest in matters of government unfolding beyond the bounds of their own province. In fact, the political unrest that kept Mexico City in perpetual turmoil throughout this era confirmed New Mexicans in the belief that they should manage their own affairs with as little outside interference as possible. As it turned out, they were able to achieve that because the repeated and often violent changes of administration in the national capital so disrupted functioning of the central government that outlying areas of the country were left for long periods of time to their own devices.

If New Mexico's citizens experienced any genuine elation over the break with Spain, the reason lay primarily with the pos-

---

3. David J. Weber, editor, "An Unforgettable Day: Facundo Melgares on Independence," *New Mexico Historical Review* 48 (January 1973):28.

sibility they now saw for the opening of free trade. They had for so long been at the mercy of Chihuahua's sharp merchants, had for so long been denied the opportunity of dealing with French- and English-speaking traders from the East, that removal of commercial barriers loomed as the most promising benefit to be derived from independence.

Word had scarcely reached Santa Fe that Spain no longer ruled before New Mexican officials announced an end to the old restrictive policies. Foreigners were now at liberty to enter the province for the purposes of trade. Even as the two-hundred-year-old bars were being pulled down, a Missouri trader stood on the doorstep rattling to get in.

He was William Becknell, a famed Indian fighter and veteran of the War of 1812, who had left Arrow Rock, Missouri, on September 1, 1821, with twenty-odd men and a pack train of goods for the New Mexico market. By mid-November, he and his party were in Santa Fe, basking in the cordial welcome provided by government officials and briskly selling their small stock of merchandise to an eager throng of buyers. When Beck-nell repeated his success the following year, this time with wagons, and again carried an enormous profit back to Missouri, he opened the floodgate for a steady flow of caravan traffic to New Mexico. His initiative and enterprise in pioneering the main road linking the Mississippi valley with the far Southwest would eventually lead historians to ennoble him with the title "Father of the Santa Fe Trail."

The story of travel and trade on the Santa Fe Trail forms one of the great epics of the American West. For a quarter-century, the road served as an international highway between the United States and Mexico. And then, after conquering armies followed it westward in 1846, the trail became the nation's southern gate-way to California. Many venturesome men made their fortunes carrying freight and driving livestock over the Santa Fe route; others equally daring lost their last cent and, on occasion, even their lives to the hazards of the trail. Among the latter was ex-plorer and trapper Jedediah Smith, lanced to death by Co-manches in 1831.

The Santa Fe trade and life on the trail was exemplified in the life of one extraordinary participant, Josiah Gregg. He came to know the Hispanic Southwest, not as American trappers and soldiers did, but as a businessman, author, historian, and a gifted observer of the contemporary social scene. The book Gregg wrote of his years involved in the overland trade to New Mexico, *Commerce of the Prairies,* remains a classic of the period. He was an intellectual and a man of reflective temperament with a square, solid chin, high forehead, and a shock of dark hair. His rugged handsomeness, however, belied a weak constitution, for in his own words, he suffered from ''a complication of chronic diseases.'' [4] Believing that hardships of prairie travel might restore his health, he joined a merchant caravan in 1831 and followed the by now deeply worn wagon ruts to Santa Fe.

Work and the salubrious western air worked their cure, and Gregg gained a passion for the life of a wandering trader. Over the next nine years, he made repeated trips to New Mexico, on one of which he brought the first printing press to the territory. An excellent command of Spanish and his efforts to understand the strange society on the Rio Grande allowed him to produce the finest description we have of New Mexico during the Mexican years. Like his fellow countrymen, Gregg at the beginning displayed a prejudicial attitude toward the people, their customs and laws. But unlike others, he dug in with unflagging industry, trying to discover the how and the why of what he was seeing. In so doing, he soon found much that he could praise—for example, the care and correctness with which Spanish was spoken in New Mexico. Noting that the common people had borrowed many Indian words, he declared that their use, far from corrupting the Spanish, merely served ''to embellish and amplify this already beautiful and copious language.'' [5]

In Gregg's day, the American traders practically financed the provincial government in Santa Fe, for the excise taxes levied upon their imported dry goods and hardware went to pay the

4. Harvey Fergusson, *Rio Grande* (New York: Tudor Publishing Co., 1945), p. 162.

5. Josiah Gregg, *Commerce of the Prairies* (Norman: University of Oklahoma Press, 1954), p. 142.

many expenses of public administration. Members of New Mexico's upper, or *rico,* class also entered the trade, going to Missouri each year to purchase and freight back their own stock of goods. As Mexican nationals, they were exempted from paying the excise taxes, an advantage that gave them a clear edge over their American competitors. The latter partially offset that handicap by smuggling and by bribing customs officials.

Both Mexico and the United States had a vested interest in seeing that commerce moved freely over the Santa Fe Trail. During several years when the Indians of the southern plains were especially troublesome and harassed the caravans, the two countries co-operated in providing military escorts for the wagons as far as the limits of their own territory. By way of emphasizing the importance of the trade, the United States created a consular office for Santa Fe in 1825, and shortly afterward Congress appropriated thirty thousand dollars to pay for surveying the trail and purchasing an official right of way from the Indians.

The cordial atmosphere in which the Santa Fe trade had begun and initially prospered was of short duration. The reason could be found in the turbulent conditions within Mexico and in the strained relations that soon developed between that country and its northern neighbor. The first serious ill-feeling was engendered in 1836, when Anglo-American settlers, who had colonized the Mexican province of Texas, successfully carried out a revolution and set up an independent republic. That event, understandably, caused the government of Mexico to regard with suspicion the motives of all Americans operating within its territory. Those engaged in the Santa Fe trade were looked upon with particular mistrust; and after 1837, restrictions on their activities multiplied rapidly.

Not only did American traders in New Mexico have to contend with taxes, arbitrary customs officials, and curbs imposed upon them by the national government; they had to worry about periodic flare-ups of civil tumult that threatened their lives and property. The first serious incident occurred in the mid-1830s.

Since independence, most of New Mexico's governors appointed by the national government had come from a handful of local families who dominated provincial politics. But in 1835, Colonel Albino Pérez, an officer in the Mexican army and an "outsider," was sent to Santa Fe to assume the governor's chair. Brassy and aristocratic in manner, Pérez remained disdainfully aloof from Santa Fe society and alienated many members of New Mexico's small upper class. He also lost the loyalty of the rural poor when, in 1836, federal authorities obliged him to impose new taxes and to reduce some of the rights of self-government previously enjoyed by villages.

Anger against Pérez soon fueled a full-scale insurrection, usually termed the Chimayó Rebellion. In 1837, farming folk north of Santa Fe, joined by sympathetic Pueblo Indians, gathered an army and defeated the forces of the governor sent against them. Pérez and his cabinet, attempting to flee the capital, were captured by the rebels and brutally slain. Gregg paints a grim picture of the sequel: the governor's body was decapitated, and then "his head was carried as a trophy to the camp of the insurgents, who made a football of it among themselves." [6]

As the disorganized and victorious army occupied Santa Fe, native residents and American merchants alike quaked behind their barred shutters, expecting that a mob of soldiers would be turned loose to plunder the town. But nothing of the sort took place. The rebels quietly installed one of their number, a mixed-blood named José González from Ranchos de Taos, as provisional governor; they pledged loyalty to the Mexican Republic and asked for a redress of grievances; and they disbanded their troops and went home to begin the fall harvest.

The Americans were relieved to escape any physical harm, but some among them stood to lose financially since they had advanced money and goods to Governor Pérez and other murdered officials. They were still more concerned with the reestablishment of order in New Mexico, for no businessman can operate long in the midst of civil turmoil. As a gesture of support for stable government, Missouri merchants contributed more than four hundred pesos toward a war-chest raised on behalf of former governor Manuel Armijo. That individual

6. Gregg, *Commerce of the Prairies,* p. 93.

promised to mount a counterrevolution, drive the usurper González from office, and restore the full authority of the federal
government.

In fact, he did just that. With aid from wealthy ranchers in the
Rio Abajo district surrounding Albuquerque and from a company of regular dragoons recently arrived from Mexico, Armijo
marched north and dispersed the revolutionaries. When the hapless González fell into his hands, Armijo allowed him a brief interval for confession and then stood him up before a firing
squad. The short-lived Chimayó Rebellion was at an end.

Although it is plain that American merchants did not directly
participate in the disturbances of 1837, and in fact furnished
funds for quelling the revolt, nervous officials in Mexico City
believed it was they who had originally stirred up the tempest.
Still edgy over the recent loss of Texas, these officials thought it
plausible that foreigners in Santa Fe, resentful over the high
duties imposed on their merchandise, might try to subvert the
local populace to break away from the Republic. That suspicion, never entirely allayed, made life difficult for the traders,
but it did not discourage them from making their yearly crossing
of the prairies.

Still another episode, this one in 1841, provided added problems for Americans trying to do business in New Mexico. The
infant Republic of Texas, close by on the east, looked with envy
upon the profitable trade funneled from Santa Fe over the trail to
Missouri. Texas President Mirabeau B. Lamar, hoping to muscle in on the traffic and perhaps at the same time annex New
Mexico, dispatched a mixed company of soldiers and traders to
visit Santa Fe.

The announced intention of the expedition was to engage in
peaceful commerce, but the Mexican government, not unex-
pectedly, chose to regard it as a hostile invasion. Manuel Armijo, who had been named governor after the upheaveal of
1837, began preparations to resist the invaders, but his task was
made difficult, as he informed the Minister of War in Mexico
City, because, "Many of the people here expect better conditions from the Texans and thus refuse to help defend this

land.'' [7] From that it is evident that economic dependence upon the Americans had already begun to undermine the loyalty of New Mexicans toward their own country.

In spite of unwillingness in some quarters to answer a call to the colors, Governor Armijo assembled a motley force of mixed regulars and militia and marched eastward in September to meet the enemy. Wearing a plumed hat, a brilliant uniform strained tight by his ponderous girth, and mounted on a long-earred gray mule, Armijo resembled more a figure in a comic opera than a Little Napoleon at the head of a conquering army. Theatrical appearances notwithstanding, the governor and his men, with the aid of a little luck, were able to turn events in their favor.

The Texas expedition, poorly guided and indifferently led, had lost its way on the awesome Staked Plains. Exhausted, starved, and harried by Indians, the merchants and soldiers divided into several parties and plodded on toward the New Mexican settlements, hoping to find relief there.

It was a situation perfectly tailored for such a general as Armijo, who desired a large and impressive victory with minimal effort. One by one he scooped up the faltering companies of Texans, disarmed them, and hurried them southward to a lockup in Mexico. Largely because of a flowery report that he sent to federal authorities, filled with bombastic and patriotic references to his own part in the affair, the New Mexican governor became something of a national hero.

It should not be supposed, however, that Manuel Armijo was in any way hostile to Americans. That shrewd individual, who dominated provincial politics during the twilight years of the Mexican period, was heavily involved in the Santa Fe trade, as were his numerous relatives and friends. And he possessed close ties with the foreign community of traders in his backwoods capital. At the time of the Texan invasion, merchants who were concerned for the safety of their property received his personal assurance that they would be protected. While the governor was

7. Charles R. McClure, "The Texan-Santa Fe Expedition of 1841," *New Mexico Historical Review* 48 (January 1973):47–48.

absent on his campaign, Santa Fe ruffians broke into the house of the United States consul and gave him a severe beating. Armijo's secretary quickly restored order and apologized to the bleeding official.

By all reports, the governor was a mountain of a man, fond of rich food and pretty ladies and always ready to turn a fast peso, either at Santa Fe's famous gambling tables or in some scheme that moved sideways of the law. His most serious offense, as later history would show, involved the alienation of large chunks of New Mexico's public domain. He accomplished that by making enormous land grants—far in excess of what was legally allowed—to his cronies, many of whom had American citizens as silent partners. Problems, particularly over titles and boundaries, arising from such shady transfers of land were to plague New Mexico long after she had become a part of the United States.

Federal officials, unlike Manuel Armijo, were becoming more and more reluctant to have anything to do with the self-assertive Americans, perhaps because by the early 1840s the shadows of war were already forming on the northern horizon. Further constraints placed on the Santa Fe trade, including a brief suspension of all business activity in late 1844, offered clear evidence of the deterioration of both commerce and amiable relations between the two countries. The warning signs were not lost on the merchants, who began to brace themselves for the conflict they felt was as inevitable as it was desirable. These Missouri traders had in fact unconsciously paved the way for American conquest by carrying home word of Mexico's feeble hold on Santa Fe and of the New Mexicans' weak allegiance to their nation. As subsequent events were to demonstrate, Spain's now-long-discarded strategy of preserving the northern provinces from foreigners by building a wall around them had more merit than Mexico's liberal, open-door policy.

Another group of Americans of that period was drawn to the wilderness, rather than to New Mexico's towns and markets. The mountains of the Far Southwest had remained practically untouched by the Spaniards during their more than two centuries of rule. Colonial soldiers occasionally pursued Indian raiders into mountain strongholds, and in a few instances, such as at Peñasco and Las Trampas, southeast of Taos, small bands of farmers and stockmen late in the period occupied pocket-sized valleys below the loftier peaks. But in the main, New Mexico's high and wooded ground held little attraction for Spaniards.

It did possess, however, a special allurement for Anglo-American and French-Canadian trappers who, following independence, poured into the area, shoulder to shoulder with the Santa Fe traders. These mountain men, strange products of the western frontier, were after valuable beaver pelts, which for a brief term between the mid-1820s and early 1840s were in great demand by hat makers in the United States and Europe. The high country of the Mexican borderlands, particularly that surrounding the headwaters of the Rio Grande and the Colorado River, offered rich pickings for fur trappers, and they moved in eagerly to tap a resource utterly neglected by the New Mexicans.

The small, out-of-the-way northern village of Taos, close to the Indian pueblo of Taos, became the hub of the southwestern fur trade. From that base, brigades of hairy, buckskin-clad mountain men swarmed northward into the Rocky Mountains and beyond, returning after a lapse of months or years, when their tobacco and ammunition ran low. Here they found a congenial atmosphere in which to frolic with dark-eyed belles, pour Niagaras of local whiskey (called "Taos Lightning") down their throats, and engage in noisy and sometimes bloody brawls. In their uninhibited conduct and dedication to the rough wilderness life, the trappers demonstrated a kinship with those New Mexican pioneers condemned earlier by Spanish governors for their dislike of civilized restraints and love "of perfect freedom and independence."

About 1824, officials in Mexico City began to regard the mountain men with the same suspicion as they had the Santa Fe traders. The trappers were foreigners; they were probing into remote, unexplored corners of the country; and they were reaping profits, while the nation got nothing in return. As a result, instructions soon went to New Mexico's governor bidding him to prevent anyone but Mexicans from trapping on the streams and rivers under his jurisdiction. Some mountain men got around the ban by becoming naturalized citizens (often they enhanced their positions by marrying into prominent New Mexican families and serving in public office); but most resorted to extralegal means—smuggling out their furs or applying for a trapping license through a Mexican partner. By one means or another, the relentless harvesting of beaver went on, and all the while American hunters blazed new trails across the tablelands and through the mountains of the Southwest. Unknowingly, these men too were laying the groundwork for the not-too-distant conquest and assimilation of New Mexico by the United States.

Among the people of Spain and among those of Spanish descent, such as the New Mexicans, the seeds of race prejudice have never found fertile ground. It may be that the many racial strains, which over the centuries went into the making of the Hispanic nation, accustomed its people to living amicably alongside persons of different color and blood; or it may have happened that other prejudices—those against social inferiors or against religious deviates, for example—were so strong that little passion was left to kindle racial antagonisms. Whatever the historical cause, the fact remains that traders, trappers, and others from the United States, upon entering New Mexico, found its residents singularly free of bias against other nationalities. Many of the newcomers who settled down, raised families, and won acceptance in the local society, saw that, with the passing of years, their own hard-shelled notions of racial superiority began to fade and to be replaced by the open and easy attitude that characterized people on the Rio Grande.

In time, the resiliency of the New Mexican's tolerance was to be sorely tested, as it absorbed repeated blows delivered by English Americans elbowing their way westward. In 1841, at the hour of the Texas-Santa Fe Expedition, the governor of Chihuahua passed on to the citizens of New Mexico news he had received of the impending invasion . . . and a warning. "Do you know who the Texans are?" he asked them rhetorically.

They are adventurers who despise you as barbarians, weak minded, and corrupt men. They blaspheme your religion and scoff at your pious customs; they are grasping merchants who envy the fertility of your lands, the richness of your mines, and the clemency of your weather; some are men who distinguish their fellowmen by the color of their faces in order to impress the stamp of slavery on those who are not white . . . And they come to take possession of the land with their sword.[8]

Like most statements uttered in the heat of passion, this one contained a deal of hyperbole; but it also bore some grains of truth, and to that degree foreshadowed a trying time ahead when Anglo-Americans would become masters over New Mexico's Indian and Hispano population.

But for the moment, the middle years of the 1840s, the New Mexicans had a short breathing space during which to attend to internal affairs before the darkening clouds building on the eastern rim of their world overtook them. In Santa Fe, public-spirited citizens planted a border of cottonwood saplings around the bare, dust-choked plaza fronting the Governors Palace, and the provincial secretary, Donaciano Vigil, personally looked to their regular watering. The Comanches rode into the capital, as they had done each year since the signing of peace with Anza back in 1786, to eat, visit, and receive their annual gifts. Sundays, Governor Manuel Armijo strutted to church in full-dress uniform and medals, accompanied by his staff and a loud little band composed of two antiquated trumpets and a couple of drums.

Up in Taos, in the winter of 1844–1845, the village folk shared their piñon fires and swapped stories with a small, wiry mountain man named Kit Carson, whose marriage to a local girl, Josefa Jaramillo, had earned him admittance to the community's inner circle. The summer before, he had finished a stint as guide and hunter for the explorer John Charles Frémont's second expedition through the Far West; now having decided that

8. Sister Mary Loyola, "The American Occupation of New Mexico, 1821–1852," *New Mexico Historical Review* 14 (July 1939):258.

he "had rambled enough," Carson was laying plans to take up a farmstead in a fertile valley fifty miles east of Taos.[9]

In the spring of 1845, Bishop José Antonio Zubiría from far-off Durango braved the long trail through El Paso and Albuquerque to the up-river settlements. He came to inspect the spiritual condition of this isolated contingent of his flock, and what he found left him a troubled man. In a pastoral letter to the New Mexicans, he expressed his sadness at discovering so many persons slighting the Sacraments and at seeing the spiritual care of the Indians neglected. Many parishes had no priests, churches and missions were in disrepair, and the bishop lacked the financial resources to remedy the deficiencies. Equally bad, to his way of thinking, some of the rural folk lacking the guidance of a minister, had organized religious brotherhoods of laymen called the Penitentes, whose members flogged themselves and conducted mock crucifixions. Zubiría, brooding over the problems, started home for Durango, leaving a request that the faithful pray for his safe passage over a trail menaced by hostile Apaches.

That tribe did indeed molest travelers, exalted and humble alike, moving over the Camino Real in and out of New Mexico; but in 1845 a more general and formidable threat came from the Navajo. In Manuel Armijo's words, their war against the province, intermittent since independence, was now consuming everything and reducing the people to complete misery. Sheep ranches and settlements all along the western border fell prey to Navajo raiding parties, and only a few volunteer militia companies were able to offer resistance. The regular garrison in Santa Fe, undermanned and ill-supplied as always, could handle small brush fires, but a general conflagration lay beyond its capacity to contain. So the stoical New Mexicans suffered and endured through that year and into 1846; and the troops at Santa Fe lounged in their mud barracks, playing three-card monte and speculating about the future. Having heard rumors of the bud-

9. Milo Milton Quaife, editor, *Kit Carson's Autobiography* (Lincoln: University of Nebraska Press, n.d.), p. 87.

ding of a different war, they wondered how an army from the United States could be stopped on the east, when New Mexico had made so poor a showing against the Navajo on the west. It was something their government leaders were also pondering.

The two nations confronting each other across the Rio Grande in 1846, as successors of Spain and England, had inherited their old imperial rivalry for control of North America. But an immense gulf separated Mexico from the United States as far as ability and willingness to pursue the contest were concerned. Internally, Mexico was torn by political conflict, its army was short on morale and poorly led, and its thinly settled northern frontier was highly vulnerable to attack. Nevertheless, when war broke forth, Mexicans rallied to defend their homeland; and believing their cause was just, they expected to win.

Initially, the United States appeared to be at a disadvantage. There was no unity of sentiment in favor of war: the eastern seaboard for the most part was opposed to it; the South and the West, advocating expansion of boundaries and slavery, approved. And the country as a whole, with only a small standing army, was unprepared. But other considerations soon demonstrated that Americans, aggressively determined to grab territory, had the edge.

For one thing, there was no lack of volunteer soldiers. All along the western frontier could be found young men aplenty, used to a rough life and skilled in the handling of firearms, who were delighted to learn that a fight was in the offing. They and other Americans had caught the spirit of their country's divine mission, an idea first formed by the founding fathers, but given new emphasis by an eastern journalist in 1845. John L. O'Sullivan, writing for the *New York Morning News,* stated flatly, "Our manifest destiny is to overspread and possess the whole continent which providence has given us for the . . . great experiment of liberty." [10] If that was true, as many men fervently

10. Quoted in T. R. Fehrenback, *The Comanches, Destruction of a People* (New York: Alfred A. Knopf, 1974), p. 363.

believed, then territorial conquest could be seen to possess high purpose: that of delivering the blessings of democratic institutions to less fortunate people.

The immediate causes of the Mexican War were several: the annexation of Texas in late 1845 (Mexico had still not given up her claim to that lost province); a dispute over the international boundary; unpaid claims owed by Mexico to American citizens; but particularly land-hunger—President James K. Polk's ambition to acquire New Mexico and California. The last point proved especially nettlesome, for Polk was determined to have his way, and the Mexican government was just as determined to resist.

When an offer to purchase the Southwest territories was spurned by Mexico, the president began to look for a pretext to take the area by force. Nor did he have long to search. In April of 1846, Mexican troops crossed the lower Rio Grande and engaged American troops on soil claimed by the United States. Shortly, Polk appeared before Congress and announced that a state of war existed by an act of Mexico itself. He now had all the justification he needed for conquering New Mexico and the country beyond and for satisfying the demands of the expansionists who had become the dominant voice in the country.

From the beginning, Missourians had been among the loudest supporters of Manifest Destiny. They saw the hand of providence beckoning them toward the Pacific, and they anticipated that, with the westward rush, the lucrative New Mexican markets would pass to the United States. In such an event, the canny Missouri merchants could gain control of commerce at both ends of the Santa Fe Trail. The hitch was, they needed the acquisition to be made as peacefully as possible, so as not to disrupt their mercantile business. That point was underscored by their representatives in Washington, particularly by the influential Senator Thomas Hart Benton of Missouri, as President Polk and his military advisers were putting finishing touches on a plan for the conquest of New Mexico.

The instructions subsequently delivered to Colonel Stephen Watts Kearny, the man tagged to lead an army to seize the Far Southwest, included provision for concilitating Mexicans in the invaded territory and conditioning them to accept docilely a change of allegiance. To ease that task, the government planned to send a Catholic priest, conversant in Spanish, to accompany the expeditionary force. By such measures, the *Baltimore Sun* commented, on July 2, 1846, the "people will be prepared for a common union with us." [11]

Colonel Kearny (soon promoted to brigadier general) proved to be an apt commander for what became known as the Army of the West. A stern disciplinarian of cold reserve, he enjoyed a reputation as a skilled fighter among men of the western border. Added to that, he was an ardent patriot whose life's ambition, according to a tradition among his descendants, was to further the westward expansion of the country.

In early summer, Kearny put out a call for volunteers to reinforce his small corps of three hundred army regulars. From Missouri and adjacent states they came: frontiersmen, farmers, mechanics, artisans, lawyers, doctors, teachers, and students—the same broad cross section of society that was to fill the ranks in all of America's wars. As one impassioned young soldier told it later, "This blooming host, the elite of Missouri, was full of ardor, full of spirit, full of generous enthusiasm, burning for the battle field, and panting for the reward of honorable victory." [12]

With some sixteen hundred men, a battery of artillery, and a supply train that assembled at Fort Leavenworth in late June of 1846, the Army of the West's byword now was "Ho! for New Mexico." To the tune of "Bound to the Rio Grande," the soldiers moved out with snap and zest and a cockiness that said, "Bring on your grizzlies, any time, anywhere." One trooper, adept at rhyming, soon came up with new words for a marching song that fit the mood of his companions:

---

11. Quoted in Frederich Merk, *Manifest Destiny and Mission in American History* (New York: Vintage Books, 1966), p. 112.

12. Isaac George, *Heroes and Incidents of the Mexican War* (Greensburg, Pa.: Review Publishing Co., 1903), p. 35.

Oh, what a joy to fight the dons,
And wallop fat Armijo!
So clear the way to Santa Fe!
With that we all agree, O! [13]

Kearny, using a map furnished in Gregg's recently published *Commerce of the Prairies,* followed the Santa Fe Trail to the Arkansas Crossing in present southwestern Kansas. There the route forked. The southern branch of the trail, the shortest way to New Mexico, began with a fifty-mile waterless stretch of desert; so the commander led his men over the longer, northern route that proceeded via Bent's Fort in southeastern Colorado. That trading establishment, built by Charles and William Bent and the mountain man Cerán St. Vrain in 1833, was a supply and rendezvous point for trappers ranging the southern Rockies and for Indians and Santa Fe traders. The Army of the West, in point of fact, had a caravan of the latter following in its wake under a canopy of dust. Missouri's merchants, anxious lest they miss a season of trading in Santa Fe, had collected behind Kearny's invasion force, to be ready for business as soon as their countrymen had pocketed New Mexico.

After bracing for the expected fight ahead, the Americans departed from Bent's and pushed headlong toward Raton Pass, a high and perilous cut through a spur of mountains that gave access to the Mexican province beyond. By putting shoulders to their wagon wheels, the troops reached the summit of the pass. From there, in the thin air that made breathing difficult, they could see spread out before them, like the biblical promised land, the long, rolling plains of New Mexico, shimmering under midsummer's rays. Now all that remained, as their pleasant ditty said, was to "clear the way to Santa Fe."

In the New Mexican capital, a frazzled Governor Manuel Armijo was the center of fretful activity. Rumors buzzed about, thick as flies in the town's open market, and the first icy needles of panic had begun to discomfit the nervous populace. The word was out: *los americanos* were coming; and no one could be

13. Ottamar Hamele, *When Destiny Called* (San Antonio: The Naylor Company, 1948), p. 26.

quite sure what that meant. For a fact, Americans had long been seen on the streets of Santa Fe, Albuquerque, and Taos, and the New Mexicans had never found them over-dangerous; but now New Mexico leaders—the governor and the clergy—were sawing away at a frightening tune: the Americans have outraged our national honor, they have forced a conflict upon us, and they are advancing across our northern frontier.

With such words, Manuel Armijo and other officials sought to prepare their fellow New Mexicans for battle. The alarming news of the invasion was echoed by the vicar general, Father Juan Felipe Ortiz, who issued warnings to the faithful on July 4 and again on August 7. Some of the clergy, taking fright, had already fled south toward Mexico, and Ortiz ordered those remaining to stick to their posts during the dark days he foresaw ahead. Men in high places—it is difficult to say exactly which ones—launched a story that American soldiers were barbarians coming to plunder honest citizens, destroy their religion, and dishonor their women. The words were believed and pandemonium reigned in Santa Fe.

Wealthy families of the capital boarded up their homes and fled; some not so wealthy sent their most vulnerable women away to hide in the mountains. And curiously, those leaving town passed on the roads lines of terrified country folk streaming into the city, hoping to find safety there. At an emergency meeting, Santa Fe's municipal officials gravely debated whether they should tear down all the churches to prevent their being converted into barracks and otherwise desecrated. Fortunately, some American citizens living in Santa Fe intervened, dissuaded them from so hasty an action, and thereby saved the churches.

In that tumultuous atmosphere, Manuel Armijo went through the motions of mounting his defenses. From the province's sixty-thousand-odd population, he summoned militiamen and Pueblo Indians to support his regulars, which included a squadron of Veracruz dragoons. And he announced that he would make a stand against the Americans at Apache Canyon, some fifteen miles east of Santa Fe. Yet even as preparations for a field campaign were going forward, Governor Armijo busily burned bridges behind him.

On August 12, James Magoffin, a Santa Fe trader of long

standing, escorted by Captain Philip St. George Cooke, secretly visited His Excellency in his crumbling adobe palace. Magoffin came as an emissary of the U.S. government, and while no record was kept of the meeting, it appears that he persuaded Armijo to abandon the defense of New Mexico. Possibly a significant sum of money changed hands in the bargain. In any case, the governor had already perceived the inevitable conquest of his domain and had liquidated his extensive business interests, forced the Vicar Ortiz to hand over the meager funds in the church treasury, and packed his traveling trunks. When he set out with his makeshift army, clad in his finest plumage and headed for Apache Canyon, Manuel Armijo alone knew that he would not be returning to Santa Fe.

Eastward along the trail, General Kearny had reached New Mexico's outer perimeter of settlement. In the village of Las Vegas, he marched into the small plaza unopposed and from a flat rooftop declared to an assembled throng that he had come to take possession of New Mexico and extend over it the laws of the United States. Aware of the unreasonable fears bred by the appearance of his army, Kearny tried to allay the people's apprehension with mild words. "Not a pepper, not an onion, shall be taken by my troops without pay . . . I will protect you in your persons and property and in your religion. . . . Some of your priests have told you that we would ill-treat your women and brand them on the cheek, as you do your mules on the hip. It is all false." [14] The message, backed by soldiers bristling with weapons, had its effect. The New Mexicans grudgingly gave their allegiance to the new government.

Farther along at the villages of Tecolote and San Miguel, the ceremony was repeated, and again the people submitted. One of Kearny's company remarked that he expected them soon to be transformed into "as good democrats as can be found in Missouri." [15] For the moment, though, it was sufficient for the

14. Ralph Emerson Twitchell, *The Military Occupation of New Mexico, 1846–1851* (Denver: Smith-Brooks Company, 1909), pp. 49–50.

15. George Winston Smith and Charles Judah, *Chronicles of the Gringos* (Albuquerque: University of New Mexico Press, 1968), p. 116.

Americans to know that they were leaving no dangerous enemy in their rear.

As it developed, there was no enemy ahead, either. Armijo had gone as far as the mouth of Apache Canyon, where he directed his men to construct some hasty breastworks; then suddenly he called a conference with his officers to tell them he was giving up the game. Several of the militia captains threatened to shoot him if he didn't stand and fight, but the governor had the regular troops behind him, and he made his decision stick. With their commander scurrying ingloriously toward El Paso, his coattails flapping in the hot summer air, the volunteers rushed pell-mell back to Santa Fe to spread the unfortunate word and to look to the protection of their families.

Mid-afternoon of August 18, the Army of the West clattered unopposed into Santa Fe's narrow streets. On the central plaza, facing Armijo's now desolate palace, acting-governor Juan Bautista Vigil y Alaríd surrendered the city to General Kearny. A cannon boomed a salute, a new flag was run up, and as the red-and-blue bunting took the breeze, a thunderous cheer arose from the leg-weary men who had cleared the way to Santa Fe. It was an epic moment: the first time in its brief history that the United States had taken a foreign capital. A petite young lady accompanying the merchant caravan, Susan Magoffin, wrote effusively in her diary, "I have entered Santa Fe in a year that will always be remembered by my countrymen; and under the 'Star spangled banner,' too, the first American lady who has come under such auspices." [16]

While the giddy Susan swelled with pride, the women of the New Mexican capital—those who had been unable to flee or who had chosen not to—were overcome by a far different emotion. As the Mexican tricolor was lowered from its staff for the last time, they sent up a wail of grief, so piercing and distressful that the roistering soldiers in the plaza were momentarily silenced. It was not that the olive-skinned *señoritas* and the matronly *señoras* despaired so much over the political conse-

16. Stella M. Drumm, editor, *Down the Santa Fe Trail and into Mexico* (New Haven: Yale University Press, 1965), p. 102.

quences represented by the changing of flags; rather, the event, as they intuitively understood, meant that their old world, their familiar style of life, would never quite be the same again. Behind their cry of anguish, too, was the fear that the roguish-looking Americans, conforming to the usual behavior of con-querers, would assail their religion, assault their virtue, and steal their few material possessions. But on these counts their fears proved baseless.

General Kearny, mindful of his instructions to conciliate the New Mexicans, took pains to see that the transition from the old government to the new was accomplished in a calm, orderly, and reassuring manner. Of his soldiers he demanded perfect decorum; those who suffered a lapse in manners and affronted the defeated people, he sternly disciplined. To all who would listen, he restated his earlier message delivered at Las Vegas, Tecolote, and San Miguel: property rights and religion would be respected, and the United States would assume responsibility for protecting homes and possessions from hostile Indians. These promises, as well as the restrained conduct of the troops, had their effect. In the words of a private in the Missouri Mounted Volunteers, ''The New Mexicans had been frightened almost to death by the stories the priests and the rich (for they are the two classes that rule the country) had told them of the barbarians that were marching against them, but now after we have min-gled a few days with them, they begin to look a little more cheerful.'' [17]

To dispell any lingering notion that barbarians had claimed the country, Kearny summoned several lawyers in his ranks to prepare a fitting set of laws for the American territory of New Mexico. The document they produced rested on both American and Mexican precedents, with the strongest influence deriving from the Declaration of Independence and the Bill of Rights. This basic law, known popularly as the Kearny Code, was printed in both English and Spanish, and together with the United States Constitution, was widely distributed throughout

17. Smith and Judah, *Chronicles of the Gringos,* p. 121.

the land's towns and hamlets. The first step in Americanizing the new acquisition had been taken.

For six weeks, General Kearny worked tooth and nail to fashion a framework that would preserve New Mexico and insure its continued tranquillity, for his orders were to proceed on to the conquest of California with the main part of his army when that end had been achieved. In addition to the promulgation of his legal code, Kearny appointed a set of civil officials, including as governor the trader Charles Bent, who maintained a home in Taos. And to strengthen Santa Fe's defenses, Kearny began construction of Fort Marcy on a prominent hill a short distance north of the plaza. Finally, as a gesture toward promoting cordial relations, he became a regular attendant at Sunday Mass. On one occasion, the general even carried a candle in a religious procession, though he later confided to Susan Magoffin that he felt he was making a fool of himself.

In late September, Kearny left the capital for California, turning over military command of New Mexico to Colonel Alexander Doniphan, who remained behind with a portion of the Army of the West. Shortly, Colonel Sterling Price reached Santa Fe with reinforcements from Missouri, including a Mormon battalion of five hundred infantry. Doniphan now took the majority of these troops, leaving Price enough for garrison duty, and headed south, intending to strike Chihuahua. First, however, he made a swing into western New Mexico and arranged a peace treaty with the Navajo under Chief Zarcillos Largos. Then, back on the Rio Grande, he moved below Las Cruces, where his soldiers on Christmas Day defeated a Mexican force at the Battle of Brazito. The victory permitted Doniphan to occupy El Paso, and the following February he succeeded in capturing the city of Chihuahua, two hundred and fifty miles farther south.

While these events were unfolding, Colonel Price in Santa Fe was having his hands full trying to control an explosive and wholly unexpected situation. What promised to be a peaceful military occupation had suddenly gone sour when word leaked out that a conspiracy was afoot to rise against the Americans.

Price moved swiftly to nip the plot in the bud by arresting its leaders in Santa Fe. But plans for insurrection had already been spread among towns north of the capital. When Governor Bent went to his home in Taos in mid-January he was set upon and killed by an angry mob of New Mexicans and Indians. Other Americans in Taos and in nearby Arroyo Hondo and Mora also fell victims to the uprising.

When word of the slaughter reached Santa Fe, Colonel Price marched north with a scant 353 soldiers, among them a company of mountain men enlisted by the slain governor's partner, Cerán St. Vrain. Trudging through deep snow, the vengeful little army brushed aside superior enemy forces at Santa Cruz and Embudo and went on to encircle Taos Pueblo, where those responsible for the outbreak had fortified the mission church. That stronghold was taken by storm—a furious assault that bloodied the waters of the splashing mountain stream cutting through the heart of the village. Defeat of the Taos rebels and speedy trial and execution of their leaders effectively cooled the spirit of revolution throughout the territory. Henceforward, for good or ill, the political destiny of the New Mexicans was bound to that of the American nation.

The future of their cultural heritage and language, however, remained to be settled. The short quarter-century that the Rio Grande people had been ''Mexicans'' failed to instill in them any strong feeling of identity with the republic to the south; so, after 1846 and the jarring separation from Mexico, they went back to thinking of themselves as Spaniards. By tradition and speech, that's what they were; only now they were something more: they were Americans, too, entitled to rights and privileges won decades before by soldiers and statesmen of the Thirteen English Colonies. Some among the New Mexicans must have entertained doubts about what times ahead held for them; but not young José Leandro Perea, who lived through the unsettling events of 1846. Reflecting upon the American invasion years later, when he had become one of the leading ranchers in the territory, he declared with solemn conviction, ''Then I felt perfectly satisfied and had no tears to shed over the matter; for I knew it would ultimately result in making our people freer and more independent than they ever could be under their former government, although many years might pass before much could be accomplished." [18]

In New Mexico, children of Spain and England had at last come together in significant numbers. Would the meeting result in a blending of cultures, or would it lead to the opening of a new and more subtle conflict? The answer to that question, as Perea might also have anticipated, lay farther down the road.

18. W. H. H. Allison, "Santa Fe in 1846," *Old Santa Fe* 2 (April 1915):394.

5

The Americans

Y the Treaty of Guadalupe-Hidalgo ending the Mexican War, made public in Washington on July 4, 1848, the United States achieved its principal objectives: the acquisition of New Mexico and California and recognition of the Rio Grande as Texas's southern boundary. Along with the new territory, the nation also acquired an alien population and a basket of prickly problems. Evidently it did not occur to Americans, dedicated to republican principles, to hold the people they had conquered in a subject state. Those Mexicans who chose to remain in their homes (the treaty gave ones who did not the right to remove to Mexico) were to receive the same privileges of citizenship as everyone else.

But this was a new experience for America—taking in at one scoopful so many foreign-born—and it created a distinct unease in many quarters. What effect would Hispanic customs have on American institutions? How could questions involving land grants in the captured territories be resolved? What would be the status of the Pueblo people, accorded the rights of citizens under Mexico, but now part of a country that had not yet extended such rights to Indians? Finally, what were to be the social consequences of suddenly bestowing free institutions upon, in the view of some Americans, an uneducated race of mixed-bloods?

There were even blunt spokesmen who went so far as to

suggest that the United States had made a bad bargain, annexing New Mexico. Congressman Truman Smith of Connecticut, for one, told his fellow lawmakers in Washington that they had cheated themselves and had invited disaster by bringing people of low morals, such as the New Mexicans, into the Union. South Carolina's Senator John C. Calhoun, even before the war had ended in 1848, had bellowed and pawed like an old bull and fulminated against granting equality to "colored" races inhabiting the Mexican borderlands. "Ours, sir, is the Government of a white race," he pronounced pontifically before the Senate.[1] And that sentiment was not his alone. Some years after the Civil War, General William T. Sherman, who heartily disliked the arid country and the people of the Southwest, was quoted as saying that the United States ought to declare war on Mexico and make it take back New Mexico.

One result of such hostility was that New Mexicans for more than sixty years were repeatedly checkmated in their efforts to achieve statehood, and so their land remained until 1912 a territory whose officials were appointed from Washington. Upon that vexation were piled others—problems with hostile Indians and outlaws, problems of education and economics, difficulties involving land and water rights and territorial boundaries, and—most of all—the uphill job of adapting to a new pace and pattern of life, one ruled by the philosophy of thrift and hustle. All of these had become apparent as early as 1850, and any impartial observer, had he been asked then to assess New Mexico's prospects for the future, likely would have volunteered a dim and pessimistic view. A country and people so unlike the rest of the United States seemed to have a poor chance of adjusting to the militant demands of American patriotism and economic nationalism.

Yet things were not so black as they appeared. The New Mexicans, like most pioneers, were accustomed to living by luck and hope, and they possessed some firm traits of character, often overlooked by American newcomers, that promised to see them through the hard times of their territorial days. Perceptive

1. Merk, *Manifest Destiny*, p. 162.

Richard Weightman, New Mexico's delegate to the national Congress, recognized the moral assets of his constituents in 1852. "I have never met in any part of the United States," he declared,

> people more hospitable, more law-abiding, more kind, more generous, more desirous of improvement, more desirous that a general system of education be established among them . . . or more desirous of seeing in their own idiom the Declaration of Independence and the Constitution of the United States. Among them I have met men of incorruptible integrity, of honor, refinement, intelligence and information.[2]

Sweet words, those, and all the more welcome to New Mexican ears because they were so rare.

The Anglo-Americans entering New Mexico in the late 1840s and 1850s were small in numbers but large in influence. New merchants came, as establishment of regular stagecoach and freight service with the East led to stimulation of business. The ranks of the military swelled with the construction of forts on the Indian frontier—such posts as Fort Union (1851) and Fort Stanton (1855) on the east; Fort Fillmore (1851) and Fort Craig (1854) south of the main settlements on the Rio Grande; Fort Defiance (1851) guarding the western Navajo country; and Cantonment Burgwin (1852) in the north, a short distance from Taos.

Then, besides the merchants and soldiers, there were the lawyers in frock coats and bat-wing collars. They descended in swarms, after the conquest, eager to their shoe-soles for political power and a slice of New Mexico's vast real estate, which represented the country's most visible wealth. The influential Padre Antonio José Martínez of Taos, a man of great intellectual gifts and social consciousness, likened the hastily contrived American government in New Mexico to a burro, adding ruefully that "on this burro lawyers will ride, not priests." [3]

2. Frances Leon Swadish, *Los Primeros Pobladores, Hispanic Americans on the Ute Frontier* (Notre Dame, Indiana: University of Notre Dame Press, 1974), p. 68.

3. Erna Fergusson, *New Mexico, A Pageant of Three Peoples* (New York: Alfred A. Knopf, 1955), p. 260.

The state of New Mexican politics in the period following the Mexican War was ready-made for lawyers and opportunists of all sorts to jockey for advantage. The assassination of Governor Charles Bent and the collapse in 1847 of the civil government created by Kearny left the area under virtual military rule. That situation continued over the next several years, while Congress debated New Mexico's future political status. In the meanwhile, persons on the Rio Grande broke into two opposing camps: the supporters of a territorial form of government and the advocates of immediate statehood. In the main, Anglo-Americans, being in the minority, favored the former system. If New Mexico stayed a territory, its principal officials would be appointed in Washington. For that reason, the Hispano majority tended to lean toward statehood; with the right to elect their own officials, they could easily put native New Mexicans into the highest offices.

This political issue, which had become involved with the national question of extending slavery into the Mexican borderlands, was temporarily resolved by the Compromise of 1850. Congress, among other things, admitted California as a free state and provided for the organization of New Mexico as a territory, leaving her inhabitants at liberty to decide the future status of slavery. It was a stop-gap measure, to be sure, for many New Mexicans would continue to press for statehood, but at least for the time being it gave the region an orderly civil government.

The Compromise of 1850 also resolved another complicated matter—an old claim by Texas to that portion of New Mexico lying east of the Rio Grande. For ten million dollars' compensation provided by the United States government, Texas relinquished her claim, thus paving the way for establishment of a permanent boundary with New Mexico. The Territory, as organized in 1850, then, included the New Mexico and Arizona of later years and a part of southern Colorado.

On the south, New Mexico's border with Mexico was less easily settled. In accordance with the Treaty of Guadalupe-Hidalgo, a joint boundary commission was organized and began (in July 1849) the task of surveying a dividing line between the

two nations. The United States surveyors working with the commission also had instructions to look for a practical railroad
route to the Pacific, close to the boundary, and to ascertain the
agricultural possibilities of the new country. In the course of the
work, it was discovered that the map used to establish the original treaty line eight miles above El Paso had been inaccurate
and that the border would in fact have to be placed thirty miles
farther north. That slip meant withdrawing five or six thousand
square miles from the United States and losing a potentially rich
farming district in the Mesilla valley.

Before a serious dispute could develop, the American minister to Mexico, James Gadsden, negotiated in 1853 the treaty
that bears his name, providing for the purchase of a large tract
of desert land in southern New Mexico. The area offered an ad-
vantageous route for a transcontinental railway entirely on
American soil, and its acquisition concluded the final adjustment of our border with Mexico. The new terrain bought by
Gadsden was added to New Mexico's Doña Ana County, one of
nine counties carved out by the first territorial legislature. Large
enough to be a state in its own right, the land purchased
stretched from present eastern New Mexico across modern Arizona to the Colorado River at Yuma. Other counties showed a
similar westward sprawl, for the time was still several years
away when Congress would lop off half of New Mexico to form
the Arizona Territory.

The far-seeing statesmen at Washington who pushed the
Gadsden Purchase hoped that work would begin as soon as possible on a transcontinental railroad through the area. Since the
gold rush of '49, a flourishing center of American enterprise had
grown up on the west coast and with it a need for better communication. But the dream of seeing iron rails laid across the
windy wastes of southern New Mexico to California was not to
materialize for a generation. Dissension over slavery and the
ravages of civil war were to retard economic growth even in this
remote corner of the country.

In the meantime, with no trains yet crossing the Southwest,
new stagecoach companies moved to fill the transportation gap.
One of the most successful was John Butterfield's Overland

Mail, which inaugurated twice-weekly stage service between St. Louis and San Francisco in 1858. To avoid severe winter weather, the company marked a route for its coaches along a broad southern parabola running through Fort Smith, Arkansas, and the Indian Territory, across the plains of Texas to El Paso, thence forty miles up the Rio Grande to Mesilla, and from there over the lower reaches of New Mexico to Tucson and beyond. For its time, Butterfield's line was the longest in the world.

New Mexico's fertile Mesilla Valley, which had remained unsettled through the Spanish period, was beginning to blossom in the 1850s as the principal agricultural and population center in the southern part of the territory. When the Overland Mail coaches initially passed through the town of Mesilla, there were already more than three thousand inhabitants to cheer them on their way. Waterman L. Ormsby, a twenty-three-year-old corre-spondent for the *New York Herald* and a passenger on the first westbound stage, saw "irrigated fields groaning with the weight of heavy crops," but any favorable impression that view might have inspired quickly took flight when the refined young man gazed upon Mesilla itself. To him, the low-built adobe houses looked like "miserable dog kennels," and "the people seemed . . . to bask in the sun with the complacency of overfed ani-mals." [4]

With all the presumptuousness of youth, Ormsby speculated upon how much more productive this rich valley would prove if it were in the hands of industrious and steady eastern farmers, instead of the "lazy and indolent people" who then occupied it. Each generation of Americans, it seemed, had to learn anew what the Spaniards had discovered long before: in New Mexico, men could not recreate a life and society they had known else-where. Here, the wide and strange land shaped and reshaped human institutions to its own purposes, and one either learned to live with the blazing sun, the scarcity of water, the dust and in-terminable distances, and the whispering quiet of empty can-yons and mesas, or he admitted failure and moved elsewhere.

4. Waterman L. Ormsby, *The Butterfield Overland Mail* (San Marino, California: The Huntington Library, 1955), pp. 79, 80.

While southern New Mexico in the decade of the 1850s was undergoing its first serious development, adventuresome souls three hundred miles to the north were pushing out from the old villages of Taos and Abiquiu to plant settlements, or *plazas,* in what is now lower Colorado. The first brave settlers began building homes in the high, cold San Luis Valley as early as 1853. The next year, fifty families of New Mexicans and Americans, led by Major Lafayette Head, took up land on the Conejos River, not far from the spot where Zebulon Pike had been arrested by Spanish soldiers a half-century before. And in 1859, the same year prospectors discovered gold in the Pike's Peak region, Manuel Lucero with a small band of relatives and friends founded Lucero Plaza far along the upper reaches of the Rio Grande.

These tiny communities, and others that soon arose, were challenged in their first years by wandering parties of Utes who claimed ownership of the intermontane valleys and the majestic peaks surrounding them. Fort Garland, established under the long shadow of the Sierra Blanca in 1858, helped hold the Indians in check, as did periodic military expeditions launched from the south. But in the main, as happened all along the vast and open southwestern frontier, the pioneers themselves had to assume the major burden of defense.

The gold rush to the Rockies and the ensuing boom in population led to the formation of the Colorado Territory in 1861. As a result, New Mexico lost ground, for its northern boundary was pulled back to the parallel of 37°. The reduction meant the territory was deprived of a valuable coal-mining area around Trinidad and of jurisdiction over those outermost settlements in the upper San Luís valley created by New Mexicans in the previous decade.

In these early years of adjusting to its new place in the Union, New Mexico absorbed a respectable quota of adventurers, gamblers, speculators, and renegade whiskey-peddlers—offscourings from the eastern states—but it also got a share of those solid, upright, intelligent citizens representing the glue that held a democratic society together and gave it its strength. Among the latter appeared a fair sampling of persons dedicated to "cultured activity" and to the transplantation of American civilization to the distinctive landscape of the Southwest.

Of several breezy newspapers that shortly began printing in the territory, one, the *Weekly Gazette,* called attention in 1856 to the newly formed Santa Fe Literary Club (whose president, interestingly, was a native New Mexican, Nicholás Quintana) dedicated to the expansion of knowledge and the holding of debates on burning questions of the day. Even more lustrous was the Historical Society of New Mexico, founded in 1859, probably the first such scholarly body to appear anywhere in the Far West.

One of the guiding spirits behind the launching of the Historical Society was New Mexico's first resident bishop (later archbishop), Jean B. Lamy, a Frenchman by birth and a zealot when it came to charitable works and the mission of the Catholic Church. He was a strange man, Lamy, at least to the New Mexicans, who were unaccustomed to sober-minded clerics with a puritanical streak.

The new bishop, after his arrival in 1851, began a campaign to impose religious discipline upon the native clergy, whose lighthearted style of living caused him personal pain and scandalized the Americans. Lamy's reform measures met with fierce opposition, particularly from the redoubtable Padre Martínez of Taos, and his disdain for local custom caused despair among those determined to preserve Hispanic Catholicism. But Lamy did manage to begin a new era in the moral and spiritual life of New Mexico. Working with the energy of a whirlwind, he built in succeeding years forty-five new churches and a string of parochial schools, among them St. Michael's College at Santa Fe. Since public schools capable of teaching basic English were still decades away, Bishop Lamy's pioneer classrooms offered the first formal introduction many young New Mexicans had to the language and culture of the American nation.

Before education or the natural process of assimilation could make much headway, however, the people of the Southwest were caught up in the momentous and ugly events attending the great controversy over slavery. It was an issue in which the New Mexicans had small stake (in all the territory, there were

only twenty-one black slaves in 1861), but it was, as the down-
hill course of circumstances soon proved, a problem impossible
to sidestep.

The overriding question in national politics and the one that
dominated debate in Congress during the 1850s centered upon
expansion of slavery to the western territories—especially to
New Mexico Territory. Abolitionists had viewed the Mexican
War as a plot by Southerners to extend slavery's realm, and so,
after the war, they waged a bitter campaign to exclude the hate-
ful institution from the newly acquired borderlands. Actually,
many statesmen in Washington had long recognized New Mexico as a land unsuitable for slavery because her agriculture was
small in scale and native labor was both plentiful and cheap.
Territorial citizens themselves had approved antislavery resolutions in 1848 and 1850. But a seeming reversal in sentiment
came in 1859, with adoption of a slavery code engineered by
Miguel A. Otero, the New Mexican delegate to Congress. The
code, designed to protect slaveowners in their property, was
more an expression of Otero's own pro-Southern sympathies
than it was a sign of any fundamental shift in attitude among
territorial residents. The people, above all else, desired to be
left alone, for they saw little to be gained by joining in the great
political arguments between North and South over slavery and
the legality of secession.

When the differences became unreconcilable and the storm
broke, splitting the country in halves, New Mexico unexpect-
edly found herself part of the theater of conflict. From the outset, the newly formed Confederacy cast covetous eyes westward, where it dreamed of creating an empire that would reach
to the Pacific. The benefits to be gained by spanning the continent were enormous: the gold fields, particularly those of Colorado and California, could help the South finance the war;
seaports on the West Coast might open the possibility for an
Asiatic trade, and they would certainly diminish the Union's capacity to maintain an effective blockade; and of diplomatic significance, the Confederate States, enlarged to take in the Pacific
Slope, would attain immense prestige, perhaps enough to tip the
balance and bring recognition from European nations.

Winning the West, then, just might be a crucial step toward winning the war. But nothing could be won without a grand strategy; and when one was developed by Southern leaders, it showed plainly that as a first step toward westward expansion, New Mexico must be brought securely into the Confederate camp.

At the outbreak of the Civil War in 1861, a sweeping glance at affairs on the upper Rio Grande made it appear that the Confederate annexation of New Mexico could be accomplished with relative ease. For one thing, in the lower part of the territory there existed a hard core of Southern sympathizers—mainly ranchers out of Texas, who had settled recently in the Mesilla district, plus a flock of miners working new mineral discoveries around Tucson. For another thing, most of the ranking officers serving in the military Department of New Mexico defected to the South, bringing with them precious information on war matériel stored at several territorial forts. Then, indulging in a bit of wishful thinking, Confederate leaders imagined that they perceived a growing sentiment in favor of secession among native New Mexicans. Added to those considerations, the territory's long eastern border with Texas clearly dictated an inevitable union with the Southern cause; equally clearly, the vast distances separating her from the northern states would prevent help from arriving should she try to avoid the inevitable.

The offensive was taken almost at once by Lieutenant Colonel John R. Baylor of the Confederate Army, who, in the summer of 1861, gathered 350 recruits into a regiment called the Texas Mounted Volunteers. With these hard-bitten men, accustomed all to handling arms and sleeping on the ground in every sort of weather, Baylor marched to El Paso, where he occupied Fort Bliss and prepared to march up the Rio Grande to begin the conquest of New Mexico. A man of vindictive nature, with a sinister look about him, the colonel was, nevertheless, a decisive and forceful leader. With his war-hungry Texans, he made a swift move against Federal troops stationed at Fort Fillmore near Mesilla and pursued them in earnest as they fled eastward toward Fort Stanton.

Near the Organ Pass above present Las Cruces, Baylor managed to bag the whole lot, forcing the Union commander, Major Isaac Lynde, of Vermont, to surrender. Back in Mesilla, he took stock of his gains and the political situation in the territory.

For several years, southern New Mexicans, including those in the settlements south of the Gila River, had been discontented because of neglect by officials in faraway Santa Fe. In fact, they had held conventions at Mesilla in 1859 and at Tucson in 1860 to assemble plans for organizing a separate territory, to be called either Pimería, Gadsonia, or Arizona. But the war had intervened, and the planning ceased. Yet Baylor was aware of the strong movement for separation, as well as the Southern leanings of much of the population, so he moved to capitalize on the disquiet and out of it to gain a foothold in the West on behalf of the Confederate States of America. On August 1, he proclaimed all of New Mexico south of the 34th parallel (that is, the lower half of the territory) to be the new Territory of Arizona, with Mesilla as the capital and himself as provisional governor. That was sufficient for the moment, he decided, until the Confederate government had a chance to approve his actions and to say what the next step should be.

Preparations for taking that step were already under way in the Confederacy's capital of Richmond, where President Jefferson Davis had lent a willing ear to proposals put forth by Henry H. Sibley. A native of Louisiana, a West Pointer, and lately a U.S. Army major serving in New Mexico, Sibley came offering both his services and a plan to capture the southwestern territories. If given the authority, he would raise an army of Texas backwoodsmen and set out northward from El Paso and Mesilla to take the Union-held forts in upper New Mexico and the gold fields of Colorado. That done, he would turn west and, with ranks swelled by volunteers he expected to rally to the South's call, seize California.

President Davis was enchanted by the bright prospect. Mississippi-born Davis had served as U.S. Secretary of War, beginning in 1853, and in that capacity had come to appreciate the value of the desert borderlands acquired from Mexico. Indeed, he had been a key figure in the maneuvering that led to the Gadsden Purchase and was one of those most vocal in arguing for speedy construction of a transcontinental railroad through the Southwest. Thus Sibley's talk impressed him favorably, and he gave Sibley the authority sought, along with the rank of brigadier general. The South's dream of a dazzling empire stretching from sea to sea appeared about to be realized.

But all this while, loyal Union men had been rallying in northern New Mexico. Governor Henry Connelly at Santa Fe, one of the old-guard traders and anti-Confederate to the core, issued a call for the formation of militia companies to defend the territory. Word went also to pro-Union partisans in Colorado and California: if the disturbing rumors of an invasion from Texas by General Sibley were true, here in New Mexico was the proper place to confront the enemy.

To Colonel Edward R. S. Canby, commander of Federal forces in New Mexico, fell the task of preserving the upper Rio Grande from the Confederate threat. In a day when most men went bearded, Canby remained clean-shaven, his solid jaw and square chin giving him the look of a kind but forceful schoolmaster. His planning of strategy, too, was more academic than military—slow and methodical, rather than bold and aggressive. Canby believed in consolidating his troops, the regular soldiers and the native New Mexican militia, and holding a secure defensive position. That he elected to do at Fort Craig, a strong post situated on the west bank of the Rio Grande a few miles below Socorro and just inside the 34th parallel that Baylor was claiming as the northern border of his Confederate Territory of Arizona.

General Sibley meantime had scoured the Texas frontier and put together three regiments totaling twenty-six hundred men. They were a coarse lot, much given to raucous laughter and the playing of practical jokes, but they knew how to fight. And few as they were, they stood ready to march all the way to the Pacific if Hell-for-leather Sibley in his stiff gray uniform would lead them. So up the Rio Grande from El Paso and Mesilla they came, in February 1862, intending to dispose of Fort Craig with a slashing blow and then afterward take Albuquerque, Santa Fe, and, beyond that, Fort Union, with its valuable store of military supplies. They rode with dash and confidence, and there was a noticeable spring in the trot of their range-bred, grass-fed Texas horses, for, with this slim army, as they well knew, went Confederate hopes in the West.

Strenuous marching brought Sibley's gray column of Texan stalwarts to a point on the east bank of the Rio Grande opposite Fort Craig. From there, they could gaze across the roily waters to dove-colored adobe walls, pierced at intervals by embrasures for artillery, and beyond to the far-rising ramparts of the San Mateo Mountains. On the face of it, the Confederates had a tough chore ahead of them if they planned to take the fort by storm. But a hasty assessment convinced Sibley that an assault could not succeed. Hence he tried several maneuvers to draw the Federals into the open, away from their protective battlements. Canby, however, proved a model of caution and refused to take the bait. He had upward of thirty-eight hundred men, but many of them were grass-green militia and native volunteers, in whom he placed small confidence.

The Rebels went into camp, and a brisk night breeze carried the muffled sound of their activity across the Rio Grande to the watchful men in the fort. There, one of the officers walking the walls and contemplating the flickering pinpoints of the enemy's campfires suddenly conceived a masterful piece of strategy. Hurrying to Colonel Canby, he quickly won approval for his plan. With three men, he loaded a dozen howitzer shells into wooden crates and lashed them to the backs of a pair of decrepit old mules. With his assistants, he then set out for the Confederate camp, crossing the river under cover of darkness. Close to Sibley's line, they ignited the fuses, lashed the mules forward, and commenced a swift retreat.

The tactic, so brilliantly executed, might have brought destruction and chaos to the Confederate ranks, but for one trifling fact neglected by the Union officer and his men: mules possess a strong homing instinct, and this incendiary pair, once becoming aware that they were abandoned, turned tail and went pelting over their back trail. The escort wheeled about and beheld with horror two shadows trotting companionably behind, under a sputter of sparks. With a shout, the riders spurred their horses and raced for the shelter of the fort. The ensuing boom rocked the valley and shook awake every man, blue and gray, trying to sleep there. In the report of the incident delivered to Canby, total casualties were listed as two mules.

If that can be considered a lighter moment of the Civil War in New Mexico, then it was one of the very few. Shortly there would be only the suffering, devastation, and death that are the hallmarks of all armed conflict. And it began just above Fort Craig on February 21, with the first major battle fought between Union and Confederate troops in the Far Southwest.

On that day, General Sibley moved his army six miles up the Rio Grande to the Valverde Ford. If anything could draw Canby's forces out into the open, he reckoned, it would be a threat by the Confederates to cross to the west bank of the river. Nor was he wrong in his guessing. When the Union commander perceived the intention of the enemy, he plucked up courage and ordered out his troops to defend the Valverde crossing.

The Rio Grande, for centuries the scene of fierce struggles between Spaniards and Indians, was now invaded by the din and violence of another sort of contest—a fratricidal one, between Northerners and Southerners. The Battle of Valverde involved the bloodiest kind of tough, stand-up fighting—"terrific beyond description," one Rebel lad recalled it later.[5] The Texans, screaming like maddened cougars, made a savage charge armed with pistols, double-barrelled shotguns, and bowie knives. Some of the New Mexican militia broke and retreated, but others, particularly those under Colonel Kit Carson, who had come down from his home in the north to support the Union cause, held their ground. A battery of Federal artillery, which had been conveyed to the east shore, was overrun, but not before every man defending it had died, including its gallant officer, Captain Alexander McRae, who fell at his post "pierced with many bullets." As the day rounded to a close, Canby's men fell back toward the fort, leaving the waters of Valverde Ford tinctured with the blood of their dead and wounded. "We made the Yankees dance to our music!" the jubilant Confederates

5. Theo. Noel, *A Campaign from Santa Fe to the Mississippi* (Houston: Stagecoach Press, 1961), p. 29.

shouted to one another, and in their enthusiasm they claimed a victory.[6]

The laurels, however, were anything but clearly won. Sibley's brigade held the ford and that, together with a lift in morale, was about all that had been gained. In the debit column, Canby still occupied a strong position inside Fort Craig; and the Rebels, with only a few days' rations left in their knapsacks, could not even consider a siege.

General Sibley, therefore, found himself obliged to violate one of those age-old principles of war known to every military commander: never bypass and leave an enemy on your rear. Sibley would press rapidly on to Albuquerque in search of supplies and hope that Canby's force stayed holed up, licking its Valverde wounds. If northern New Mexico fell as planned, then the Confederates could return and deal with Fort Craig at leisure.

As it happened, several circumstances intervened to frustrate that simple scheme. First, Federal troops guarding the supply depot at Albuquerque got word of the Rebel advance in time to load many of their military stores on wagons and hurry them north. What they couldn't carry, they burned. Sibley's hungry boys laboring up the sandy, brown valley of the Rio Grande saw the telltale column of black smoke and were crestfallen. Without rations and ammunition, their invasion must inevitably grind to a halt. It would probably have done just that had not the Confederates managed to seize the small military post of Cubero west of Albuquerque on the Navajo frontier. There, enough arms, food, and medical supplies to fill twenty-five wagons had been assembled earlier for an intended Indian campaign. Captured, that equipment went to sustain the Rebel drive northward.

Whatever more Sibley needed to feed his men and horses he hoped to purchase from the New Mexicans, now that he had reached the populous sections of the territory. But in his failure to accomplish that can be found the second reason why his larger strategy soon derailed. All along, the Confederates had counted on winning over the Hispano population, but they had

6. Noel, *A Campaign from Santa Fe*, pp. 29, 59.

failed to reckon with the New Mexicans' antipathy toward Texans—an outgrowth, in part, of the Texas invasion of 1841 and more recent boundary disputes—or their unwillingness to accept Southern currency as payment for their foodstuffs. On the contrary, many of the local people had answered Governor Henry Connelly's call for volunteers, and others brought in money, mules, and provisions, placing them at the disposal of the Federal army.

Third, General Sibley seriously miscalculated the strength of Union arms opposing him in the north. On February 22, the day after the Battle of Valverde, a regiment of Colorado Volunteers with two batteries of artillery had left Denver as snow tumbled from a slate-gray sky. Plowing through heavy weather, the men crossed over Raton Pass during the first week of March and were soon billeted in Fort Union on the Santa Fe Trail. From all the feverish news that came to their ears then, it was apparent that the Coloradans would shortly be in the thick of a fight.

The Civil War in the Southwest was indeed moving toward a climax. From Albuquerque, Sibley had set half his army on the road to Santa Fe, supported by what supplies he could muster. In a close squeak, Governor Connelly, other territorial officials, and the small garrison at Fort Marcy managed to escape eastward by caravan to the relative safety of Las Vegas and Fort Union beyond the mountains. At that point, Loyalist fortunes in New Mexico appeared to be at their lowest ebb.

The Confederates, however, still lacked a decisive victory; mainly, they needed to grab the Federal arsenal at Fort Union, to resupply their ranks and to prevent their invasion from running out of steam. The issue was decided, not at the fort, but in Glorieta Pass located above the mouth of Apache Canyon, fifteen miles east of Santa Fe—the same area Governor Manuel Armijo had refused to defend when Kearny approached, back in 1846.

On March 27 and 28, 1862, regular troops from Fort Union, supported by the Colorado Volunteers, met the Rebels at Glorieta, in what would become known as the Gettysburg of the West. The first day of sharp combat ended in a draw, but the second indisputably went to the men in gray, who won control of the canyon. Nevertheless, final victory was snatched from their hands when Major John M. Chivington of the Volunteers delivered a wholly unexpected thunderbolt. Two years later, Chivington would lead a hideous massacre of peaceful Cheyennes at Sand Creek, Colorado; but at this juncture, he was the Union's man of the hour.

Taking a detachment of Coloradans and guided by Colonel Manuel Chaves of the New Mexico Volunteers, Chivington followed a difficult mountain trail that carried him behind the battle in the pass. Discovering the Confederate supply train, which had been left weakly defended at the rear, he drove off the guard, bayoneted eleven hundred mules, and burned sixty-four wagons. Chivington's successful foray, it soon became apparent, completely reversed the fortunes of war in New Mexico.

For Sibley's Texans, the loss of their field supplies at Apache Canyon was a first-class disaster, forcing them to abandon all consideration of an assault on Fort Union. Indeed, the Confederate command realized that the roof had collapsed on their ambitious plan to turn New Mexico into a launching ground for Southern expansionism in the West. Like a good soldier, General Sibley thought first of the safety of his army. With provisions unavailable and with the Colorado Volunteers and well-fed Federal troops arrayed against him, he began to withdraw down the Rio Grande.

At Peralta, a few miles below Albuquerque, the Rebels encountered Canby and his soldiers, who had at last ventured forth from the security of Fort Craig, looking for a scrap. Here was fought the third and last battle of the Civil War in New Mexico—really little more than a skirmish and a reminder to Sibley that by heading south toward El Paso he was going in the right direction. Canby followed the retreating Texans for a time, but it was clear to him that in their present destitute condition they no longer offered a threat to the territory. Lean as grey-hounds, hungry as December wolves, and clad in tattered butternut uniforms, the downcast and defeated invaders formed as ragtag an army as the New Mexican sun ever blistered. A fitting epitaph for the entire painful campaign was uttered not long after its close by one of the survivors, who wrote, upon his return to Texas, "[No more for us] throwing our lives away in endeavoring to obtain possession of a country which is not worth the life of one good man, of the many who have breathed their last upon its arid sands." [7]

Defeat of the Sibley Brigade meant also the demise of the rump government at Mesilla and dissolution of the Confederate Territory of Arizona. The end was assured when California Volunteers under Colonel James H. Carlton occupied Tucson in June of 1862 and then advanced on the Rio Grande. Just a few months before, when the Rebels were riding the crest of their wave in New Mexico, Confederate Governor Baylor had boasted, "So far Mr. Lincoln is not making much headway in suppressing the rebellion. He has got himself thrashed at every fight from Manassas to Mesilla, and today we dare them to attack us at any point." [8] But by early summer, Baylor was no longer making dares, for, with other pro-Southern men, he was in full flight and glad for the chance to get out of New Mexico with his shirttail intact. The debacle at Glorieta and the retreat to Texas scuttled for all time Confederate hopes for an empire in western America.

One consequence of the Civil War in the Southwest was that the U.S. Congress finally turned its attention to the creating of another territory here. From the western half of New Mexico, Arizona was carved in 1863 and launched on the political sea. Officials in Santa Fe showed little reluctance at the reduction in size of their jurisdiction, for what they lost was at that time too remote and too thinly populated to be of much economic significance. Moreover, they could draw an easy breath that the fruitful Mesilla valley by this arrangement would remain with New Mexico.

Another and more sanguinary result of the war was that it left the frontier open to attack by hostile Indians. Tribes seeking plunder or bearing old grudges were quick to note that the white men were fighting among themselves, abandoning forts, and

7. *Beeville* (Texas) *Countryman,* June 7, 1862.

8. William A. Keleher, *Turmoil in New Mexico, 1846–1868* (Santa Fe: The Rydal Press, 1952), p. 143.

withdrawing troops for service in the East. For many, the opportunity to step up their raids was too enticing to be ignored. The ensuing bloodshed brought nightmare days to New Mexico and other western territories.

When James Carlton, having been promoted to brigadier general, reached the Rio Grande with his Union army of Californians, he assumed command of the Military Department of New Mexico, replacing Canby. Since the flight of the Confederates removed all promise of formal battle, Carlton turned his attention to the Indians pillaging the border settlements. He had several thousand troops ready for action and certain fixed notions about how to deal with raiders. The program he presented to Governor Connelly, Chief Justice Kirby Benedict, and other territorial officials was direct and harsh: wage merciless war against all hostile tribes, force them to their knees, and then confine them on reservations where they could be Christianized and instructed in agriculture. Manifestly, it was a policy designed to bring quick results.

The Mescalero Apaches of southern New Mexico were first to feel the effects of Carlton's strategy. Placing Militia Colonel Kit Carson in charge of troops in the field, the general sent his men to harry the tribe into submission. By March 1863, the campaign was completed, and Carson brought four hundred warriors with their families to the new Bosque Redondo Reservation on the Pecos River in southeastern New Mexico. Here Fort Sumner, constructed by Carlton, stood guard.

Next it was the turn of the Navajo, a people numbering at that time some ten thousand and inhabiting the crumpled and rock-strewn lands of western New Mexico. They lived by herding huge flocks of sheep, tending small gardens and orchards, and by plundering the New Mexican settlements. For years, Spanish and Mexican expeditions had tried to bring them to bay, but the Navajo proved too nimble, fading into the remote canyonlands whenever their enemies gave chase. Kearny's subordinate, Colonel Alexander Doniphan, had arranged a peace treaty with Chief Zarcillos Largos in 1846, but that document had become a dead issue within a year. As General Carlton saw it in the spring of 1863, nothing but total war could cause the Navajo to capitulate.

Again, he handed the job to Kit Carson, a man who knew the country and the habits of the Indians. Recent critics have condemned Carson for his conduct in the campaign that followed, charging that his tactics were unnecessarily brutal and that his actions showed him to be an oppressor of the Indians. But that view, under scrutiny, fails to hold water.

Colonel Carson, in point of fact, had no desire to be in charge of a campaign to crush the Navajo, and he asked several times to be relieved of the task. But Carlton, who knew the right man for a job when he saw one, was persistent, and Carson's sense of duty would not let him refuse. His reluctance stemmed from the military's avowed intention of forcing the Indians to choose between unconditional surrender or extermination, a policy originally formulated by Canby. That appeared to leave no room for compromise, but Carson felt that, in the end, his participation might act as a moderating influence.

During the last half of 1863, government troops marched and countermarched through Navajoland, destroying crops and orchards and capturing livestock. They fought no major battles, but their campaigning left the Indian economy in ruins. In January of 1864, Kit Carson led his men into the depths of Canyon de Chelly, where, for the first time, he encountered a large body of Navajo. They were exhausted and starving, and at that point disposed to listen to a man who was known to be trustworthy. The tribe would have to emigrate to a government reservation at Bosque Redondo, Carson told them, but that was preferable to annihilation. Under the circumstances, the majority of the Indians agreed, and they surrendered.

Over the succeeding months, other destitute bands gave up and were conducted eastward on a dolorous journey to their new reservation along the Pecos River. That trip into exile, remembered in Navajo tribal history as the "Long Walk," had a parallel in the tragic Trail of Tears, when Indians in the southeastern United States during the 1830s were obliged to give up their homes and move west of the Mississippi.

General Carlton was now hailed by the territorial press as the savior of New Mexico. He felt pleased that his strategy had helped reduce the danger from Indian raids, and he was eager to prove that confining the Navajo and Mescalero Apache at Bosque Redondo was the best way to keep the peace. But his reservation experiment did not pan out.

The barren land in the Pecos valley could not support the nine thousand Indians crowded there, most of whom were not interested in farming, anyway. The drinking water turned out to be disagreeably rich in alkali, having a stronger effect on the stomach than castor oil, as a soldier stationed at Fort Sumner wrote his wife. The federal government failed to provide adequate supplies to support the Indians during the period that they were getting established. And putting the Mescalero and Navajo—traditional enemies—together on the same reservation was soon recognized as a colossal blunder. When Bishop Jean Lamy came down from Santa Fe to check on possibilities for developing a mission school, he was appalled by the misery he found among the captive people.

The Mescaleros, being in the minority and suffering the most, soon kicked over the traces and melted into the mountains and plains of the south, where they resumed the old pattern of raiding. Not until the 1870s were they finally defeated and confined to a new reservation in the Sacramento Mountains.

The agony of the Navajo at Bosque Redondo lasted until 1868, at which time they were allowed to return to their beloved homeland in the west. Retracing the trail made five years before on their "Long Walk," many of the Indians were overcome by emotion as they caught a first glimpse of their familiar mesas and smoke-colored mountains beyond Albuquerque. Their war days over forever, they resolved now to adapt to changed circumstances and rebuild the traditional pattern of life disrupted by their enforced exile on the Pecos.

With the end of the Civil War in the East in April 1865, regular troops were again available in large numbers for service on the western frontier. By late 1866, General James Carlton had given up command of New Mexico, and his California Volunteers, who had enlisted to oppose the Confederates—and ended up fighting Indians—were disbanded. But the war on hostile tribes was still far from over.

On the eastern plains, Comanches and Kiowas, occasionally abetted by far-ranging Cheyenne and Arapaho war parties, threatened New Mexico's vital supply line, the Santa Fe Trail.

Military patrols from Fort Union worked feverishly to provide protection for caravans and travelers, but in spite of their valiant efforts, Anglo-Americans venturing forth in the decade after the Civil War did so at considerable risk to their lives and property.

It was a different story for the Pueblos and Hispanos, who, in the midst of this flurry, continued to hunt buffalo and trade on the plains as they had always done. The reason, of course, was that the all-powerful Comanche remained their friends, a legacy of Governor Juan Bautista de Anza's peace treaty made back in 1786. In one notable case, hostile Kiowas surrounded a roaming party of *cíboleros* (New Mexican buffalo hunters—picturesque types, armed with lances, dressed in leather suits, and wearing peaked caps topped with a feather) and prepared to massacre them to a man. But a band of Comanches happened upon the scene at this critical moment, rescued the New Mexicans, and escorted them to safety.

The Plains tribes held their ground until the early 1870s, when the full pressure of United States military might was brought against them. In the Red River War of 1874, cavalry units, including troops from Fort Union and Fort Bascom, north of modern Tucumcari, converged on the forbidding reaches of the Texas Panhandle. There the red men were hounded from one hiding place to another, until their spirit was broken, and they agreed to accept reservations in the Indian Territory. With the end of hostilities and the virtual extermination of the buffalo, which quickly followed, the vast grasslands of eastern New Mexico were suddenly thrown open for settlement.

That left only some stray Apache bands in southwestern New Mexico to be dealt with, but defeating them proved to be the most difficult chore of all. In 1879, Chief Victorio and some of his warriors bolted from their reservation and cut a bloody path across the Rio Grande and into Arizona. Their rampage lasted until Victorio's death in 1881. His son-in-law, Nana, half-blind and crippled by rheumatism, but still capable of riding seventy miles a day, then took up the hatchet and continued the war. Nana fought eight battles against the Americans and won them all, before coming into the San Carlos Reservation in eastern Arizona.

In 1885, Nana broke out with Geronimo and raided until the

final Apache surrender the following year. The most troublesome Indians were placed on a train at that time to be sent to
Fort Marion, Florida, as prisoners of war. At Deming, cowboys
stormed the train, intending to drag the Apaches onto the plat-
form for a lynching. But soldiers poured from the cars to defend
the captives, and a tragedy was averted. A mournful blast from
the engine's whistle cleared the tracks, and at the same time put
a period to the last chapter in the long history of New Mexico's
Indian wars.

While the nomad tribes were suffering defeat and confine-
ment on reservations, the Pueblo people were preoccupied with
adjusting to life under American rule. Soon after Kearny's conquest in 1846, the Pueblo village governors had visited Santa Fe
to swear fealty to the new regime and learn the nature of its
policies. What they found out was not altogether reassuring.
Mexico had recognized them as citizens and had provided special attorneys to protect their property rights, but it appeared
now that the United States was unprepared to grant them these
privileges or to make any legal distinction between Pueblos and
the warlike nomads. Anglo-American thinking, firmly wedded
to stereotypes drawn from contact with Indians in the eastern
woodlands and the Mississippi valley, tended to resist any policy that looked toward the elevation of the native people to full
rights of citizenship.

New Mexico's first Indian agent, James S. Calhoun, recognized the special problem as early as 1849. He informed Washington that the industrious Pueblos were model subjects and
urged that they be extended voting rights and that their land
grants given by Spain be protected. The last point was particularly important, because the Indians, holding some of the best
irrigated agricultural lands in the territory, were constantly bothered by trespassers and squatters. The U.S. Surveyor General
did confirm original Pueblo grants after 1854, a ruling reaffirmed by the Congress. But the duty of the federal government
to intervene actively to protect Pueblo Indian lands from encroachment—the policy Spain had pursued—would not be recognized until 1913.

Through most of the late nineteenth century, the Pueblos suffered unconscionable neglect. One observer after another reported their great need and desire for formal education, but illiteracy remained the rule. Special Agent William F. Arny told the Interior Secretary in 1870 that several villages had scraped together enough pennies to hire inept teachers, and others had offered to donate land and build a school if they could obtain some assistance from the government. But thus far their initiative had brought no response from small-minded officials.

Part of the problem was that the Pueblos, along with those Indians recently conquered and shoved onto reservations, were the hapless prey of disinterested or dishonest agents, corrupt territorial officials, and thieving supply contractors. One rare, unprejudiced Indian agent, taking a candid look at some of the ills, placed blame on congressmen and the public. "The American people," he declared bitingly, "like humbug as a duck does water. They won't believe the truth. There is so much interest used in Washington to get big appropriations, and the estimates needed are greatly exaggerated . . . And meanwhile the Indian school business and all is mere humbug; to use money for other purposes than that designed." [9] The agent's complaint, made in 1884, has a distinctly modern ring.

By and large, the Pueblos had to wait until the opening decades of the twentieth century before much notice was taken of them, but one small gesture acknowledging their existence was offered in 1863—by Abraham Lincoln. As early as 1620, the Spanish government had presented silver-tipped canes, or staffs of justice, to the Pueblo Indian governors as a symbol of authority. The canes, carefully preserved, continued to be passed down from one official to another long after Spain had given up her hold on New Mexico. President Lincoln, hearing of the custom and wishing to honor the Pueblos for remaining neutral during the Civil War, prepared a new set of canes, each with a silver crown upon which was engraved the name of the pueblo, the date of 1863, and the signature *A. Lincoln*. Presented to the villagers by Indian Superintendent Michael Steck, these gifts

9. John Ayres, "A Soldier's Experience in New Mexico," *New Mexico Historical Review* 24 (October 1949):263.

were honored alongside the original Spanish staffs, and today, when the Pueblos inaugurate their governors each January 1, the canes—one given by a king and the other by a U.S. president—are ceremoniously conveyed to the new officials.

Once the slavery issue was resolved beyond the borders of New Mexico, the maturing American nation found itself confronting other unsettling problems: what to do about reconstruction? How to bring the freed Negroes into society? Where to put the remnants of western Indians as they were crowded off their hunting range? How to regulate predatory businessmen—the empire builders and the moguls of the outspreading railroads? But most of all, there remained the questions of how to relieve the great pain left by the Civil War and how to restore unity and national spirit.

For New Mexico and other western territories, just beginning an unprecedented period of development and growth, memory of the tragic conflict faded quickly and was replaced by a boisterous enthusiasm generating a conviction that prosperity lay right over the next mountain. Throughout the Southwest, railroad promotion was in the air, and in New Mexico's scarped and rock-ribbed mountain ranges, prospectors with picks and hammers were beginning to uncover deposits of gold, silver, copper, and other minerals. The ancient dream of Coronado and Oñate of finding El Dorado on the Rio Grande arose phoenixlike to animate a new generation of fortune seekers. And for those men for whom railroading or mining held little attraction, the territory's plains and basins, from which the last hostile Indians were then being cleared, provided abundant room for staking out a princely sheep or cattle ranch.

In 1868, the year the telegraph reached Santa Fe, the New Mexico Territory had a population of twelve thousand to fifteen thousand Anglo-Americans. With their bustle and ambition, they sparkplugged the new economic boom, but enterprising Hispanos were soon catching the spirit and seizing opportunities for personal enrichment. From their old settlements in the Rio Grande and Upper Pecos valleys, native New Mexicans fanned out eastward, crossed the Canadian River, and planted tiny

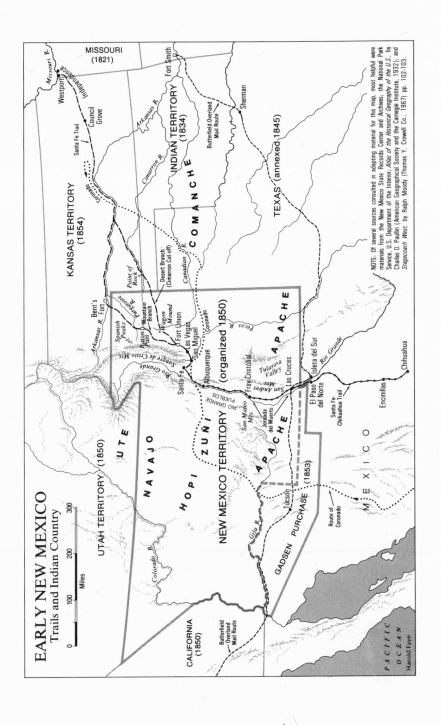

EARLY NEW MEXICO
Trails and Indian Country

MISSOURI (1821)

Missouri R.

Westport
Independence
Santa Fe Trail
Council Grove

Fort Smith

INDIAN TERRITORY (1834)

Arkansas R.
Cimarron R.

COMANCHE

Butterfield Overland Mail Route

Sherman

TEXAS (annexed 1845)

KANSAS TERRITORY (1854)

Point of Rock
Desert Branch (Cimarron Cut-off)
Canadian R.

Bent's Fort
Arkansas R.
Spanish Peaks
Raton Pass
Mountain Branch
Wagon Mound
Fort Union
Las Vegas
San Miguel
Coronado

Sangre de Cristo Mts.

Pecos R.

APACHE

Santa Fe
Albuquerque
Rio Grande
Fray Cristóbal
Tularosa Valley
San Andres Mts.
Las Cruces
Isleta del Sur
Rio Grande
Santa Fe del Sur

(organized 1850)

RIO GRANDE PUEBLOS

San Mateo Mts.
Jornada del Muerto

El Paso del Norte

Santa Fe-Chihuahua Trail

Encinillas

Chihuahua

UTAH TERRITORY (1850)

UTE

NAVAJO

HOPI

ZUÑI

NEW MEXICO TERRITORY

Colorado R.

Gila R.

Tucson

GADSEN PURCHASE (1853)

Route of Coronado

M É X I C O

CALIFORNIA (1850)

Butterfield Overland Mail Route

Miles
0   100   200   300

PACIFIC OCEAN

Harold Faye

NOTE: Of several sources consulted in adapting material for this map, most helpful were materials from the New Mexico State Records Center and Archives; the National Park Service, U.S. Department of the Interior, Atlas of the Historical Geography of the U.S., by Charles O. Paullin (American Geographical Society and the Carnegie Institute, 1932); and Stagecoach West, by Ralph Moody (Thomas Y. Crowell Co., 1967) pp. 102-103.

communities and sheep camps as far as the Staked Plains of Texas. Others trickled into the southeastern part of the territory, and by the late 1860s had built adobe homes along the Rio Hondo, an affluent of the Pecos. Another wave of Hispanic pioneers moved westward—from Socorro to the gemlike valley of the Rio San Francisco close to the Arizona boundary; and from the old villages in the Chama valley to the San Juan Basin in the Four Corners. Finally, a few of the more venturesome drove seed flocks northward in the 1870s, stocking the emerald-green ranges of the Rocky Mountain states with New Mexican sheep.

The expansion of the sheepmen had not progressed far before cattle ranchers, mostly from Texas, began to drift into the territory and compete for the choicer pasture lands. As early as 1865, beef contractors for the Bosque Redondo Reservation were encouraging stockmen to drive cattle from the plains of west Texas up the valley of the Pecos River to feed the captive Navajo. Charles Goodnight and Oliver Loving, among the early participants in that activity, took their first herd of longhorns to New Mexico in the summer of 1866. Even though their route up the Pecos had been blazed by others, it soon became known as the Goodnight-Loving Trail, and when in succeeding years it was extended to Colorado and beyond, it came to rank with the Sedalia and the Chisholm trails as one of the great cattle thoroughfares of the American West.

Conspicuous among the pioneer stockmen was John S. Chisum, an early associate of Goodnight, who in 1873 began building a ranch of baronial dimensions along the middle Pecos River. From his headquarters near modern Roswell, Chisum sent out a hundred cowboys to tend some eighty thousand head of cattle grazing on ranges that extended, according to one local newspaper, "as far as a man can travel, on a good horse, during a summer." [10] The massive size of the operation soon earned Chisum the title "Cow King of New Mexico," and for a time in the late 1870s, he was probably the largest cattle raiser in the United States.

The demand for beef at Bosque Redondo and other Indian

10. *Las Vegas Gazette,* November 25, 1875.

reservations had first drawn ranchers to New Mexico, but it was not long before boomtowns in newly opened mining districts throughout the territory offered even more promising markets. The sudden stampede of people to out-of-the-way mountain valleys, where most of the mineral discoveries occurred, created unparalleled opportunities for a cattleman to trail in a small herd and sell it at a considerable profit.

New Mexico at that time already possessed one of the oldest mining industries in America. In the Cerrillos Hills south of Santa Fe, Pueblo Indians for centuries had worked open-pit turquoise mines, removing some one hundred thousand tons of waste rock, with nothing more than muscle and primitive tools. The Spaniards showed little interest in turquoise, but they did extract lead, coal, and considerable copper from the Santa Rita del Cobre Mines near Silver City. During the Mexican period, a short-lived gold rush drew fortune seekers to the Ortiz Mountains south of the Galisteo Basin, but the finding of spectacular bonanzas awaited the influx of prospectors that occurred at the end of the Civil War.

Many of General James Carlton's California boys, once they had finished with Indian fighting and been mustered out of service, decided to stay in New Mexico. Some of them, familiar with the gold fields and mining methods in their home state, took up pans and picks and began prospecting in the more secluded valleys and sierras of the territory. That vanguard was soon joined by new ranks of hopeful men, fresh from the overcrowded diggings in Colorado.

The late 1860s witnessed important gold strikes at Pinos Altos, below the Mogollon Range, and in the nearby Pyramid Mountains, and at Elizabethtown, situated high on the western slope of Baldy Mountain in the Sangre de Cristos. In the following decade, dramatic gold and silver discoveries created a minor frenzy among promoters and investors and gave swift birth to such new towns as Hillsboro, Chloride, Georgetown, and White Oaks. One of the richest finds was made in 1878, not far south of Hillsboro, at Lake Valley—a vaulted cavern of horn silver so pure that miners sawed and cut the ore into blocks, instead of blasting it free.

The crescendo of New Mexico's mining boom had passed by the early 1890s, but while it was in its noisy prime, it pumped much-needed wealth into the territorial economy. It also lent credence to those wispy legends of colonial days, now a part of American folklore, that suggested that the wind-battered mesas and mountains of New Mexico were storehouses of treasure. The wealth proved real enough—just not large enough to fulfill the extravagant dreams of those who pegged their hopes on a never-ending supply of precious metal. In the wake of the bust, the high country was left littered with ghost towns and abandoned tunnels whose only occupants were swarms of shrieking bats.

Coinciding with the peak of the mining excitement, railroads had thrust across New Mexico, finally tying the lower half of the nation together. The Atchison, Topeka, and Santa Fe, besting its rival, the Denver and Rio Grande Western, for possession of Raton Pass, became the first to lay rails into New Mexico from the east. Following the heavy ruts of the Santa Fe Trail, it reached Las Vegas early in 1879. Continuing westward, the railroad bypassed Santa Fe with its main line and curved down the Rio Grande valley to Albuquerque. Thence it reached south to a division point at Rincon. There, one branch was extended to El Paso, while the other ran to Deming, where, in 1881, it forged a transcontinental link with the Southern Pacific that was building eastward from California. Soon other major railroads, short lines, and spurs spread a vast web of track across the territory to serve the newly prosperous farming, ranching, and mining interests.

A surveyor, helping to lay out a rail bed in western New Mexico had exclaimed with vehemence to his tent-mates one evening in 1880 that surely "This was God's country because no one else would have it." [11] He was wrong, of course, for with improved communication and promotion of New Mexico's bountiful resources, more and more people from the far corners of the nation began arriving to stake out and claim a piece of the territory for their own.

11. Henry Allen Tice, *Early Railroad Days in New Mexico, 1880* (Santa Fe: Stagecoach Press, 1965), p. 9.

Among them, inevitably, were those who came because the palmy days of the mining camps, the railroad towns, and the cattle ranches promised easy picking for any ruthless and violent gent willing to prey on his neighbors. It was a time—from the end of the Civil War to the end of the century—when most men wore a gun belted to the waist and when dance hall keepers installed signs that read, "Don't shoot the musicians, they are doing the best they can." The New Mexico Territory was an outlaw haven, and, in the phrasing of Emerson Hough, a popular writer of the day, "was without doubt, as dangerous a country as ever lay out of doors." [12]

Political corruption, range wars, feuds, land frauds, and cattle rustling—the assembly of irritants that plagued America's western frontier from beginning to end—brought their full measure of grief to New Mexico's citizenry. The Colfax County War (1875–1878), one of the more prominent disturbances, pitted claimants of the nearly two-million-acre Maxwell Land Grant against squatters who had settled on what they regarded as public domain. At the center of the tumult, which included a string of shootings and several hangings by enraged vigilantes, rode the notorious Texas gunman, Clay Allison. The Santa Fe Ring, a Republican political machine that dominated territorial affairs from the late 1860s to the mid-1880s, also had a hand in the Colfax affair, as did Governor Samuel B. Axtell.

The bloody disorders in southern New Mexico that came to be known as the Lincoln County War (1878–1881) attracted even greater attention. There, within the 27,000 square miles embracing the largest county in the United States, rival factions composed of merchants and cattlemen fell to feuding. Complete lawlessness soon reigned, as rustlers and gunfighters arrived from all parts of the Southwest to take advantage of the turmoil. Among them was the young firebrand William Bonney, alias Billy the Kid.

In the fall of 1878, President Rutherford B. Hayes declared Lincoln County in a state of insurrection, and a federal investigator, Frank W. Angel, was sent to inquire into the sources of

12. John H. Vaughan, *History and Government of New Mexico* (Las Cruces: Privately printed, 1931), p. 184.

the hostilities. He found territorial affairs a shambles, with officials including the United States Attorney, the Surveyor General, and Governor Axtell deeply embroiled in Lincoln's troubles. Even the courts were in disarray. Numerous murder cases,
for example, never reached trial, for preliminary hearings resulted in a stock verdict: "The deceased came to his death ac-
cidentally after having given due provocation." [13]

Angel's report to the president led to the removal of Governor Axtell and the resignation of other territorial officials, most
of them members of the scandalous Santa Fe Ring. General Lew
Wallace of Indiana was then appointed as governor to clean up
New Mexico and bring peace to Lincoln County. Wallace, a
veteran of the 1862 Battle of Shiloh and at one time the
youngest major general in the Union army, was a sensitive man
of artistic temperament who had a fondness for painting and for
writing novels. In Santa Fe, he discovered a congenial climate
for both of those pursuits (parts of his classic work *Ben Hur*
were composed in the old adobe Governors Palace). But in the
matter of politics and reform, the atmosphere proved highly
combustible and unfavorable to the task of restoring stability.

For three years Governor Wallace worked to suppress violence, disperse the bands of desperadoes, and root out corrupt
politicians. Not only did he have little to show for his efforts, he
lived under constant threat of harm. Billy the Kid, for one,
openly boasted, "I mean to ride into the plaza at Santa Fe, hitch
my horse in front of the palace, and put a bullet through Lew
Wallace." [14] Perhaps with that threat in mind, the governor's
wife, Susan, wrote to their son in 1879: "My Dear—General
Sherman was right. We should have another war with Old Mexico to make her take back New Mexico." [15]

Burdened by the day-to-day frets of his job, Wallace resigned
in 1881 to take an assignment more suited to his nature, that of
ambassador to the Ottoman Empire. By the time he left, the
Lincoln County War was burning itself out, and during the sum-

13. William A. Keleher, *The Fabulous Frontier*, revised edition (Albuquerque: University of New Mexico Press, 1962), p. 57.

14. Calvin Horn, *New Mexico's Troubled Years* (Albuquerque: Horn and Wallace,
1963), p. 208.

15. Horn, *New Mexico's Troubled Years*, p. 208.

mer of that year the last phase came to an end when Sheriff Pat
Garrett shot down Billy the Kid at Fort Sumner. But the imposition of order throughout New Mexico was far from complete.

Ahead lay a series of blood-stained episodes fated to keep the
land on edge for another full generation: a cattlemen's war
around Farmington in San Juan County; a gunfight in which
Deputy Sheriff Elfego Baca alone stood off eighty cowboys for
thirty-six hours in the village of Frisco; reigns of terror by such
merciless bandit leaders as Mariano Leiba of Bernalillo and
Vicente Silva of Las Vegas; raids by the Gorras Blancas (White
Caps), a secret Hispano group in northeastern New Mexico,
organized to protect communal lands from encroachment by
Anglo ranchers; the murder of a controversial political figure,
Colonel Albert Jennings Fountain of Las Cruces, and his young
son as they were crossing the empty wastes of the White Sands;
and in the next century an attack by the Mexican revolutionary
leader, Pancho Villa, on the border town of Columbus during
March 1916. With experiences like those, and others equally
racking, it is apparent that New Mexico's road to maturity was a
long and painful one.

Even in the midst of civil strife and political storms, New
Mexico was edging toward a social and cultural transformation.
But the changes beginning to take place and the society that was
emerging showed only marginal similarities with the develop-
ments then going on in other areas of America's West. New
Mexico, despite immigration from the eastern United States,
steady economic growth, and a gradual increase in educational
institutions—all of which drew the territory closer to the main-
stream of national life—still remained a land apart.

Much of the reason resided in the continuing dominance of
the Hispano population. Throughout territorial days, and indeed
until the 1940s, descendants of the colonial Spaniards consti-
tuted a majority of New Mexico's people. In the other bor-
derland provinces acquired from Mexico in 1848—Texas, Arizona, and California—the original inhabitants, by contrast, had
quickly been swamped by incoming Anglo-Americans and their
Hispanic culture either buried or relegated to small, isolated
islands within the new English-speaking society.

In the eastern United States, where the rise of industry lured wave after wave of European immigrants, it had become fashionable and appropriate to speak, by the 1880s, of the national melting pot. Accurate as the metaphor may have been for most of the country, it just did not apply to the sons of the conquistadors on the upper Rio Grande. Simply put, the New Mexicans refused to melt; and at every turn, they repulsed attempts to make them give up their language, their folkways, and their traditional style of life.

Gradually, of course, by a process of accretion, American ways made inroads. Yet the framework of Hispanic culture was kept intact and continued to serve as the principal point of reference by which the people viewed their past and measured the future. It was a situation similar to that experienced by the Pueblos subjected to Spanish rule in the seventeenth and eighteenth centuries. The Indians, when under pressure, had taken up certain external features of the new alien culture, but at the same time they held fast to those ancient practices that were the heartbeat and pulse of their traditional world.

For a long time in the nineteenth century, New Mexicans were allowed to move along at an unhurried pace, and to follow their Old World customs without interference because other Americans were hardly aware of their existence. The desert Southwest was a land virtually unknown to New Englanders, southerners, or midwesterners. Indeed, many labored under the assumption that that part of it known as New Mexico belonged to a foreign country.

It was a curious, peripatetic New Englander named Charles F. Lummis who was the first to tell easterners something about the strange and virtually unknown corner of their country that had been settled three centuries before by the Spaniards. Lummis initially passed through New Mexico in 1884 on his way from one newspaper job in Ohio to another in Los Angeles. Young and of a romantic frame of mind, he quickly fell victim to a spell cast by the colorful land and its exotic people. In more than a dozen subsequent books, he glorified the Hispano and Indian cultures of the Southwest, extolled them as valuable adjuncts to American civilization, and chided his fellow countrymen for paying more attention to decadent Europe than to some of the bright and unusual places in their own nation.

Hammering away at his theme, Lummis coined the expression "See America First," by which he meant New Mexico and the Greater Southwest. The Santa Fe Railroad, eager for passengers on its new track through the territory, picked up the phrase and used it, along with Lummis's books, in a promotional campaign to attract permanent settlers as well as tourists. Plainly, the day had passed when any American could speak, as General Sherman had, of New Mexico's worthlessness and recommend that it be given away.

One testing still remained to confirm Americans in the belief that New Mexicans were loyal and worthy sons of the republic. At the outbreak of the Spanish-American War in 1898, President William McKinley sent a telegram to Governor Miguel A. Otero, Jr., at Santa Fe, asking him to assist in recruiting stalwart young men who were good shots and good riders. Otero, the first Hispano to serve as governor of the territory, knew he was on the spot. "Many newspapers in the East," he later told an interviewer, "were dubious about our loyalty we having such a large Mexican population." [16] Some of these papers published inflammatory statements, claiming that New Mexico was filled with Spanish sympathizers and that one group of partisans had raised the flag of Spain over a church north of Santa Fe.

Hoping to lay suspicions to rest, Governor Otero issued a call to every town and ranch in the territory for volunteers and offered his own services, if needed. The response from both Hispanos and Anglos was so generous that afterward Theodore Roosevelt would claim that half the officers and men of his famous Rough Riders Regiment came from New Mexico. One of note was young Captain Maximiliano Luna, among the first to plant the guidon of his company upon the summit of Cuba's San Juan Hill. He was later killed while serving in the Philippines.

The patriotism of New Mexicans was reaffirmed during World War I. On the bloody fields of France, Hispanos and Indians formed a third of New Mexico's contribution to the great army that stopped the German spring drive of 1918. But by that

16. Marion Dargan, "New Mexico's Fight for Statehood, 1895–1912," *New Mexico Historical Review* 14 (January 1939):11.

time, the people of the Southwest had already won the ultimate recognition that made them full participants in the American political system: in 1912, both New Mexico and Arizona achieved statehood, as the forty-seventh and forty-eighth states, respectively.

For New Mexico, the event marked the end of sixty-two years of territorial status and the successful conclusion of a long and hard-fought campaign by a small group of statehood advocates. The delay, in part, had been caused by many New Mexicans themselves who, over the years, had protested that the people were too poor to bear the taxes needed to support a state government. Conservative businessmen also lined up with the opposition—not out of consideration for the poor, but because they felt that federal control from Washington was preferable to "home rule" by unscrupulous politicians. Then there was the fear and some prejudice on the part of eastern congressmen who believed that until English had been made the language of the courts and schools, New Mexico would not be ready for democracy. That obstacle began to dissolve in 1898, after Congress passed the Fergusson Act providing for the foundation of a public school system in the territory.

The active and vocal minority supporting statehood included politicians aspiring to one of the two Senate seats that would be created; owners of large land holdings who hoped that admission would lure investors and boom the value of real estate; and those progressive citizens who believed that New Mexico, with its large population (327,301 in 1910) was honor bound to accept her responsibilities and become a state.

When the matter could no longer be evaded, Congress passed the Enabling Act, signed by President William Howard Taft on June 20, 1910, which provided for the calling of a constitutional convention in New Mexico. The conservative document that body drafted was ratified by voters early the following year, and on January 6, 1912, New Mexico formally became a state in the Union. William C. McDonald, a rancher from Carrizozo, was elected governor. The Senate seats went to Thomas Benton Catron, once a power in the old Santa Fe Ring, and to Albert Bacon Fall, who nine years later, as U.S. Secretary of the Interior and the first New Mexican to achieve cabinet rank, would suffer disgrace in the wake of the Teapot Dome scandal.

At the White House ceremony for the signing of the statehood bill, President Taft, after laying down his pen, said to the small group of New Mexican dignitaries ringing his desk, "Well, it is all over. I am glad to give you life. I hope you will be healthy." [17] The same hope was with the people of the new state. As the word was flashed by telegraph to Santa Fe, citizens assembled in the plaza facing the old Governors Palace and on the same spot where Spaniards and Indians had fought in 1680, where Mexicans celebrated their independence in 1821, and where ranks of Confederate soldiers rode in 1862, they set up a chorus of rousing cheers for the just-born state of New Mexico.

17. Robert W. Larson, *New Mexico's Quest for Statehood, 1846–1912* (Albuquerque: University of New Mexico Press, 1968), p. 304.

6

All Together . . .
but Not Quite

ON the year 1922, the small Indian pueblo of Tesuque eight miles north of Santa Fe closed its doors to the outside world and prepared to starve in protest to the Bursum Bill then pending in Congress. In the year 1957, a crusty rancher named John Prather took up his rifle to defend his land from the United States government, which wanted to add it to the White Sands Missile Range. In the year 1966, a band of armed Hispanos invaded the Echo Amphitheater Park in northern New Mexico, administered by the National Forest Service, and declared it to be the free and independent Republic of San Joaquin. Three events wholly unrelated, it would seem. But were they?

It is doubtful that the participants—Indian, Anglo, and Hispano—in each of these incidents saw beyond the small circle of their own immediate troubles and perceived that they had become enmeshed in a larger problem inherent in the workings of the democratic process. That problem, foundation-cracking in its implications, was one that worried founders of the republic and has continued to perplex just men to the present day. And it is this: how can individuals and minorities be protected in their basic freedom and rights if an overbearing majority chooses to treat them capriciously? Beginning with the Bill of Rights, successive laws were formed to curb despotic tendencies on the part of government (which enforces the will of the majority) and to maintain a climate in which personal initiative and the creative impulse could thrive.

But from the outset, the safety of those who differed in some particular from their fellow men depended more on public tolerance than on laws, for laws are easily set aside. After all, it was God-fearing, self-righteous men, members of the democratic majority, who held up slavery in the South as a noble institution and who persecuted the Mormons, driving them from Missouri and Illinois into the deserts of Utah. After much bloodletting and social wrenching, those and similar wrongs were eventually righted, but from it all there emerged no guarantee that dissidents, nonconformists, and minorities of whatever stripe would not in times of stress suffer new oppressions.

It has been said of the twentieth century that it offers no room for the individual: he has been trampled upon, submerged, and swallowed up by the corporate state, corporate business, corporate labor. Even the collective weight of public opinion is often insufficient to halt the growth of massive bureaucracies, monopolies, and cartels. And on every hand men are heard to bewail their own impotence and entrapment in "the system." Yet, a residue of hardy individualism remains—a legacy, many scholars believe, of our frontier experience—among people in every economic and social class in the fifty states. And to that may be attributed those periodic flare-ups in which persons alone or in small groups resist being reduced to ciphers in a statistical chart and risk all in defense of their essential humanity. Each state, each region, has seen such episodes, and none perhaps more than New Mexico.

The Pueblo Indians' fight against the Bursum Bill, John Prather's private war to keep his ranch, and the Hispano's Republic of San Joaquin (founded as part of a continuing struggle to recover lost land grants)—all were expressions of the view that the little man in a democracy has a right to be heard and to survive. These three cases are singled out, because in each one people were ready to lay their lives on the line for what they believed.

The struggle of the Pueblo people to maintain their islands of individuality and culture in the great sea of conforming pressures that twentieth-century America had become reached a point of crisis when New Mexico's Senator Holm O. Bursum in 1922 introduced his congressional bill. That measure was designed to settle the claims of white squatters on Pueblo land, but it did so to the detriment of the Indians. When the full details of the Bursum Bill became known, the Pueblos and their friends in the white community mounted a full-scale attack upon it, creating a controversy that soon gained nationwide attention.

The source of the trouble lay back in the nineteenth century. By terms of the Treaty of Guadalupe Hidalgo, ending the Mexican War in 1848, the Pueblos' property rights over some seven hundred thousand acres had been guaranteed. The point was reaffirmed after 1854 by the surveyor-general and by the United States Congress. Notwithstanding, the Indians were continually bothered by trespassers and squatters moving upon their valuable irrigated lands, because the Supreme Court had decreed in 1876 that the Pueblos, owing to their advanced culture, were not wards of the government, as other tribes were, and hence were not entitled to government protection. It further declared that they had complete title to their lands, could dispose of them at will and that federal Indian laws were not applicable to them.

That decision proved most damaging for New Mexico's Indians. The Spanish regime had diligently protected their property boundaries, upheld the doctrine that their lands were inalienable, and provided free legal services. Now the Pueblos found themselves thrown on their own meager resources and deprived of the supporting arm of the government. Also, it soon became apparent that, without federal protection, there was nothing to prevent individual tribal members from selling off small parcels of the lands that heretofore had been held in common. As a result of that situation, some thirty percent or more of the Pueblos' best acreage shortly passed into non-Indian hands.

The land base would have continued to erode had not the court in 1913 reversed its earlier stand and ruled that the United States was in fact responsible for the welfare of the Pueblo people, just as it was for other Indian tribes in the country. Official guardianship, the court held, should have been continuous since 1848, and therefore all losses of original Pueblo lands to encroachers or purchasers were illegal. A victory for the Indians, or so it appeared.

The fly in the ointment was that, by this time, some three thousand Hispanos and Anglos had claims to former Pueblo farmlands and irrigation rights. Both they and the state were unwilling to see that property given back to the Indians without a fight. Much of the land indeed had been acquired by the current owners in good faith; some of it had been lived upon by non-Indians for two or more generations.

Although the court had said that the government must move to recover the Pueblos' lands and water rights from outsiders, suits to quiet title and delays interposed by the Interior Department kept the matter festering year in and year out. In the meantime, several pueblos such as Tesuque, San Ildefonso, and San Juan, which had suffered the greatest losses, were forced by circumstances to take government rations. Drought added to their woes. With the state of uncertainty, tensions mounted, and isolated instances of violence began to erupt between Pueblos, Anglos, and Spanish settlers. That was the situation in 1921 when New Mexico's own Albert B. Fall was appointed Secretary of the Interior by President Warren G. Harding.

Fall genuinely wished to defuse the explosive land controversy in his home state, but in so doing he hoped to strengthen his own political hand. The settlers were loudly defending their claims; moreover, they represented an important block of votes. The Indians, on the other hand, defended themselves with milder words, appeared to have few supporters outside their own communities, and had no power at the ballot box, since they were still denied the right to vote. Not surprisingly, Secretary Fall chose to follow a course highly unfavorable to the Pueblos.

In May of 1921, Fall asked Senator Bursum to draft a bill to resolve the land crisis. The final measure that emerged after much tinkering and revision was designed to confirm all non-In-

dian claims of title held for more than ten years prior to statehood in 1912.[1] The Indians were delivered an additional blow
by another provision of the bill proposing that future challenges
to Pueblo water rights and land should fall under the jurisdiction
of the unfriendly state courts. By inference, this could be taken
to mean that all internal affairs of the Pueblos came under authority of the court system. Should that prove true, it would
suggest that judges could force native priests, governors, and
other principal men to provide information on the most secret
aspects of Pueblo life or face contempt citations. Since all the
Indians' affairs, political as well as economic, were closely
bound up with religion, and village customs were protected by
an inviolable rule of secrecy, any such invasion of their privacy
by the state would quickly lead to dissolution of Pueblo society.
The Bursum Bill, then, pending before Congress in 1922, carried with it the potentiality of disaster for New Mexico's village
Indians.

Shut up in their mud pueblos, two thousand miles from
Washington, they nearly missed hearing about the bill altogether. No reports of it appeared in the local press, no public
official called it to their attention. In fact, it seemed there was a
deliberate conspiracy of silence on the part of the Bureau of Indian Affairs to keep the measure quiet until it had become law.
But the Pueblos had friends of whom, until this point, they had
been unaware, and those friends now came to their aid with ad-
vice, money, and political muscle.

The earliest and most vocal supporters of the Indians sprang
from the colonies of artists and writers that had grown up in
recent years in Santa Fe and Taos. The same enchanting landscape and Old World atmosphere that had inspired Governor
Lew Wallace to pursue the avocations of painter and author also
drew and exhilarated others of artistic and intellectual ability.
Two of the pioneers were Ernest L. Blumenschein and Bert
Phillips, who landed in the isolated Shangri-La of Taos in 1898.
They stayed, they painted sublime canvases of Indians and of

    1. Kenneth Philp, "Albert B. Fall and the Protest from the Pueblos, 1921–23,"
Arizona and the West 12 (Autumn 1970):240.

mountains, brilliant with sunlight; they attracted others; and in 1914, they formed the Taos Society of Artists. Their work, constituting a distinctly New Mexican school, was disseminated and publicized by the Santa Fe Railroad, and it put their little colony on the nation's art map.

Where the painters led, writers and other intellectuals had soon followed. Mable Dodge Sterne, who dabbled in letters and had once run a salon in Greenwich Village, arrived in Taos in 1917. To her wide circle of acquaintances in the East, she wrote effusive letters filled with praise of New Mexico's lustrous viewscapes and multicultural people. At her urging, a young New York poet, John Collier, came, as did D. H. Lawrence from England, and others. The high country of northern New Mexico became a refuge for literary exiles, many of whom developed a strong feeling of kinship with their Pueblo neighbors.

It was the youthful and intense poet John Collier who learned of the onerous Bursum Bill before Congress and sounded the alarm. With Mabel Sterne's new husband, Taos Indian Tony Luhan, as his interpreter, Collier met far into the night with the Pueblo elders, explaining the full implications of Senator Bursum's legislation. Of their reaction, he wrote later, "The old men of the tribe moaned, knowing it was a sentence of death." [2]

Collier carried his warning down the Rio Grande to the remaining Pueblos. They listened in astonishment and reacted swiftly. Messages went out, just as they had 242 years before, at the time of the great Pueblo Revolt, summoning the Indians to unite. Delegations from each village came together at Santo Domingo, north of Albuquerque; they formed an All-Pueblo Council and pledged to use every resource available to defeat the Bursum Bill. The little pueblo of Tesuque went further, declaring that its people would barricade themselves behind dirt walls and starve before surrendering their traditional sovereignty.

Now that the Indians had joined battle, their allies began to

2. John Collier, *Indians of the Americas* (New York: W. W. Norton & Company, Inc., 1947), p. 250.

rally in legions. The artists and writers of Taos, and those who had spilled over to Santa Fe, issued a stinging manifesto, grandly titled "Proclamation to the American Public," in which they eloquently defended Indian rights.[3] Uniting under the slogan of "Let's Save the Pueblos," they unleashed a blitz of paper and words, inundating newspapers and magazines across the country with protest resolutions, letters, and articles. Many of their friends in the eastern intellectual community were persuaded to join the struggle though they had never seen New Mexico or a Pueblo Indian. The rising chorus of protest was becoming fierce.

But more was yet to come. The General Federation of Women's Clubs, with a national membership of two million, threw its full weight behind the Pueblo cause. The energetic president, Mrs. Stella Atwood of California, raised money, hired lawyers, and set up an effective lobby in Washington. Her fellow club members, at her prompting, showered their congressmen with telegrams and letters. She visited meetings of the Pueblo Council and trod the halls of Congress, where she reasoned, pleaded, and threatened retaliation at the voting box. And with all her travels and thunderings, Mrs. Atwood raised the Indians' plight to the level of a national issue.

The usually reticent Pueblos, too, were now carrying the banner plainly for all to see. They had drafted their own appeal to the people of the United States, condemning the Bursum Bill as a threat to their way of life, and they had raised $3,500 to send a delegation to Washington to present their case. The Pueblo spokesmen traveled across country accompanied by John Collier and carrying the venerable Spanish and Lincoln canes as symbols of their authority. At major cities, they appeared before huge gatherings of sympathetic citizens and won new partisans; and in Washington they stood toe-to-toe with stern-faced senators whose votes would decide the fate of their villages.

The intensity of the furor dumfounded Secretary Fall. It appears never to have occurred to him that anyone gave a penny

3. Philp, "Albert B. Fall and the Protest from the Pueblos," p. 244.

for what happened to the Indians. But now he learned differently.

The campaign on behalf of the Pueblos began to take effect. In Congress, the Bursum Bill was recalled from the House by unanimous consent, with the explanation that its intent had been misrepresented to the lawmakers. Then further hearings on the entire question were undertaken by the Senate Subcommittee on Public Lands and Surveys. Finally, in 1924, the matter was judiciously settled with passage of the Pueblo Lands Act which set terms for the eviction of—and, in some cases, compensation for—squatters on patented Indian grants. The ancient land rights extended to the Pueblos by Spain were at last recognized as perfect and unimpaired.

The heated debate over the Bursum Bill had aroused broad interest in Indian rights and had focused attention on New Mexico and its people, as well. Even more fundamental was the shift in government policy that ultimately resulted. Before the affray, the Bureau of Indian Affairs had actively worked to discredit the culture and religion of the first Americans and to bring about their speedy assimilation. Now, with defeat of the bill and clear evidence of widespread support for the Indians' effort to maintain their tribal integrity, a more tolerant attitude began to make itself felt among government policy-makers and administrators. President Franklin D. Roosevelt added the crowning feather when, in 1933, he appointed John Collier to be Commissioner of Indian Affairs, with the understanding that the red men would be accorded the respect and responsibility to which they were entitled as members of a free nation.

The Pueblos' exertions in the 1920s, while paving the way for better treatment of all American Indians, did not, of course, prevent new controversies from arising in succeeding years. That first all-out fight, however, did show them how to get a hearing for their grievances and where to find backers when a forceful push was needed to make their point. Such valuable knowledge was later put to good use by Taos Pueblo in a long bout to gain title to the sacred Blue Lake located on national forest land high in the mountains above the village.

Largely at the urging of Commissioner Collier and New Mexico's senators, Congress in the 1930s directed the Secretary of
Agriculture to issue the Taos people a special permit that would
give them exclusive use of the Blue Lake shrine and to instruct
the Forest Service to prevent any desecration of the surrounding
wilderness area. That arrangement worked fairly well until the
1960s. Then, however, population pressures brought increasing
numbers of outdoorsmen into the high country, resulting in
numerous instances of vandalism; and Forest officials grew lax
in maintaining the wilderness character of the lake, allowing,
for example, the inroads of logging companies.

To the Taos Indians, who felt the security of their religion
was at stake, the situation became intolerable. They therefore
decided to petition Congress to grant them title to the lake and
to a wide belt of adjacent lands to serve as a buffer. The claim
they put forward was based on use and ownership before the
coming of the Spaniards and was substantiated by both Indian
tradition and archeology.

In 1965, a bill was offered that, if passed, would have separated the Blue Lake watershed from surrounding federal land
and placed it under the Department of Interior as trustee for the
Indians. But Congressional approval was delayed another five
years by opposition in the Senate. In the interval, Taos leaders
labored tirelessly to win confirmation, repeatedly following the
now well-worn path to Washington. Again, as they had done
forty years before in the Bursum Bill affair, friends of the Indians rattled the drums in support and spoke with determined
voice to their elected representatives. The news media throughout the country, sensing the awakening interest in America's Indian heritage, gave front-page coverage to the issue and on occasion editorially defended the Taos position.

Resistance in Congress finally crumbled, and President
Nixon, on December 15, 1970, signed a bill placing 48,000
acres of Carson National Forest, including Blue Lake, in trust
for the sole use of Taos Pueblo. That victory for the Indians not
only reaffirmed basic principles of justice, but demonstrated a
strong sentiment among the Anglo community for protection of
divergent cultural and religious enclaves within the larger fabric

of society. Exactly how much straying from conformity's road a democracy could tolerate was still not definitely answered; but at least this case had shown it could stand some, without toppling into ruin.

A hundred miles below New Mexico's southernmost pueblo, battling John Prather won the same point and in a manner not wholly unlike that of the Indians. Prather's name is not one generally found in formal history books. But it deserves to be, just as the stand he took deserves to be pondered by all thoughtful people.

In 1883, John Prather and his brother Owen came to New Mexico on horseback, from Texas. As part of the last wave of the western movement, they were seeking free land at a time when most of the prime land had already been claimed. The Prathers were stockmen, and as they rode, they looked with admiration upon the grassy plains of southeastern New Mexico. But other Texans had got there first, twenty years before, with their beef herds, and even now they were being pressured by a new sort of migration—rangy, hollow-eyed men driving patched-up wagons loaded with plows, fencing tools, and hollow-eyed children. These dry-farmers out of Texas, Oklahoma, Arkansas, and Missouri would try, and try again, over the next decades to bring in a crop in a country that had adequate rainfall on an average of once every three years. Some of them would always be going broke and pulling up stakes for California, but others would hold out until the dust-bowl days of the thirties.

In any event, the Prather brothers caught the drift of things there on the plains and, having no desire to compete with either the established ranchers or the encroaching sod-busters, they kept moving. Beyond the Pecos, they followed a pass through a ridge of mountains and emerged upon the western slope to see, dipping before them, the shimmering expanse of the Tularosa Basin and the distant dark ridge of the San Andres Range.

What they had entered, after their trip over the plains and through the cool mountain forest, was a different world—a kingdom whose pebbly soil could support only a thin mantle of grass and scattered clumps of yucca and greasewood. Gypsum flats and lava beds covered great sections of the land, and summer's blazing light and dry heat shriveled every living thing. The White Sands, a lake of shifting, glittering gypsum dunes, reached fifty miles north and south down the center of the basin and served as a playground for little whirlwinds, called dust devils, whose antics could be followed by anyone with a perch in the mountains fifty miles away. A typically Spanish landscape, people called it; but that description wandered considerably from the truth. Nothing in Spain, even in the bleakest parts of Andalucía, could quite match the desolation and forlornness of that portion of New Mexico extending from the Tularosa Basin west across two mountain chains to the Rio Grande.

Such hard, inhospitable country—much of it then in Lincoln County—attracted a certain breed of men. Restless and roistering men were drawn to it, especially those who felt uncomfortable in crowds, shunned society's constraints, and were at ease with solitude. And men like the Prathers, hereditary pioneers with no other frontier than this to go to. In those early days, almost everyone else was prepared to leave the Tularosa kingdom to the Apaches and the jackrabbits; and they joked, after seeing natives grubbing roots for fuel and bringing water on burros from the mountains, that this was the only place on the continent where men, reversing the usual order of things, dug for firewood and climbed for water.

But it was here that John Prather, after some shifting about, settled on a spot with fair grass below the Sacramento Mountains and went to raising cattle. Owen, nearby, began developing a sheep ranch. Decades crept by, wars and depression bedeviled the outside world, and all the while under the flaming New Mexican sun, John Prather worked his stock and continued to improve his property of some four thousand deeded acres and an additional twenty thousand acres leased from the government. For all the hardships, there were compensations: the burning flush of indescribable sunsets, the smell of summer rain on the desert, the display put on by giant yuccas each spring when for a few weeks they send forth a tall stalk and clusters of snowy blossoms—like hominy ice cream on a stick, according to one old-timer. But best of all, in the view of John Prather and of the few hundred other scattered souls who scratched out a living in this desert world the size of one or more New England states, it was a place where a fellow could go his own way, unfettered by many of the shackles that had been clamped on modern life, and where he could still enjoy the satisfaction of benefiting directly from his own labor.

Then World War II changed all that for the Tularosa country and for all the off-the-path pockets in New Mexico that had kept one foot planted in the nineteenth century. Even Albuquerque, the state's transportation hub and largest city, was to have its character permanently altered by events of the 1940s.

The war was hard on New Mexico, too, for reasons other than those having to do with fast and irritating change. In proportion to the scant population, New Mexicans—Indian, Hispano, and Anglo alike—experienced the highest casualty rate of any state during the opening years of the conflict. Two of their regiments were at Bataan in the Philippines, and after Bataan fell to the Japanese, they endured the infamous "Death March" and three years of imprisonment. Some of the survivors, keeping a vow made during that harrowing time, later undertook a pilgrimage on foot to the rustic adobe Santuario de Chimayo, a popular Hispano shrine north of Santa Fe that dates from colonial days.

Another course of events during the war was to make an even deeper impression on New Mexico and at the same time would start John Prather on the road to his small rebellion. It had its beginning on the pine-clad summit of the Pajarito Plateau west of Santa Fe. Upon the plateau in 1943, the U.S. government sealed off a tract of land and built the secret city of Los Alamos around an atomic energy laboratory. Scientists living with their families in almost complete seclusion soon produced the first atomic bomb and tested it on July 16, 1945, at the Trinity Site in the desolate White Sands of southern New Mexico. The full significance of the project was not known to the public until the bombing of Hiroshima and Nagasaki revealed to the world the arrival of the nuclear age.

The explosion of the atomic bomb at the White Sands Proving Ground (now the White Sands Missile Range) was felt over much of New Mexico in that summer of 1945. But it was what followed that proved more disturbing to the residents of the Tularosa Basin. The military was in need of land, a great deal of it, for the testing of rockets and the training of their crews, a program deemed crucial for national defense. To expand the range, hundreds of thousands of acres were ordered withdrawn from the public domain and from private ownership, which meant condemnation proceedings were instituted against surrounding ranchers. Many of these people waged fierce court battles and appeared at congressional hearings in a bid to keep their land, but one by one, over succeeding years, they lost out and were displaced.

Then, in 1955, the government, as it crept eastward toward the Sacramento Mountains swallowing up chunks of ground in whale-sized gulps, ran straight into eighty-two-year-old John Prather. His land, which he had held and worked for fifty years, was not for sale, Prather announced. And anyone who tried to put him off might get hurt. In the U.S. District Court at Albuquerque, a condemnation suit resulted in a ninety-day eviction notice for John Prather and his neighbors. The old man's response to that action was to issue a public statement: "I'm going to die at home." [4]

The army found itself in an awkward position. Prather, with all his stubbornness and independence, was an authentic pioneer who had a personal hand in taming the West. He was a survivor of that frontier stock whose experience had come to be viewed by Americans in romantic and heroic terms. If he stood by his guns, as he was threatening to do, the whole affair might be ballyhooed to the skies by the news-hungry press and the army made to look like an oppressive monster. The situation demanded gentleness and tact, and government officials mustered every ounce of that they could.

The army reasoned and cajoled. It offered this thorn in its side the sum of $200,000 for his ranch. It warned him that

4. C. L. Sonnichsen, *Tularosa, Last of the Frontier West* (Old Greenwich, Conn.: The Devin-Adair Co., 1972), p. 286.

missiles, enough to scare any man, would be shot over portions of the property, and his life would be in danger. To the offer, John Prather said no. And to the warning, he replied, "I'm not afraid of missiles. I've raised mules all my life." [5]

By now, August 1957, the episode was spread across the front pages of the nation's leading dailies, and reporters were pouring into El Paso, where they looked for transportation northward to the Tularosa Basin. At the ranch, Prather's kin had arrived, twenty-five in all, and they joined in fortifying the main house in preparation for a siege. As jeeps brought in army officers and newsmen over a dusty, washboard road, it appeared the basin's first battle since the days of the Apache wars was about to be fought.

Officials, however, had had enough. Public opinion was clearly swinging to the side of the courageous old rancher, and since he could not be moved, short of force, a directive from Washington ordered military personnel to withdraw from the Prather Ranch. The army then went back to court and obtained a new writ exempting the ranch house and fifteen surrounding acres from confiscation; the remainder of the land was forthwith annexed to the military reservation. If John Prather raised no further fuss, he would be left alone.

That ended the matter. Prather had lost his ranch, but he had also won a victory of sorts. Standing firm, he had forced the U.S. government to compromise and in so doing had chiseled himself a niche in the history of southern New Mexico. As one writer later explained it, John Prather reacted as his forebears had reacted against invasion of their independence and property rights. His was the code and the psychology of the eighties, and he was the last of his kind. [6]

The upheaval in New Mexico produced by World War II, by the growth of postwar defense installations and industries, and by the sudden influx of population—all of which hastened the end of John Prather's world—also contributed to rising social and economic problems among Hispanos in the mountains of

---

5. Sonnichsen, *Tularosa,* p. 287.
6. Sonnichsen, *Tularosa,* p. 290.

the north. Again, as in the cases of the Pueblo Indians and the ranchers of the Tularosa Basin, a struggle for land became the focus of a human drama, bringing private citizens into conflict with established authority.

Descendants of the Spaniards, particularly those dwelling in rural areas, had managed with some success to cling to the core of their culture and language during the early decades of the twentieth century. They continued to farm in traditional ways, to pursue the yearly observance of ancient religious practices, to speak a lilting and archaic Spanish, and to perform folk plays and to sing songs brought to this land three hundred years earlier by their ancestors. But after 1940, the modern world— swiftly, inexorably—began closing in, with its powerful pressures for assimilation into the dominant stream of national life. People left their adobe villages in droves to look for high-paying jobs in industry outside the state or to seek work in suddenly booming Albuquerque or in the uranium mines that opened in the Grants area in the early 1950s. Many communities, bereft of their young and middle-aged, were abandoned to the care of a few old people; schools and small businesses closed; village life declined and family unity was sundered.

There is nothing new, of course, about a migration from farm to city, and the stresses such a movement can cause are well known. But for New Mexico's Hispanos, the difficulties were compounded because leaving home also meant leaving their language and culture behind. To enter into confident, prosperous, urban America and gain a measure of success, one needed to become a homogenized American. Many New Mexicans in fact made that transition and in time dropped the ties to their native villages. Their children grew up speaking only marginal Spanish, or none at all, and the pride once held in their Hispanic heritage seeped away.

Yet, there were others, perhaps the majority, who still felt a powerful kinship with the past, and who never lost, in the midst of smog and noise and the clutter and clatter of the city, a longing to return to the places of their birth and once again to work the land and smell the crisp winter air heavy with piñon smoke. Often they did go back for a day—arriving from California or

Texas or beyond—to a kind of symbolic homecoming on the feast day of the village's patron saint, and afterward taking the long road back to their new homes and jobs. Some of those who had settled in Albuquerque, Bernalillo, Santa Fe, and Las Vegas, only a few hours' drive from their country places, could go on weekends to look after small fields or a few head of live-stock, maintaining that one small link in the chain of their former lives. And, finally, there was that handful for whom the pull of their homeland was too strong, and they gave up city life altogether to return to their mud houses in what had become known as the "poverty pockets" of the northern mountains.

The rub was that the land base of the Hispano villages had been eroding for a hundred years, and what remained was scarcely enough to provide a minimal livelihood even for the small population still engaged in farming or stock-raising. As with Pueblo lands, the problems of Spanish land grants had commenced soon after the American conquest of New Mexico. The 1848 Treaty of Guadalupe Hidalgo with Mexico provided for the protection of property rights of those persons who had suddenly become citizens of the United States. The difficulty of fulfilling that guarantee became apparent only later, as dif-ferences in Spanish and Anglo concepts of law and land tenure began to raise complex legal questions. The most flammable of these involved the old community land grants which had been made by Spain and Mexico. Originally, under terms of such grants, settlers had received individual title to the small amount of farmland available along the irrigation ditches, while the remainder of the grant was held in common for purposes of grazing and wood-gathering. The boundaries of the community holdings, in the absence of surveyors, were inexactly deline-ated, using such natural landmarks as large rocks, prominent trees, springs, and arroyos. Within a short time after establish-ment of the American legal system, complications arising from these Hispanic practices produced a tangled web of claims and counterclaims and opened the way for speculators to obtain, often through deceit and fraud, a controlling interest in some of the most valuable grants.

Early, Congress took a sidelong look at the exasperating

problem and then handed it to the Office of the Surveyor-General, which was created in 1854 for the specific purpose of adjudicating Spanish and Mexican land titles. At the time, New Mexico had more than one thousand claims awaiting settlement, some of them dealing with the community grants and others with large private grants that had once been allotted to individual Spaniards. The first surveys showed that many of the old boundaries could no longer be accurately defined and that often the grants had overlapping claims. Legitimate descendants of grantees seldom possessed their original papers, and some of those who did, through fear or distrust of the alien legal procedures now imposed upon them, failed to bring the documents forward to receive new patents for their lands.

In the forefront of those who profited from such a situation were the lawyers—the class of men who Father Martínez had predicted in the 1850s would supplant priests as the real power in New Mexico. For clearing titles, they exacted huge fees. These fees were usually paid in land from that held in common, so that, within time, as seemingly endless litigation over titles continued, sharp-eyed American lawyers and their associates acquired possession of prodigious sections of the Spanish grants. One Santa Fe attorney, for example, was reported by a local newspaper in 1894 to have an interest in seventy-five grants and to own outright nearly two million acres.[7]

Commented one of New Mexico's leading land-grant authorities, "Only a few claims were confirmed and patented under the Surveyor-General, and by the 1880s speculation in the grants had reached the point of a national scandal."[8] As a result, a Court of Private Land Claims was established in 1891 in a bid to settle the many controversies by judicial means. Although that body succeeded in adjudicating all claims by 1903, it sowed the seeds of future discord by accepting and continuing a precedent regarding community grants that had been laid down by earlier courts.

7. Quoted in Howard Roberts Lamar, *The Far Southwest, 1846–1912* (New Haven: Yale University Press, 1966), p. 150.

8. Myra Ellen Jenkins and Albert H. Schroeder, *A Brief History of New Mexico* (Albuquerque: University of New Mexico Press, 1974), p. 61.

Unfamiliar with Spanish law protecting and preserving village commons, American judges had ruled that the ancient common lands could be partitioned and divided among the numerous grant-claimants. That meant that vast areas of upland pastures and mountain woods, of which villagers had made free use for generations, were now allotted to individuals who could put them up for sale if they chose. Not surprisingly, surrounding lands soon slipped from the grasp of community members and passed to the control of outsiders—often cattlemen from Texas—or into the public domain, where much of it was placed under the National Forest Service. A similar pattern of land loss was experienced by a number of American Indian tribes in the twentieth century, when by Congressional Act their reservations were broken up and the land granted in severalty, thereby destroying the common-property base of community existence.

In response to social and economic frustrations and to lingering resentment over land problems, disaffected Hispanos in the late 1950s began to be drawn to a strange folk movement with revolutionary undertones. Its spokesman and leader was a man of rare charisma—Reies Lopez Tijerina, a Mexican-American fundamentalist preacher who came to New Mexico and found in the long-unresolved land issue a cause upon which to build a personal crusade. As Tijerina saw it, the Hispano people's diminishing lands and loss of a sense of community were leading unavoidably to surrender of control over their own destinies and to eventual cultural extinction. To reverse that unhappy process, Tijerina advocated a concerted push, via the courts, to obtain equal rights in education and employment—which, he declared, federal and state governments had been remiss in providing. But more to the point, he called for restitution of the community land grants that, to his view, had been usurped and illegally dispersed when the U.S. government failed to protect them under an obligation imposed by the Treaty of Guadalupe Hidalgo.

The better to disseminate his ideas and attract followers, Tijerina founded the *Alianza Federal de Mercedes* (Federal Alliance of Land Grants), usually referred to simply as the *Alianza*. He delivered heated speeches with messianic fervor, making the sweeping claim that members of his organization were the rightful heirs of millions of acres of land now in possession of the Forest Service and Anglo ranchers. And he asserted that twenty thousand people had joined the *Alianza* to participate in a common struggle for their lost rights. (A more accurate figure, perhaps, would be a quarter of that number.)

Through the mid-sixties, the militancy of the *Alianza* increased, as its demands became more shrill, and mounting resentment found an outlet in mass meetings and protest marches. Then, in October 1966, Reies Tijerina, with 350 followers, many of them armed, made a dramatic and unprecedented invasion of the Kit Carson National Forest northwest of the village of Abiquiu. At a popular tourist park called the Echo Amphitheater, located just inside the forest boundary, the *Alianzans* seized control and proclaimed establishment of the Republic of San Joaquin del Cañon de Rio de Chama—a new city-state founded on land alleged to have been once part of the nineteenth-century Spanish land grant of San Joaquin. The people set up tents and built campfires, elected government officials, erected a pole and upon it raised the blue-and-gold banner of their "republic." When Forest Service rangers attempted to intervene, the *Alianzans* arrested them for trespassing. It was a grandstand play engineered, as Tijerina admitted later, to gain publicity and to bring the old matter of land grants into the courts for airing.

After occupying their campground for several days, the *Alianzans* left quietly, believing that they had scored a point and won attention for their cause. In time, Tijerina and several of his lieutenants would be charged by federal authorities with assaulting forest rangers and with conversion of government property. State officials too were taking another look at the movement and assessing its potential for stirring up added trouble. Governor David Cargo from Santa Fe spoke out emphatically, "I can sympathize with the people involved. . . . They are very, very poor. . . . It's the right of every citizen to petition government. However, I will not tolerate violence or destruction of property." [9]

---

9. Michael Jenkinson, *Tijerina* (Albuquerque: Paisano Press, 1968), p. 69.

But both the note of conciliation and the warning contained in the governor's words went unheeded. In June 1967, the combative *Alianza* unleashed its now celebrated raid on the Rio Arriba County Courthouse at Tierra Amarilla. It was a frenzied shooting attack by Tijerina's partisans, who captured and held the town and courthouse for two hours, wounding two officers and taking a pair of hostages, in an episode ripped from the pages of the Old West. Afterwards, the attackers—labeled insurrectionists by much of the nation's press—fled to the mountains. New Mexico's lieutenant governor (in the absence of Governor Cargo, who happened to be out of the state) called out National Guard tanks, 40mm cannons, helicopters, and masses of troops in trucks and on horseback to pursue the offenders—the largest manhunt in the history of the Southwest. Some *Alianza* members, mainly women and children, were taken, but most managed to elude the searchers. In the days and weeks that followed, they were identified and arrested, one by one, among them Reies Lopez Tijerina. Brought to trial in Albuquerque, Tijerina conducted his own defense with consummate showmanship and, in a stunning verdict, won acquittal. Tried again on different charges stemming from the Echo Amphitheater incident and related matters, he was later convicted and served a two-year term in a federal prison and a short term in the state penitentiary.

The power and influence of the *Alianza* dwindled rapidly after the Tierra Amarilla affair. Awaiting trial, Tijerina tried to broaden his appeal for justice by merging with the nationwide civil rights movement; he traveled to California to confer with labor organizer Cesar Chávez and to Atlanta, where he met with Martin Luther King, Jr. As leader of a Chicano contingent to the Poor People's March on Washington in 1968, Tijerina gained attention as one of the loudest and most dedicated spokesmen for social reform. But back in New Mexico, his standing with his followers was on the wane, and others in the Hispano community, particularly militant youth, began to look for answers in new directions.

Meanwhile, as the 1970s opened, land problems and poverty continued to plague northern New Mexico—the "Appalachia of the Southwest," some observers had labeled it. However, nu-

merous federal programs and a renewed willingness on the part
of Hispanos of all ages to work for the revitalization of village
culture gave promise of a more productive future. As yet, however, New Mexico's distinctive Hispanic heritage has not received the recognition and respect that it deserves as one of
America's oldest and most creative wells of human experience.
Whether that error will ever be fully corrected remains to be
seen.

In recent decades, many New Mexicans have campaigned
vigorously, though without the violence of the *Alianza,* to promote a variety of causes that they believe to be fundamental for
the preservation of their state's distinctive character and envi-
ronment. Beginning in the 1920s, residents of Santa Fe em-
barked on a program to revive the use of Pueblo architecture
and the old territorial building style, a movement insuring
that the flavor of the past, at least in that city, would not be
buried under a tasteless modernity. Throughout the northern part
of the state, a clandestine group of artists, known popularly as
the "Billboard Vigilantes," periodically conducted nighttime
excursions to remove from the highway advertising signs that
sullied the landscape. When, in the late 1960s, plans were announced to build a pulp mill on the Rio Grande, aroused citizens banded together in newly formed conservation organiza-
tions to protect the area's principal water course from pollution.
After stopping construction of the proposed mill, they went on
to challenge land promoters who were subdividing huge tracts
of desert into "jackrabbit estates" to be sold to gullible easterners. And they took on a new wave of strip miners and began
working in the Four Corners to correct the hazards associated
with huge power plants whose stacks spewed tons of fly ash into
the clouds.

New Mexico's Indians too have entered upon a new period of
activity in which, more and more, they are looking outward and
participating in community, state, and even national affairs.
Tribal members campaign for positions on local school boards,
run for legislative offices, and win appointments in state government. The Jicarilla Apaches on their capacious northern reserva-

tion and the Mescalero Apaches on their well-timbered lands in the south have demonstrated resourcefulness and initiative in developing business enterprises and sponsoring programs that promote economic self-sufficiency and foster tribal unity. The largest Indian group in America, the Navajo, occupying a far-flung reservation from New Mexico across northern Arizona and into Utah, continue to show amazing adaptability to changing conditions while maintaining, perhaps to a greater degree than any southwestern tribe, their native language and customs. The new Navajo Community College, for example, helps prepare young people for life in today's world, but at the same time it places strong emphasis on the Indians' cultural heritage.

What now seems clear to all thoughtful New Mexicans is that they must keep looking for ways to preserve the old alongside the new. And in the face of diminishing resources, they must seek to perpetuate some measure of that reverence for the land and its waters that was characteristic of the best among both Spanish and Anglo-American pioneers and among the original Indian inhabitants.

The sense of dust-laden timelessness that seems to hang over all New Mexico, from Clayton in the northeast to Lordsburg in the southwest and from Shiprock in the northwest to Hobbs in the southeast, carries with it the accumulated experience of centuries, the sum total of the lives of Indians, Spaniards, and Americans who left their imperishable mark on this big, dry, windy land. Forgetting either their achievements or their failings as we lurch into the future can only bring an impoverishment of spirit that modern man can ill afford.

A Personal Epilogue

*T*HROUGHOUT its long history, New Mexico has meant many things to many people. To the Pueblos, the Navajos, the Apaches, and the Spaniards who knew it when time and space were of a different dimension, the arid country along the Rio Grande was filled with mystery, unseen forces, and hidden terrors, but also with dreamlike days, summer and winter, when the clear and empty wilderness in its rugged beauty stirred the imagination and lifted men's souls.

Early American settlers, even with a far different view of the world and the workings of nature, still were struck by New Mexico's brooding silence, in which all things, physical and nonphysical, real and unreal, seemed encrusted by time.

Later, the descendants of those first settlers came to call New Mexico the "Land of Enchantment"—not with any overgrown sense of pride or out-of-hand boasting, but simply because the phrase fit so uncommonly well. Newcomers, especially in this fast-paced age of ours, often miss catching at first glance the shapes and tones and delicate pigments that combine to produce the full picture of enchantment. But that is understandable, and perhaps forgivable, for such things are elusive and not easily perceived.

"If this is the 'Land of Enchantment', you would have to prove it to me!" The man speaking was one of my fellow passengers, offering his opinion in loud voice as our airliner winged over mile after mile of dun-colored, cheerless New Mexican landscape.

"You call this enchanting?" a seat-mate on the Super Chief asked me in accusative tone on another occasion. He was pointing at the *malpais,* the lava beds, that cover so much country east of Grants like frozen waves of black rock.

I would be the first to admit that the casual visitor traveling the main road, rail, and air routes through New Mexico is not likely to be overwhelmed by ever-changing scenes of enchanting beauty. There are too many dust storms, too many stretches of monotonous brown wasteland, and now too many places where men have mishandled and abused the land.

Still and all, the words of the motto are apt. New Mexico has the power to enchant people the way Arizona and California and even Texas never can. I'm speaking here of reflective and imaginative persons; not everyone is equally susceptible to spells. But, one could reasonably ask, what is the source of this power, and why is it concentrated in lands bracketing the upper Rio Grande?

Artists and writers, those who have come here and found a congenial atmosphere, seem to understand the answer. They live in exile, if we can believe a remark once made by the novelist Conrad Richter. He wrote, "New Mexico is like that. You never know in what obscure canyon or on what sun-baked mesa you will find an artist or scholar in exile." [1] While "hid out," they soak up the land's enchantment, and in their several creative ways, try to communicate to others the spirit, the feel, and the meaning of New Mexico.

There's no escaping it. New Mexico *is* different. Call that difference enchanting, if you will. But don't stop there, as the impetuous chambers of commerce do, with their flashy folders and catchy phrases designed to snare the tourist and his dollar. Go beyond and get a glimmer of what that exiled artist in his canyon or that scholar on his mesa sees in his self-imposed solitude. With a little effort, the occasional rubbish staining the landscape can be overlooked. Then the human eye can reach

---

1. *The Mountain on the Desert* (New York: Alfred A. Knopf, 1955), p. 4.

beyond and get a clear, untarnished vision of mountain peaks
rammed shoulder to shoulder, dark gorges where water rushes
foaming and bright, high pancake plains tilting toward Texas
and comprising one of the finest natural pasturelands in North
America, islands of pine and spruce forest, and the blue vault of
sky, best seen when autumn days are laced with sparkling air.

And if that is not enough, the mind's eye can be stretched to
even greater limits by merely looking backward, instead of forward, as we are so accustomed to do. That extraordinary in-
strument of vision can take in the pageantry and drama of the
past and, by the happy process of blending imagination with
mastery of fact, can even resurrect the men, great and small,
who helped make New Mexico the enchanting, beguiling, seductive place that it is.

Men like Coronado, whose name will forever be linked to the
myth of the Seven Cities of Cíbola; like the reconquistador
Diego de Vargas and the Pueblo warrior-chiefs Popé and Tupatú. Like Governor Anza, whose army slew the Comanche
leader Cuerno Verde; and Pedro Bautista Pino, the only New
Mexican ever to sit in Spain's parliament. Or men like Josiah
Gregg, the Santa Fe trader, or the peerless Kit Carson, or young
Captain Alexander McRae, who gallantly died defending his
cannon at the battle of Valverde. Even men like Billy the Kid,
and the land-grant leader Reies Tijerina—even they had a role
in the shaping of New Mexico.

I sometimes wonder what unseen forces brought this extraordinary gallery of persons—and those just mentioned are a paltry
sampling—to this gaunt and uncommon land. Perhaps it has to
do with that same tug I felt when, as a schoolboy many years
ago, I motored out of Texas and first saw Tucumcari Mountain.
It's not much, as mountains go, in the Southwest. But it is the
first one you see, coming in off the tiresome Staked Plains. If
you happen to be of the proper temperament and are heir to a
romantic frame of mind, that flat-topped mound of rock and
earth may speak to you and let you know, without equivocating,
that New Mexico has just gained another loyal son.

Today my own small exile camp, made with adobe in the old
style, lies tucked away in the badlands south of Santa Fe. Right

where I put up a corral, burro shed, and blacksmith shop, Castaño de Sosa rode by in 1591, on his way to the Tano Pueblos in the upper Galisteo Basin. Awhile back, a neighbor stopped in and gave me a strange rusted horseshoe nail he had taken from a pack rat's nest under a rock ledge. Its club head and thick shank identified it as Spanish. No question there. But who lost it and when? Since no one can dispute me, I like to think that one of Castaño de Sosa's horses threw a shoe hereabouts, and this solitary nail remains as the only record of a little mishap nearly four hundred years old.

Mementos of New Mexico's past, whether a small horseshoe nail or shard of Indian pottery, an imposing mission ruin or a crumbling cavalry fort, are plentiful—so much so that one is seldom far from some tangible reminder that history here is not remote and dead, but very close, and its effects still strongly with us. That too is an ingredient in the recipe for enchantment.

Nor are all the reminders merely inanimate museum specimens. Hidden away here and there amid mountains, mesas, and deserts can still be found a remnant of those picturesque and zestful folk who enlivened New Mexico's last free-wheeling days before staid maturity and the beginnings of artereosclerosis set in. In their lives something of an earlier day remains.

Attend a native trade fair or ceremony far out on a reservation, off the main visitor route, and you will find them—a handful of authentic frontier types, spontaneously drawn together by an event that would have been familiar to their grandfathers. There will be elderly Indians of several tribes, stoop-shouldered and weathered, wearing bright blankets, braids, and beaded moccasins; Hispano ranchers and farmers with gnarled hands, with faces the color of saddle leather—an occasional one among them still sporting the conical sombrero fashionable a hundred years ago. And you'll see Anglo cowboys in boots with two-inch heels—meant for riding, not show—and in hats that bear the marks of hard work and hard weather. In the way these persons look, and walk, and dress, and talk, it is plain that they are linked to the past in a way modern man never can be.

The wish to know such people better and to learn more about the land that bred them led me one October morning to stuff my

saddlebags full of books and maps, load a packhorse with bed-
ding and grub, and ride out of my camp, headed west. I had in
mind to visit an isolated slice of New Mexico whose history has
always fascinated me, the valley of the Rio Puerco. Here is a
country that, for a brief spell in the middle colonial period and
again in the nineteenth century, held a population several times
larger than it has today. This valley of phantoms is now an
eroded and tortured wasteland, scarred with washed-out roads
and nearly deserted mud towns melting back to dust. It is a
place of silent, empty spaces and buried hopes. Much of it can
be seen only on foot or on horseback, which means that its
haunting beauty is untouristed, unexploited, unlittered.

The first day, I rode down the narrow valley of the Galisteo,
over the same route that Coronado used in the spring of 1541,
when he went east to the plains seeking the mystery of Quivira.
Late in the evening, I crossed the Rio Grande with tired horses
and reached Cochití Pueblo on the west bank. I feasted on hot
chile stew and afterward climbed a ladder to a mud roof that offered a likely place to spread bedroll and tarp. Under a sky
washed white with stars, I listened to the muffled throb of a
drum coming from one of the council houses and caught the
faint perfume of piñon smoke left over from the evening's cook-
ing fires. In the last moments before I drifted off to sleep, the
derisive words of that up-to-date fellow on the Super Chief
skipped through my mind: "You call this enchanting?"

On the following day, I climbed over the Jemez Mountains
and camped in a grassy glade ringed with kingly ponderosas.
The next day saw me thoroughly lost, as a hundred-year-old
trail descending the western slope gradually pinched out and
then completely vanished. A good rule in such cases is to follow
any canyon downstream to get out of the high country. The one
I took led right down to Jemez Pueblo, precisely where I wanted
to go, for I had friends to look up there.

It was late. The streets of the Indian town were inky dark, except where the glow from windows formed yellow pools in the
dust. The clop-clop of my horses' feet made little echoes and
caused faces to peep from doorways to see who was passing.
The shadow of a small girl wearing a shawl flitted by in the

night. I threw a hurried question: "Could you point the way to my friend's house?" Courtesy still flourished here, for the shadow turned aside and beckoned me through an alley that opened on another street. I followed and found the house.

My friend was home. In fact, he was holding court. The Pueblos, as they have always done, run their own internal affairs and dispense justice in time-honored ways. Elected as governor for the year, this gentleman had summoned other officials to hear the case of a fellow tribesman. I apologized for the intrusion.

"No matter! No matter!" he said, with a warmth and simple dignity that put me at ease. His little grandson would find a corral and feed for the horses and a room in the pueblo for me. Then, later, when official business was out of the way, I should come back for supper. Before I left next morning, his daughter favored me with a warm, round loaf of bread freshly drawn from an adobe oven. It traveled with the books in the saddlebags.

Beyond Jemez stretch twenty or so hard miles to the Rio Puerco. At one point, the route cuts across the concrete highway that angles up from Albuquerque, heading for Farmington and the Four Corners. But past that, the twentieth century is left behind. When the dry Puerco valley unfolds before you, it is suddenly a world where distance and history count for much, and time and the march of progress for very little.

The Puerco is properly a river when it rises in the San Pedro Mountains farther north, but by the time it reaches the middle valley here, the waters have seeped into the sand, leaving only a damp and deeply entrenched stream bed. The old floodplain, where Spaniards used to farm, extends on either side to the foot of sharp-edged mesas capped with basalt. Looking down from those heights, you can easily pick out the dim traces of fields and irrigation ditches. Who could believe now, seeing the thorny desert scrub and shifting dunes, that for a time, in the 1700s, acres of wheat, corn, and other grains greened this valley floor? Sheep and cattle in abundance once grazed behind the fields, and in the years of drought, they stripped away the ground cover down to the roots. When the rains came, then, nothing held the soil, and water ran in furious torrents through hundreds of little channels that sliced their way to the Puerco. Over-grazing and arroyo-cutting ruined the Puerco valley. Here, one of the tragic sides of history, man's abuse and neglect of the land, is preserved in an open-air museum for anyone who cares to study it. It's an old story, often repeated in the South-west.

I steered my horses down the winding valley and through decaying towns whose only adornment lay in the sonorous names they still wore: San Luís, Cabezón, Guadalupe, Casa Salazar. One main street after another presented the stereotyped picture of a western ghost town complete with sagging doors on creaky hinges and banks of tumbleweeds blown up against rotting walls. Long ago, a good road had carried oxcarts, then stagecoaches, and finally even a few of Mr. Ford's Model Ts. But the arroyos took that, too. The few ranchers who still enter, to tend property given their ancestors by Spain, have four-wheel-drive rigs. They make their own roads, twisting back and forth to avoid the cuts—after every rain, picking a new way.

I camped on a high spot with a view and staked out the horses. Alone in such a place, at dusk, the imagination, unbidden, tries to call up departed spirits of Spanish farmers and merchantmen, Navajo and Apache raiders, cowboys and cavalrymen. Each shifting shadow or shrill bark of a coyote raises a new apparition, and a determined act of will is needed to prevent a bad case of the dismals from developing. Good medicine is a friendly campfire of juniper sticks, accompanied by a bubbling coffee pot. That combination has served New Mexican travelers well for hundreds of years; and as a source of cheer, it has been nowise diminished by onslaught of the modern age.

Early in the morning, I prepared to cross the Rio Puerco. The channel's quicksandy bed is notorious, but stories of humans, livestock, and even pick-up trucks disappearing into its devouring depths are probably exaggerated. Nevertheless, I took precautions at a likely-looking ford. Uncoiling my catch rope and tying it fast to the saddle horn, I had me a solid line to hang on to. As an added safety, I gathered up an armload of stones, and with the horses trailing a few feet behind, walked slowly across the soft bed. Casting the stones ahead and avoiding the places where they went under with a gentle sucking sound, I got my little caravan to the other side without mishap. Mountain men used the same trick when they moved through the Southwest hunting beaver long ago; I wondered if anyone but myself had recently benefited from it.

Leaving the Puerco, I ascended one of its western tributaries, the Rio Salado, a salty little stream that would be called a river only in New Mexico. On one of its bluffs, I came upon a small ranch that looked deserted. It sat alone and forlorn, a low rock-and-mud building with a scatter of pole corrals behind. No truck or jeep was in sight, though a few head of horses grazed in a small, fenced pasture. Then I saw smoke coming from the stovepipe.

Riding in, I took the two Hispano cowboys by surprise. They hadn't seen another soul for weeks. One was old, the other young and brash, and they were starved for talk. I was starved for the beans and new-made tortillas they offered, so over a plank table in the house we made a fair swap. A jar of jam from my pack pinch-hit for dessert, disappearing faster than cake at a birthday party.

The *patrón,* they said, came once a month from Bernalillo to get a report on his cattle and to bring in grub and kerosene. He also hauled drums of drinking water, for the thin trickle in the Salado was too salty for humans, though the stock managed to get by on it. The nearest fresh spring lay miles away, too far to pack water conveniently on horseback.

The men had a tough bit of work cut out for the next day. Half a hundred cows had been grazing on the Mesa del Chivato for the summer, and they planned to make a gather and drive them down to a handy pasture near the ranch. Later in the month, the *patrón* would arrive and help move these and other cattle in easy stages to the upper Puerco, where trucks would be waiting to haul them to market. They could use help on the mesa, and they tempted me with descriptions of wild country. I could even take one of the horses out of their remuda, if I didn't mind a little bucking, first thing in the morning.

The old man—small, energetic, with dark-socketed eyes and

a set of thin gray whiskers—possessed an untapped well of lore concerning the Puerco Basin and surrounding country. He had listened to the stories, legends, and songs of this pocket-sized world apart and had known the men who saw it in better days. With only occasional prodding from me, he talked into the night, while I scribbled notes by the oil lamp. Later, before turning into our bunks, the pair asked me to read from an Old Testament. Both men were illiterate. The copy was coverless, tattered, and in Spanish. I read a half-dozen of my favorite Psalms; they thanked me and bid *Buenas noches.*

The trail to the summit of the Mesa del Chivato was the worst I ever encountered. My two companions lived by the old cowboy rule, *Never walk when you can ride.* But the last stretch before the top was too rough, even for them. We dismounted and climbed hand-over-hand, leaving the horses with loose reins to find their own way. I glanced back and saw them clamoring like goats, their shod hoofs ringing on the brittle rock. The vista at the end made the effort worth it.

A hundred square miles of broken and seamed country, riven by the Rio Puerco, sprawled beneath us. The cowboys, breathing hard, stared with me, though they had seen it all from this point many times before. Here, as elsewhere in New Mexico, the scene is forever changing, always volunteering new patterns of light that put old and familiar features of geography in different dress. For the first time I got a clear view of the basin's most spectacular landmarks, the collection of volcanic plugs or necks, each one a column of congealed lava, rising mountainlike in splendid isolation above the valley floor. These geologic ghosts of extinct volcanoes are fitting monuments in the graveyard of the Puerco. The northernmost, Cabezón Peak, holds a Navajo shrine on its crest. Indians say that the peak was formed after the legendary War Twins killed a giant. When they cut off his monstrous head, it turned to black stone.

The cattle we wanted were scattered over several miles of mesa top. The elevation caught summer rains blown off Mount Taylor to the west and supported a healthy stand of pines interspersed with open grassy meadows. The spring calves had grown fat and sassy. As we made a gather and began working toward the south, they kept breaking from the bunch to frolic and throw their tails in the air.

On the lower end of the mesa, we came to an easy trail leading to the bottom. The cattle seemed to know they were leaving good grass, and they balked. We whooped and hollered at them, pelted rumps with our ropes, and rode back and forth like demons, trying to shove the leaders over the edge. All we managed to do was dissolve our neat herd into dispersed knots of threes and fours. It was gut-busting, sweaty, exhausting work, but this was the way it had always been on cattle ranges in the West.

The old man finally called a halt and let us know there was a better way to do the job than wearing out good horseflesh. We got together a parcel of ten head or so that we could handle, forced them on the trail, and moved about halfway down the mesa to a little pocket that formed a natural holding place. While the old man kept them checked there, the youngster and I rode back up to the rim. In less than an hour, we had the remaining cows grouped again. When they picked up the bawling of their herdmates down below, they took the trail so fast we had to push to keep up.

We bottomed out in a little canyon that descended toward the ranch, so that, even though dusk was closing in, it was a simple matter to reach the new pasture. After closing the gate on the cows, we still had a two-mile ride back to headquarters. I couldn't see my saddle horn in the darkness and worried, knowing the tricky path ahead followed close to the edge of steep-walled arroyos. *No te preocupes!*—"Don't worry," the cowboys said. "These horses can see, even if we can't. They'll take us home." And they did. I still wonder how.

A few days later, I caught up my own horses, preparing to leave the Rio Salado ranch. The younger fellow helped me throw a diamond-hitch on my pack. "If you'll change your mind and stay," he said earnestly, "we'll put in a good word for you with the *patrón*. I think he'll hire you." I smiled at his eagerness and told him again that I was just riding through, getting a feel for enchanted country, *tierra encantada*. He looked a little puzzled . . . but let it go at that.

As I rode out, a jet streaked and roared across an otherwise flawless October sky, a reminder that the world of the machine had already displaced an older time when muscle and spirit weighed most in the human equation. But quickly the jet and its feathery tail of vapor were gone, and I was alone again, jogging eastward toward the distant Rio Grande and the blue-black shadow of Sandia Mountain.

Suggestions for Further Reading

The historical literature pertaining to New Mexico is vast, and beginning readers sometimes have difficulty finding an appropriate place to start. One good introduction to the state's past is Edward P. Dozier's *The Pueblo Indians of North America* (New York: Holt, Rinehart and Winston, 1970). A sympathetic treatment of the life of a modern Pueblo woman is found in Alice Marriot's now classic *María: The Potter of San Ildefonso* (Norman: University of Oklahoma Press, 1950). For information on two of New Mexico's non-Pueblo tribes, the reader may consult C. L. Sonnichsen, *The Mescalero Apaches* (Norman: University of Oklahoma Press, 1958); and Frank McNitt, *Navajo Wars* (Albuquerque: University of New Mexico Press, 1972).

Spanish exploration and settlement of New Mexico have received attention in scores of studies. For historical drama and authenticity, Herbert E. Bolton's *Coronado, Knight of Pueblos and Plains* (Albuquerque: University of New Mexico Press, 1949), remains unsurpassed. An interpretation of the early colonial period, showing a strong anti-Spanish bias, is Jack D. Forbes's *Apache, Navajo and Spaniard* (Norman: University of Oklahoma Press, 1960). Serious readers will wish to consult the writings of France V. Scholes, representative of which is *Troublous Times in New Mexico, 1659–1670* (Albuquerque: University of New Mexico Press, 1942). A good source on the later colonial years is Alfred B. Thomas, *Forgotten Frontiers* (Norman: University of Oklahoma Press, 1932).

On the Santa Fe Trail, Josiah Gregg's matchless *Commerce of the Prairie* stands at the head of the list. Two splendid works offer a look at the fur trade and the life of the mountain men: David J. Weber, *The Taos Trappers* (Norman: University of Oklahoma Press, 1971); and David Lavender, *Bent's Fort* (Garden City, N.Y.: Doubleday and Co., 1954).

Among the many illuminating books on New Mexico's territorial and modern periods, the following are of special merit: Howard Roberts Lamar, *The Far Southwest, 1846–1912* (New Haven: Yale University Press, 1966); Robert W. Larson, *New Mexico's Quest for Statehood, 1846–1912* (Albuquerque: University of New Mexico Press, 1968); A. M. Gibson, *The Life and Death of Colonel Albert Jennings Fountain* (Norman: University of Oklahoma Press, 1965); and Miguel Antonio Otero, *My Life on the Frontier, 1864–1882* (New York: Press of the Pioneers, 1935).

Two novels speak with exceptional eloquence about New Mexico as it was. One is Willa Cather's *Death Comes for the Archbishop* (New York: Knopf, 1955), which serves up in fictional form a faithful portrait of Archbishop Jean B. Lamy. The other is Eugene Manlove Rhodes's much-praised cowboy novelette, *Pasó Por Aquí* (Norman: University of Oklahoma Press, 1973). Agnes Morley Cleaveland presents an Anglo woman's view of New Mexico ranch life in *No Life for a Lady* (Boston: Houghton Mifflin Co., 1941). The Hispanic side of ranching is given by Fabiola Cabeza de Vaca in her picturesque chronicle, *We Fed Them Cactus* (Albuquerque: University of New Mexico Press, 1954).

Index

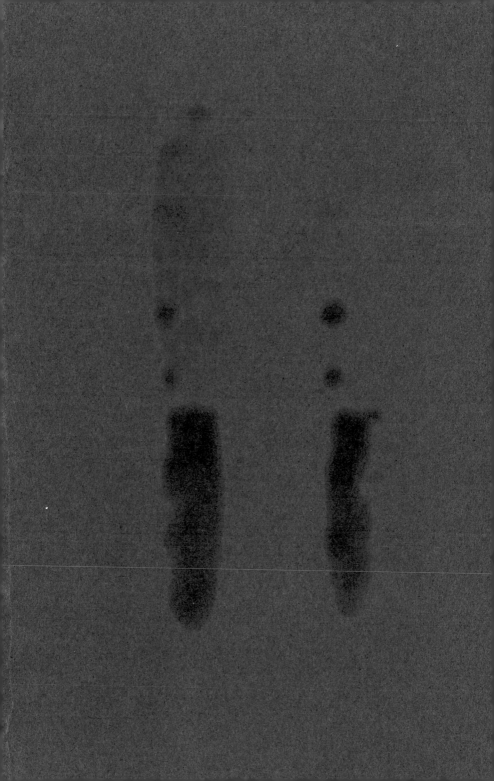

507643